MW00626246

# BECOMING A
# *Great*
# MISSIONARY

*A Training Manual*
*for*
*Missionaries, Members, and Priesthood Leaders*

# BECOMING A *Great* MISSIONARY

*A Training Manual*
*for*
*Missionaries, Members, and Priesthood Leaders*

Kevan Kingsley Clawson

*Foreword by Anne Pinnock*

Walking the Line Publications  South Jordan, Utah

Other books by Kevan Clawson
*Psalms to the Lord*
*The Atonement of Jesus Christ*
*The Second Coming of Jesus Christ*
*A Life of Miracles*

Books by Kevan & Terri Clawson
*Obtaining Your Calling and Election*

Cover Design: Jaime Clawson
Electronic Page Makeup: Jennifer Asplund
Editing: Terri Clawson and John Hopkins
Printer and Binder: Printed in the USA by Morris Publishing, 3212 E. Highway 30, Kearney, NE 68847, (800) 650-7888

This book is not an official publication of the Church of Jesus Christ of Latter-day Saints. All opinions expressed herein are the author's and are not necessarily those of the publisher or of the Church of Jesus Christ of Latter-day Saints.

©2002 Kevan Kingsley Clawson. All rights reserved.
Published 2002
Printed in the United States of America
Distributed by Walking the Line Publications, P.O. Box 95645, S. Jordan, UT 84095–0645
www.walkingthelinebooks.com
Copying or reproducing this publication in whole or in part violates U.S. Federal copyright law.
All rights reserved.

ISBN 0-9714540-5-1

*Dedicated to Hugh W. Pinnock,*
*mentor, hero, and friend.*

# Foreword

Kevan Clawson was a legend in the Pennsylvania Harrisburg Mission during the time Elder Hugh W. Pinnock served as its president. Given his proven success as a missionary, Elder Clawson is credible with the principles he discusses in this book. He knows how missionary work can be done successfully.

President Pinnock was a wonderfully motivating teacher to Elder Clawson and 608 other missionaries who served under him during the three years he served as their leader in the Pennsylvania Harrisburg Mission. With his perpetual smile and his gift as a teacher, President Pinnock stimulated a desire within his elders, sisters, and grand couples to serve more faithfully and to learn to find joy in the principle of hard work.

President Pinnock never asked his missionaries to do anything he hadn't done himself. At one point, he shared his experience with some of the more dedicated missionaries about his own 100-hour work-week. Elder Clawson, with his companion Elder Ben Casper, decided they wanted to experience working a 100-hour week. They requested and received special permission to serve with adjusted rules. They caught up with their washing, got up earlier in the morning, and came home to their apartment later than usual in the evening. They even took sandwiches in their pockets so they could save time at lunch. Elder Clawson and Elder Casper did everything in their physical power to use their time prudently. They trusted that the Lord would bless them if they were extra-mile elders.

At the end of that special 100-hour week, Elder Clawson and Elder Casper had taught over 70 discussions! President Pinnock counseled that it wasn't wise for them to persist in the 100-hour week, but promised that if they continued their sustained faithful effort the blessings would follow. During the six months they labored in the Altoona Pennsylvania area they persisted in teaching high numbers of discussions (they averaged over 30 discussions a week), setting the pace for other missionaries in the mission.

In the pages that follow, Elder Clawson shares the principles he found bring success to any faithful missionary. He was a model about whom President Pinnock would often refer over the next 25 years when he was encouraging and training other missionaries. Elder Clawson was called as a seventy and a ward and stake mission leader after completing his full-time mission. He referred frequently to the "how-to" notes he took at President Pinnock's training sessions. This missionary manual is comprised of those notes and Elder Clawson's recollections of his training by President Pinnock.

The profound effect President Pinnock had on the missionaries who served under him continued well after their time together in the mission field. At the completion of our mission, President Pinnock and I worked as a team to keep the missionaries united by publishing a missionary newsletter for several years and through reunions and temple sessions. I would gather the missionaries and President Pinnock would touch the gathered group with his mighty spirit. President Pinnock became Elder Pinnock when he was brought into the First Quorum of the Seventy. He kept track of his missionaries and counseled them if they listed from their course. As a result, they have achieved a united bond and still enjoy sharing the missionary spirit in great numbers each year. Even after the untimely death of their President, they persist in their desire to gather and renew their missionary spirit.

President Pinnock was admired and loved by all of those who served under him. This great love and dedication to the principles that President Pinnock taught can be seen through the success that followed him. Wherever Elder Pinnock served, and whenever he trained missionaries, the missionary work in that area flourished.

Elder Clawson feels a need for all missionaries to have access to these success principles and the enthusiasm he continues to feel for missionary work. He knows how success can be achieved and is passing on these principles to help all those wonderful missionaries who are desirous of achieving success and blessing the lives of those who search for truth.

*Sister Anne Pinnock*

# Contents

x

# Preface

The purpose of this book is threefold. Its primary purpose is to prepare young men and young women to become *great* missionaries by giving them a realistic view of mission life and very specific things they can do to increase their effectiveness as missionaries. The second purpose of this book is to give Church members information on how they can help the full-time missionaries in their work and how their efforts tie into the work the missionaries are doing. It will teach members how to become missionaries themselves and how they can prepare nonmembers to accept the full-time missionaries into their homes. Its final purpose is to help priesthood leaders understand their role in missionary work and how best to coordinate the responsibilities of local ward leaders with the responsibilities of the full-time missionaries. Missionary work is most successful when all three of these groups (missionaries, members, and priesthood leaders) work well together. Sisters, in reading this book, you will not find reference to men *and* women but take no offense. It would simply be too cumbersome to write everything to properly address both sexes. Please understand that all references, outside of the application of priesthood ordinances, refer to both elders and sisters. This book is of value to *all* missionaries, and you can certainly be counted among the great!

I present the information in this book with great confidence, because I have had the opportunity to serve as an effective and dedicated missionary for over 15 years. My experience as a missionary began with my friends, as an excited convert to the gospel of Jesus Christ. I then served a full-time mission in Pennsylvania, which was shortly followed by my ordination as a seventy. With the discontinuation of local seventy quorums, I was ordained a high priest but continued to serve as ward mission leader. I was then called into the stake mission presidency. Over the years, I have been privileged to participate in almost every possible activity a missionary might experience.

The Lord blessed me to become a successful missionary by giving me a great leader: Elder Hugh W. Pinnock. He was my mission president, mentor, hero, and friend. He was a man who listened to the Lord. Elder Pinnock took my overwhelming desire to serve my Lord and Savior, directed it in a positive way, and helped mold and shape my talents and character to become a true servant of God. Most of the information contained in this book has the handprint of Elder Pinnock.

I have attempted to clearly differentiate the types of missionaries with whom I have worked and taught during my many years of missionary work in an effort to bring to light certain principles and characteristics that make missionaries truly successful. For example, I write about the difference between good and bad missionaries. Let me make it clear from the start that I am not passing judgment on people who have these characteristics, because we all have qualities that can be improved upon. Part of the challenge of life is to see ourselves clearly—to see ourselves as God sees us—and to change those things we need to change in order to become prepared to serve God and live in His kingdom. I am using this contrast as a tool to help those who read this book see more clearly the qualities that produce success. I also write about the difference between good missionaries and *great* missionaries. Again, this is done only to help those who read this book see clearly the specific traits, qualities, beliefs, and actions that will help all missionaries become everything God intended them to be.

I feel the need to comment on the many stories I have included in this book to teach certain principles through events that I have either witnessed or in which I have participated. I am now getting older and my memory of these events, many of which happened over 20 years ago, may not be what it once was. Thus, those who know and have worked with me may have different perspectives concerning those events. All I can say is that I have endeavored to recount the missionary experiences in this book as accurately as my memory permits. Over the years, some events may have become magnified and others diminished, and details of these events may have been lost altogether. Regardless of any failings that I might have had in telling these stories, the purpose behind the telling is what is important; learning the lessons that will make someone an effective missionary.

Though all of the stories told in this book are true, I have changed the names of the people I talk about to protect their privacy. Therefore, most of the names are fictitious. However, I have left intact the names of the places where these events occurred so those who participated in these wonderful experiences can relive them again through my words. Occasionally, where the story has a negative tone, I have simply left out both names and places to avoid any embarrassment to those who were involved.

Most of the experiences I have shared are personal and some are sacred. Only recently has the Lord prompted me to share with others the many wonderful miracles I have had the privilege to experience. I learned long ago to listen to the promptings of the Lord and, as in my youth I felt *compelled* to speak to others about the gospel, in my old age I now feel *compelled* to share with others the gifts and blessings that God has given me over the years. God has so greatly blessed me that I cannot go to the grave without documenting, and thereby humbly witnessing to others, His power in my life. Truly, I feel like Ammon in the Book of Mormon:

> *And it came to pass that when Ammon had said these words, his brother Aaron rebuked him, saying: Ammon, I fear that thy joy doth carry thee away unto boasting. But Ammon said unto him: I do not boast in my own strength, nor in my own wisdom; but behold, my joy is full, yea, my heart is brim with joy, and I will rejoice in my God. Yea, I know that I am nothing; as to my strength I am weak; therefore I will not boast of myself, but I will boast of my God, for in his strength I can do all things; yea, behold, many mighty miracles we have wrought in this land, for which we will praise his name forever.* (Alma 26:10–12)

As you read this book, keep in mind that every mission and every missionary is different. Not every problem, or solution, will apply in every case. The book is designed to be a general handbook that gives a basic framework of how missionary work should be conducted and provide ideas of how to expand missionary work using different finding and teaching techniques. My hope and prayer is that this book will be useful as you strive to preach the gospel to those who are prepared to hear, and that it will motivate you to find the success that  can only be obtained by understanding and using the POWER of God.

Finally, it is important to understand that this book is not in any way an official publication  of the Church of Jesus Christ of Latter-day Saints. I have no authority to speak for or on behalf of the Church and all ideas, suggestions, and/or doctrine presented in this book represent my personal opinion and do not necessarily represent the views of the Church or the publisher.

# BECOMING A *Great* MISSIONARY

# One
# Why Go On A Mission?

*T*he first qualification for becoming a great missionary is to go for the right reason. I cannot begin to tell you the problems that arise in the mission field as a result of young men going on full-time missions ill prepared or for the wrong reasons. They are disasters waiting to happen. Unprepared and un-motivated missionaries not only harm themselves, they prevent their companions from progressing, or, worse, encourage detrimental be-havior among an even wider group of missionaries. They can even hinder the work of the Lord and at times actually cause prospective converts to reject the Gospel—with obvious eternal consequences.

So, why go on a mission? There are really only two righteous reasons to go on a mission:

*1. Go on a full-time mission out of a sincere desire to serve the Lord.*

You should have a desire to serve the Lord, a desire that has been kindled by a burning testimony of the Gospel of Jesus Christ. You should have a testimony of the gospel that has been nurtured by parents, teachers, and, most importantly, by your own prayers and study of the sacred scriptures.

1

## Becoming a Great Missionary

2. *Go on a mission out of duty to the God who gave you life.*

Duty is not a bad reason to go on a mission. Remember Duty, God, and Country? Remember the Scout code of honor: I will do my best to do my duty to God and my country? Doing one's duty is a time-honored and respected reason for doing anything! So, yes, do your duty. Go on a full-time mission out of duty and obligation to your God, your Church, and your family. The great rewards will be the same. But understand that *duty* is more than saying, "I'm going because they want me to." A true desire to do your duty still requires a *desire* to serve faithfully, work hard, and a commitment to obey the mission rules.

Missions are very difficult and anyone who goes should have a strong desire to go and do a good job. Just going and filling time is *not* doing your duty! The Church does not want any "Beetle Baileys" in the Army of God—men who enlist and then do everything they can to get out of work and are content to be mediocre. That might be humorous in a comic strip, but it is devastating in real life!

If you feel you do not have a strong testimony of the gospel but have a desire to go on a mission and serve faithfully because of all that your parents, teachers, and your God have done for you, then go! Work hard, serve faithfully, and you will receive the same blessings as those who are spiritually better prepared. When you serve *faithfully,* the blessings will be the same because of the nature of the work. It is the S*pirit* that testifies; it is the S*pirit* that converts. God simply needs faithful servants to spread the word and He takes care of the rest. Whether you go on your mission as a spiritual giant or a spiritual midget does not matter. What matters most is that you go on your mission committed to *serve* faithfully and work hard. The Lord will take care of the rest!

◆◆◆

2

As for me? My desire to serve the Lord and serve a full-time mission was a way to repay my Savior for saving my soul. You see, I was a sinner. Not your everyday, garden-variety sinner, either. My descent into darkness and sin almost destroyed my soul. I was saved by Jesus Christ. The story is as old as Adam and Eve but as fresh as a person's last sin. I was saved by the loving grace of Jesus Christ and convicted by the Spirit of God that fell upon me. That same Spirit brought clarity to my mind: I saw the current state of my soul and realized that if I didn't change my life, if I didn't repent with full purpose of heart—and fast—I would, in fact, suffer eternal damnation. For months I lived in a terrible, overwhelming fear of death. If I died before my repentance was complete, I was doomed.

Once I was accepted back into full fellowship within the Church, the Spirit of the Lord began to work upon me, like Paul of old:

> For though I preach the gospel, I have nothing to glory of: for necessity is laid upon me; yea, woe is unto me, if I preach not the gospel! (1 Corinthians 9:16)

I felt I was under the same necessity to preach the gospel. There was no joy in it, not yet anyway, but only a sense of duty and fear of God. The joy came later, as service in the fields of the Lord permitted the Spirit of God to work through me to others. As the Spirit brought knowledge and joy to those I taught, it also brought joy to me since I was the conduit the Lord used to touch others.

I began, not by force of circumstance that a full-time mission places upon us, but by a desire just to start, to be actively moving towards the God who saved me. I began with my friends; lost souls like myself who knew me and had seen the change in my life. It was hard to confront my friends—embarrassing at times, and awkward.

## Becoming a Great Missionary

But I said the words and even though they smirked and wondered and said, "No way!" the Spirit forced me to continue. Then it happened, the moment every missionary waits for. I found a listening ear in one of my best friends. He was a member of the Church, and like me, had long ago been drawn away by the temptations of the world. Nonetheless, he still had that tiny spark which, with work, was ready to burst again into flame. As he listened, the Spirit of the Lord began to work within me for the first time and the words that I spoke often were not my own. My dialog was full of false doctrine (What did I know? I had never even taken the discussions!), and often I did not know what I was doing or what I was saying or where the discussions with my friend were taking us. But God *always* works through imperfect servants (remember, all have sinned and fall short of the glory of God), and, as I was to find out later, people are not converted by words but by the Spirit of God.

Once begun, I could not stop and I soon saw with clarity the next great step in my progression: I had to go on a full-time mission. I knew with all my heart that this great step would truly wash away my sins and prepare me to live with Jesus Christ, the Savior of my soul. You can see how it was; necessity was laid upon me. Woe to me if I did not preach the gospel of my God!

Now we let the other shoe drop: What are the reasons *not* to go on a mission? They are too numerous to list, but a few will do. Sometimes the best thing a person can do for himself, his family, and even his God, is to stay home and follow another fruitful destiny. The call for every young man to serve a mission is a general statement, not a specific prophecy or call to the individual. Only serious prayer and fasting can bring the right answer to your own heart.

As you review the reasons *not* to go on a mission, remember that most people's lives are in a constant state of flux—situations and people change all the time, especially when they are young. Just because a young man is not ready to go on a mission *now* does not mean he will not be ready to go in a few years or even a few months. There is nothing sinful or wrong in *waiting* until you are truly ready to go on a mission! In fact, by waiting and spending the time you need to properly prepare, you show your maturity and integrity.

Here are just a few reasons *not* to go on a mission, or at least to postpone your mission until you are ready to go for the *right* reasons:

*1.  Don't go on a mission if you are overly involved with a girlfriend.*

Boy, this is a tough one. Many young men have girlfriends prior to leaving on a mission. Young men are supposed to have girlfriends. But if you are following the counsel of the prophet, you have not yet gotten "serious" because you are too young and have other commitments to fill before you will be ready to fully commit to any young woman.

Why does having a serious girlfriend cause problems? The reasons should be obvious. At best, having a serious girlfriend can interfere with your becoming totally committed to serving the Lord. At worst, a girlfriend can become a serious obsession leading to sin and deception. This is precisely why Paul recommended that those called into the service of God not be married, as any time spent developing or maintaining a relationship takes away from the time and energy that should go into serving the Lord.[1]

---

[1] 1 Corinthians 7:29–33 JST.

# Becoming a Great Missionary

For example, it is not uncommon for young men to fall into sin and then, due to pressure from parents or others, be coerced into going on a mission. Pressure to go on a mission can overwhelm some young men, causing them to lie, even to their bishop. These young men end up carrying a terrible burden throughout their mission (or until they finally break down and confess to the mission president).

One sister told me that while she was in the Missionary Training Center, some missionaries with serious girlfriends started to do very bizarre things. Some got T-shirts with their girlfriend's picture on the front and wore them under their suits. Others went so far as to have pictures of their girlfriends printed on their pillowcases so they could "sleep" with them during their mission. Others spent hundreds, even thousands, of dollars calling their girlfriends from their mission or spent hours of wasted time writing their girlfriends every day. The list goes on and on!

And then there are the "Dear John" letters. I know of very few missionaries whose girlfriends actually waited for two years. Most young women find someone else to marry and end up sending a "Dear John" letter to their missionary. In some cases, this is the best thing that can happen, as the missionary can finally settle down and focus on the reason he is supposed to be there in the first place— serving the Lord. But in other cases, the missionary becomes bitter and ends up depressed and moody the rest of his mission.

When you consider all of the negative things that can, and do, happen as the result of having a serious relationship with a girl prior to going on a mission, it is better for a young man to decide immediately whether he really wants to go on a mission or stay home to develop a permanent relationship with his girlfriend. At the very least, such a young man should be told to postpone his mission to gain time to resolve this important issue.

2. *Don't go on a mission if you are going just to please your parents.*

Being forced, coerced, bribed—you pick the verb—to go on a mission is not a reason to go. At best, you will spend your time regretting the absence of your friends, thinking about all of the things you could be doing, or thinking about all the things you will do when you get home. We used to call this being "trunky" (another word for homesick). Being trunky is normal for missionaries about to go home, but too often we see missionaries who are trunky from the first day they arrive in the mission field. It is a symptom of a missionary who came out for the wrong reasons. At worst, you will continue with your normal life while on your mission by not following the mission rules; i.e., watching TV, playing video games, spending endless hours at some gullible member's home, etc. You will end up wasting both your own time and the sacred time of any companion you are given. If you really do not want to go on a mission, then be a man and have the courage to say so to your parents. Stay home and live your life. It will be better for you and much better for your future mission companions who will have a better chance to be paired with a companion willing to work hard and live the mission rules. Besides, remember that life often changes! Who knows whether, in a few months or a few years, you *will* be ready to serve a mission for the right reason. Again, there is nothing sinful or wrong in *waiting* to go on a mission until you are sure you are ready!

3. *Do not go on a mission to get off drugs or to overcome bad habits.*

Don't laugh, it happens *all* the time! Oh, if you could hear the stories from the Missionary Training Centers of the baggage missionaries bring with them! One missionary I worked with came on his mission to get off drugs. He was hooked and wanted to get clean. He knew he would never get clean without help, so he went on a mission. Once in the Missionary Training Center, he began to go through withdrawal with hallucinations, tremors, etc. and was sent to the hospital. When I met him, he was wearing dark glasses (he always wore dark glasses—I think his eyes were permanently dilated from all of the drugs he took) and loved to talk about his past: his drug days, his fast cars, and the life he left behind. One night, in tears, he asked me to help him become a better missionary. I have no doubt about his desire. He really wanted to be like those faithful young men with whom he constantly rubbed shoulders, but he could not. He was not prepared. By the end of his mission, he may have become a good missionary, but by then it was too late . . . his mission was over. The time this missionary spent on his mission was wasted, compounded by all the time wasted by each of his companions and the district and zone leaders who spent their time dealing with this problem elder. All that wasted time and effort. . .

4. *Don't go on a mission to escape or cover your sins.*

Far too many missionaries go on their missions burdened with sin. Sometimes they have not taken enough time to repent properly, or some authority figure thought this was "just what was needed" to bring them around, as though they were sending these young men to a military academy to straighten them out. Sometimes missionaries have hidden their sins and lied during their interviews. These sins, if not confessed and repented of properly, become a millstone around their necks that drag down them and all those around them.

One missionary I knew came on his mission carrying a terrible burden of sin. He was a homosexual who had never truly overcome this serious problem. He had repented and fallen several times before coming on his mission. In fact, while in the mission home he committed sin again with a visiting friend. Of course he was sent home, but a couple of years later was permitted to try again. On the eve of his final interview with the stake president, he sinned again. Out of fear and shame, he lied to his stake president and soon found himself on a mission. I found out about his problem because his guilt and desire to sin again made him act strangely. His companion confided to me his strange behavior and then, during a split with this missionary, I confronted him. Fortunately, the Spirit of the Lord was with me, and I was inspired to ask just the right questions. He soon spilled his soul to me, flooding the street we walked upon with pain and suffering. I called my mission president immediately and the next day this young man was transferred to the mission home. I don't know what happened to him after that. I *do* know that he should never have come on a mission in the first place and was a burden to himself, his companion, and the mission.

A young man himself who is not ready to go on a mission must have the moral courage to say so, regardless of any pressure being exerted by those around him. Unprepared young men should not be sent on missions! Remember, there is nothing immoral or improper in delaying a mission call until a person is ready!

5. *Don't go on a mission if your obligations at home don't permit it.*
It isn't often that home obligations keep a young man from going on a mission, because the Lord is careful to prepare the way for those who desire to go on missions, but there are exceptions to every rule. Where a young man is the only son and provider for a family, it could be improper for him to leave. Wards will sometimes take on this responsibility for those in need but all things must be done in wisdom. If your heart is in the right place, but you are unable to go due to life's circumstances, then God will uphold your decision. There are always other ways you can serve your Lord and God. Missions are important, but they are not the only way one can serve!

# Becoming a Great Missionary

*6. Don't go on a mission if you are called into the military.*

Here is a righteous reason not to go on a mission. God and country. The military is an honorable and worthy calling for any young man to pursue. Should your country, or your heart, take you into the military instead of the mission field, God will uphold your decision. I remember a young family in Hartford who went through this dilemma with their son. As ward mission leader, I had been involved in bringing this family into the Church. As their home teacher, I helped them grow and gave them counsel in matters about the Church they as yet did not understand. This was one of them. Their only son had been preparing to go into the military for years. His father had been in the military, and there was a long military tradition in the family. More importantly, the young man *wanted* to go into the military. After the family joined the Church, they all desired to fulfill the commandments of God. But what should they do? War would soon be coming (a short time later the Gulf War began), and this righteous young man was confused about his feelings and desires. The family was split between whether he should go on a mission or go into the military. They turned to me for counsel. Actually, it was easy for me. I knew within my heart that both paths were worthy and righteous paths for this young man to take. I expressed to them my feelings and told them that this young man should fast and pray and find out for himself what the Lord wanted him to do. One week went by. When I met with this family again, they told me the young man had made the decision to go into the military. I instantly knew that this was the right decision for this young man and his family and I told them so. They were all so happy! About six months after entering the service, this young man was married in the temple. He served his country and fellowman

**10**

faithfully and righteously. I have absolutely no doubt that he was blessed just as much for the decision he made to go into the military as he would have been by going on a mission.

For those who hesitate to equate service in the military with going on a mission, I need only remind you that many of the greatest men recorded in the scriptures were military men first, before they were called into the service of God. Let me name just a few: Enoch,[2] Moses,[3] Joshua,[4] David,[5] Captain Moroni,[6] Helaman[7] (remember the 2,000 stripling soldiers?), and *General* Mormon,[8] who served first and foremost as the leader of the Nephite armies and only between that great service wrote the Book of Mormon.

No one in the Old Testament was closer to the kind of man the Lord wanted us to be than King David, a man after the Lord's own heart,[9] who was first and foremost a soldier. And who can possibly deny that the work that Captain Moroni did in saving the Nephites from being overrun by the Lamanites was any less important than the work that Helaman was doing with the Church?

---

[2] "...it is interesting to note that what John saw was not the establishment of Zion and its removal to heavenly spheres, but the unparalleled wars in which Enoch, as a general over the armies of the saints, 'went forth conquering and to conquer.'...Truly, never was there a ministry such as Enoch's, and never a conqueror and general who was his equal! How appropriate that he should ride the white horse of victory in John's apocalyptic vision!" (Bruce R. McConkie, *Doctrinal New Testament Commentary,* Vol. 3, pp. 478–479).

[3] "The Ethiopians, who are next neighbors to the Egyptians, made an inroad into their country...So Moses, at the persuasion of the king himself, cheerfully undertook the business, because Moses was to be their general. When he therefore proceeded thus on his journey, he came upon the Ethiopians before they expected him, and joining battle with them he beat them, and deprived them of the hopes they had of success against the Egyptians, and went on in overthrowing their cities, and indeed made a great slaughter of these Ethiopians" (Josephus, *The Antiquities of the Jews,* 2.10.1–2).

[4] Exodus 17:13; The Book of Joshua.

[5] I Samuel 18:5.

[6] Alma 43:16-17.

[7] Alma 53:17-22.

[8] Mormon 2:1–2.

[9] 1 Samuel 13:14; 16:7.

## Becoming a Great Missionary

> *Yea, verily, verily I say unto you, if all men had been, and were, and ever would be, like unto Moroni, behold, the very powers of hell would have been shaken forever; yea, the devil would never have power over the hearts of the children of men.*
> (Alma 48:17)

7.  *Don't go on a mission if you are ready to raise a family.*

This is an extension of reason number one. If you are older, have a serious girlfriend, or have a strong desire to start a family, don't go on a mission. There is nothing wrong with getting married in the temple of the Lord and starting a family. You will have other opportunities to serve God. This can be a tough decision; one that can only come after much prayer and fasting. But if by going on a mission you will end up ineffective and distracted, don't go. If you can stand before your God at the last day and say that even though you did not serve a mission as a young man, you were married in the temple, served faithfully in Church callings, sent children on missions, and perhaps served a full-time mission later in life, do you really think you would stand condemned before God? I don't. I think He would happily accept such a person into His Kingdom. Remember, there are other ways to serve God. If you go on a full-time mission, make sure it is the right thing *for you*!

Full-time missions are incredibly difficult and no one should be called to go, or accept a call to go, who is not prepared and going for the right reasons. If you are old enough to go on a mission, you are old enough to make your own decision. Don't let anyone force you to go if you are not ready. Don't let anyone or anything *prevent* you from going if you are ready! I had great fears that I would not be permitted to go on a mission because of my past, but I was determined to do whatever I had to do to go. I had to wait 18 months just to turn in my mission papers while I continued to repent and correct those things in my life that were out of line. Then, for another six months, I had to go through numerous interviews with my bishop and stake president. I had to go to a psychologist and special medical doctors. I even had to be interviewed by a General Authority! But I persevered for two long years and overcame all obstacles in my path. When I received my mission call, I was ready. Make sure you are ready also.

> *We do not wish a man to enter on a mission, unless his soul is in it.* (Discourses of Brigham Young, *p. 322*)

Many people simply do not understand how important it is that missionaries are properly prepared, worthy, and capable of fulfilling a full-time mission. In October 1993, the First Presidency issued new, more specific instructions concerning who should and should not be sent on full-time missions. Due to the importance of this directive, and since so few people seem to understand the specific qualifications required to be worthy of the privilege of serving a mission, I have decided to reprint the full text of this directive in order to inform all parents, prospective missionaries, and priesthood leaders.

THE CHURCH OF JESUS CHRIST OF LATTER-DAY SAINTS
OFFICE OF THE FIRST PRESIDENCY
SALT LAKE CITY, UTAH 84150

March 4, 1993

To:  General authorities; Regional Representatives; Stake, Mission, and District Presidents; Bishops; and Branch Presidents

Dear Brethren:

*Full-time Missionary Service*

# Becoming a Great Missionary

Full-time missionary service is not a right, but a privilege for those who are called through inspiration by the First Presidency. Missionary service is for the benefit of the Lord and His Church to fulfill His purposes. Its objective is not primarily the personal development of an individual missionary, although righteous service invariably produces that result.

To assist you in fulfilling your heavy priesthood responsibility to recommend worthy and qualified individuals for full-time missionary service, we provided the accompanying policies, which re-emphasize and clarify long-established principles. These policies will also help orient and prepare youth for missions. Please review the suitability of potential full-time missionary candidates by carefully considering these policies before submitting a recommendation for missions.

We are grateful for the unselfish response of those who prepare themselves to be spiritually, physically, emotionally, and morally qualified to be called as full-time missionaries. We thank you for your generous, devoted service in strengthening the Church and proclaiming the gospel.

Sincerely your brethren,
Ezra Taft Benson
Gordon B. Hinckley
Thomas S. Monson
The First Presidency

**March 1993**
**Policies Related to Full-Time Missionary Work**
For General Authorities; Regional Representatives; Stake, Mission, and District Presidents; Bishops; and Branch Presidents

As priesthood leaders, you have the sobering responsibility to help identify and prepare worthy, qualified individuals for the sacred responsibility of full-time missionary service. Additionally you have the privilege of inspiring youth to resist the evils that surround them and to live worthy, exemplary lives. The following policies, based upon previously emphasized, long-established principles, are provided to assist you in these heavy responsibilities:

**Emotional Stability:** Candidates recommended for missionary service who have previously had significant emotional challenges must be stabilized, confirmed to be fully functional, and not totally dependent on medication for emotional disabilities prior to submitting their recommendation for missionary service.

**Moral Worthiness:** Individuals who have established a predatory pattern of repeated serious moral transgressions are not acceptable for missionary service.

To ensure the requisite worthiness, an individual who has committed serious transgression must have fully repented according to the criteria established by the Savior. The candidate must be completely worthy to enter the temple before being recommended for missionary service. Please confirm that the individual is free of transgression for sufficient time to manifest true repentance and to prepare spiritually for a sacred mission call. This period could be as long as three years for multiple serious transgressions, and should not be less than a year from the most recent transgression.

**HIV Positive:** Individuals who have become HIV positive will not be called and alternate methods of Church service should be suggested.

**Divorce:** Persons 19 to 26 who have been divorced are not called to serve as full-time missionaries.

**Other:** Our hearts are touched by those who are struggling with serious physical, mental, and emotional problems, who feel an obligation to complete full-time proselyting missionary service. Missionary work is extremely demanding and is not suitable for persons whose serious physical limitation, mental handicap, or emotional disability prevent them from qualifying for the demanding rigors of full-time missionary life. Moreover, significantly limited missionaries place unfair and often unreasonable demands on their mission leaders and companions, reducing their effectiveness and spiritual development.

Please communicate to individuals with serious physical, mental, and emotional limitations, our gratitude for their desire to be called. Explain that because of their circumstance, they are honorably excused from full-time missionary service for their benefit as well as to avoid undue demands on missionary companions. We are confident bishops and stake presidents will be inspired to find meaningful local opportunities for these choice individuals to experience the joy of service and personal growth compatible with their individual condition.

**Special Circumstances:** Individuals involved in any of the following situations will not be called on full-time missions and should be encouraged to accept other meaningful opportunities to serve in the Church locally.

*Abortion.* Young men who have encouraged, paid for, or arranged for an abortion resulting from their immoral conduct will not be called on full-time missions. Sisters who submit to abortions growing out of their immoral conduct will not be called on full-time missions.

*Child out of wedlock.* If a prospective missionary has fathered or given birth to a child out of wedlock, regardless of whether there is any current legal or financial responsibility for the child, he or she will not be called on a full-time mission.

# Becoming a Great Missionary

*Homosexual activity.* If a prospective missionary was victimized or participated in early-age experimentation and if there is no current indication of homosexual tendencies, the candidate may be considered for missionary service.

Homosexual tendencies can be contained. Homosexual activity can be forgiven through sincere repentance. If the candidate has participated in homosexual acts *during or after* the last three teen-age years, he or she would not be considered for missionary service unless there is strong evidence of complete repentance and reformation, with at least one year free from transgression.

Please carefully consider each potential full-time missionary candidate using these policies before submitting a recommendation. Such review will avoid the devastating feelings that would result if a recommendation were returned for failure to meet these standards.

**As a bishop, branch, stake, or mission president, should you discern unusual circumstances or situations judged to warrant consideration of an exception, they may be submitted for consideration by the First Presidency.**

Please caution candidates that to qualify for the needed guidance of the Spirit, resolution of transgressions must be made prior to entering the mission field. Further, every case of a missionary found to have entered the mission field without resolving serious worthiness concerns with the bishop and stake president will be reviewed by General Authorities. Unless there are unusually extenuating circumstances, the missionary will be returned home.

THE CHURCH OF JESUS CHRIST OF LATTER-DAY SAINTS
OFFICE OF THE FIRST PRESIDENCY
SALT LAKE CITY, UTAH 84150

October 21, 1993

To: General authorities; Regional Representatives; Stake, Mission, and District Presidents; Bishops; and Branch Presidents

Dear Brethren:

Full-time Missionary Service

Our March 4, 1993, letter on full-time missionary service reemphasized long-established principles and also provided counsel to orient and prepare youth for missions.

We sincerely appreciate the efforts each of you has made to implement this counsel. The results have been most encouraging.

The accompanying procedures will also help to further clarify the direction to be followed to assist missionaries called since the issuance of the earlier letter.

Sincerely your brethren,
Ezra Taft Benson
Gordon B. Hinckley
Thomas S. Monson
The First Presidency

## 14 October 1993
## Implementation of the First Presidency Letter on Full-Time Missionary Service

For General Authorities; Regional Representatives; Stake, Mission, and District Presidents; Bishops; Branch Presidents

On 4 March 1993 the First Presidency issued a letter on full-time missionary service to reemphasize long-established principles and to correct increasing departure from those principles. It was also to be used to orient and prepare youth for missions. **While the letter notes that some First Presidency approved exceptions may be warranted, the integrity of the principles it communicates must be maintained by prayerful, consistent application of the policies set forth therein. Unwarranted exceptions will undermine this effort to adhere to long-standing principles of worthiness.**

The First Presidency has established the following procedures to clarify how that policy letter should be administered to missionaries called since its issuance. They are intended to provide guidelines within which priesthood leaders may act in harmony with the Spirit.

All missionary recommendations must be rigorously reviewed to assure full compliance with the requirements of the First Presidency letter. Do not knowingly make exceptions to these policies.

Candidates who have resolved serious transgressions according to policy need not receive a General Authority clearance before they are recommended for missionary service. (This modifies the statement on special clearances on page 7-1 of the *General Handbook of Instructions*.)

**Belated confessions:** The First Presidency letter states, "Every case of a missionary found to have entered the mission field without resolving serious worthiness concerns with the bishop and stake president will be reviewed by General Authorities. Unless there are unusually extenuating circumstances, the missionary will be returned home."

A belated confession occurring in the mission field is handled by the mission president with his Area Presidency. If it is decided that the missionary should return home (there were no "unusually extenuating circumstances"), the mission president will coordinate the return with the Missionary Department. The department will then advise the home stake president for a missionary serving in the United States and Canada. The Area Presidency will advise the home stake president for missionaries serving elsewhere. (This policy supercedes instructions on belated confessions in the *General Handbook of Instructions* and the *Mission President's Handbook*.)

**Possible return to the mission field:** A stake president may recommend to the Missionary Department that an individual sent home after a belated confession return to the mission field after having "fully repented," but this must not be "less than a year from the most recent transgression." All other requirements of the First Presidency letter must also be met. Such a recommendation must include an explanation of why it is considered justified.

**Emotional or physical disability:** A missionary overcome by a disabling emotional or physical challenge in the field that prevents effective missionary service will be returned home for treatment. When the bishop and stake president have confirmed (from written evaluation by competent medical authority and their own thorough review) that the individual qualifies, a recommendation for return to the mission field can be submitted. If evaluation indicates the individual qualifies for missionary service, the Missionary Executive Council will reassign the missionary. Should the individual later fail to withstand the demands of missionary service he or she will be given an honorable release.

**Request for exception:** The First Presidency letter states: "Should you discern unusual circumstances or situations judged to warrant consideration of an exception, they may be submitted by the stake or mission president for consideration by the First Presidency." Any request for exception should include the specific details considered to warrant its approval. The following circumstance is one that is deemed appropriate for consideration by the First Presidency:

(a) The potential missionary was the parent of a child born out of wedlock, (b) the child was placed for adoption, and (c) the candidate has satisfied all financial obligations and otherwise completely fulfills the conditions of the First Presidency letter.

> **Missionaries Called Before 4 March 1993:**
> Missionaries who received their mission calls prior to the 4 March 1993
> First Presidency letter will be allowed to serve without applying the new
> criteria.
>
> *(Reprinted from Missionary Preparation, Religion 130, pp. 16–19.)*

Although it may seem that I have emphasized the reasons *not* to go on a mission, let me make it clear that I believe what the Prophet Spencer W. Kimball taught: *all* worthy young men [and I would add all worthy *couples*], should be preparing to serve full-time missions:

> *Again the Lord answers the question: "And that every man should take righteousness in his hands and faithfulness upon his loins, and lift a warning voice unto the inhabitants of the earth; and declare both by word and by flight that desolation shall come upon the wicked." (D&C 63:37)*

> *Did you note that said "every man," and every boy that is becoming a man? Of course, we do not send a young man steeped in uncleanness and sexual or other sins. Certainly such a one would need to be cleansed by deep repentance before he could be considered. And so we repeat it: Every LDS male who is worthy and able should fill a mission. (Spencer W. Kimball, "Planning for a Full and Abundant Life," General Conference Address, April 6, 1974)*

## Finding Yourself

If you're on your mission now and you came out unprepared or came for the wrong reasons . . . what do you do now? Hopefully it won't come to the point of deciding to go home, but decisions *must* be made, and you are the only one who can make them! You can either choose to find yourself—your true self—or you can continue your charade of being a missionary and cause harm to yourself and every companion with whom you serve. You can either find out for yourself if the Gospel is really true, or you can continue in your hypocrisy: teaching others about something in which you, yourself, do not believe. You can either decide to be a man and face up to BIG decisions and BIG challenges, or you can continue to be a child, led around by others and simply doing what you are told, or perhaps continue to be disobedient as a way of showing your independence in a situation in which you really do not want to be.

You can see how it is. Men make decisions and then have the courage to stick by them, take the consequences for them—good or bad—and know that the course they travel in life is of their own making. Children are afraid to make tough decisions, so they let others make the decisions for them, either directly or by default as a result of their inability or unwillingness to make these decisions themselves.

If you find yourself on a mission unprepared and unsure of your own beliefs, then you need to decide to find out for yourself if the gospel is true. This seems to be a simple enough decision to make, but as all who have gone through the process know for themselves, it takes a lot of hard work to find out the truth for oneself. But there it is—you must do whatever it takes to find out the truth for yourself! And how do you do this? You're a missionary! Do exactly what you have been teaching others to do. Read the Book of Mormon and then follow Moroni's promise to pray and receive an answer from God. If you learn nothing else from this process, you will learn this one principle: God does answer prayers! There is a reason that the Prophet of God has directed all people to find the truth through this process of reading the scriptures and then praying to know if they are true—because it works! Just like a scientific experiment that can be replicated time and time again, this process, this "experiment," will work every time it is tried. So do for yourself what you ask others to do! Find out for yourself if the gospel is true. Once you do this, everything will change. The following words of wisdom come from Elder Boyd K. Packer in a talk given to new mission presidents on 25 June 1982:

> There is something else to learn. A testimony is not thrust upon you; a testimony grows. We become taller in testimony like we grow taller in physical stature; we hardly know it happens because it comes by growth. It is not wise to wrestle with the revelations with such insistence as to demand immediate answers or blessings to your liking. You cannot force spiritual things. Such words as compel, coerce, constrain, pressure, and demand do not describe our privileges with the Spirit. You can no more force the Spirit to respond than you can force a bean to sprout, or an egg to hatch before it's time. You can create a climate to foster growth, nourish, and protect; but you cannot force or compel: you must await the growth.
>
> Do not be impatient to gain great spiritual knowledge. Let it grow, help it grow, but do not force it or you will open the way to be misled.
>
> It is not unusual to have a missionary say, "How can I bear testimony until I get one? How can I testify that God lives, that Jesus is the Christ, and that the gospel is true? If I do not have such a testimony, would that not be dishonest?" Oh, if I could teach you this one principle. A testimony is to be found in the bearing of it! Somewhere in your quest for spiritual knowledge, there is that "leap of faith," as the philosophers call it. It is the moment when you have gone to the edge of the light and stepped into the darkness to discover that the way is lighted ahead for just a footstep or two. "The spirit of man," as the scripture says, indeed "is the candle of the Lord." (Proverbs 20:27) It is one thing to receive a witness from what you have

# Becoming a Great Missionary

*read or what another has said; and that is a necessary begin-*
*ning. It is quite another to have the Spirit confirm to you in*
*your bosom that what you have testified is true. Can you not see*
*that it will be supplied as you share it? As you give that which*
*you have, there is a replacement, with increase!*

*To speak out is the test of your faith. Bear testimony of the*
*things you hope are true, as an act of faith. It is something of*
*an experiment, akin to the experiment that the prophet Alma*
*proposed to his followers. We begin with faith—not with a per-*
*fect knowledge of things. That sermon in the thirty-second*
*chapter of Alma is one of the greatest messages in holy writ, for*
*it is addressed to the beginner, to the novice, to the humble*
*seeker. And it holds a key to a witness of the truth.*

*The Spirit and testimony of Christ will come to you for the most*
*part when, and remain with you only if, you share it. In that*
*process is the very essence of the gospel. (*Ensign, *Jan. 1983,*
*51–56)*

Even if you fail to get the answers everyone expects you to obtain, at least you have an answer with which you can make additional decisions! If you find out that there is no God and the gospel
is not true, you can decide to return home with full confidence that
you made the right decision, based upon *your* own efforts instead of
simply relying on others. I can make this statement without fear because in my twenty-plus years of missionary work I have never once
seen the process fail! If I can get anyone to finally take the time and
make the effort to seek the truth for themselves, God will answer
their prayers. The process works!

If you find yourself on a mission for the wrong reasons, you
must go through a similar process of coming to the point of making
BIG decisions for yourself. For example, if you came out on a mission with a serious girlfriend, you must make a very difficult decision

concerning what to do with that relationship now that you are on your mission. If you want to be a great missionary, you must find a way to put that relationship on hold. This means that you *change* your relationship so that you can focus on the work of the Lord. This may mean that you no longer write to each other or cut down on your letter writing to once a month. No phone calls or weekly care packages from anyone but your extended family. I think you get the picture. If a girlfriend is distracting you then you must do whatever it takes to prevent that distraction from occurring. Will this mean that your relationship will be destroyed forever? Who knows? You must trust God and yourself! If, after two years, you find yourself still attracted to the one you left behind, then good. If not, God will provide another who will completely fill that need. Is this difficult to do? Of course! But so what? You are now a man, expected to make tough decisions and bear the weight of those decisions like a man. And no matter how it all comes out in the end, one thing is sure—you will become a better person, a stronger and more capable adult for having made those tough decisions when you had to rather than simply continuing to "go along" and in the process never growing up, never having the courage to make tough decisions, and remain a lukewarm and ineffective missionary for two years! What kind of husband and father will you be when you do get home and marry her? I shudder to think of it!

> *Nothing you do as a missionary should get in the way of your important message: not your dress, you hair length, or your attitude; not your deportment; and not your girlfriend at home. I do not wish to be insensitive to the natural affections between a fine young man and a lovely young woman. However, if a missionary receives a letter from his girlfriend stating that her affections for him have changed (we used to call that a "Dear John" letter; some of us have gotten those), I commend the good counsel given some years ago by Elder LeGrand Richards, who*

# Becoming a Great Missionary

said, "There's a new group of girls every year! And the new group is just as good as the old group." (James E. Faust, "What I Want My Son to Know Before He Leaves on His Mission," General Conference Address, 6 April 1996)

If you find yourself on a full-time mission unprepared and for the wrong reasons, there is a way to make something of yourself. It is not easy, and it is much more difficult than it would have been had you made these same decisions *before* you left on a mission, but it works nonetheless. The sooner you find the courage to make these tough decisions, the better off you will be, and the more time you will have to make a difference in the lives of those you are there to serve.

But how does this relate to finding your true self? It works this way. All of us have extraordinary talents and abilities, character traits and qualities that are a part of us because of the fact that we are children of God. Unfortunately, there is only one way for us to find out what these traits are—we must be placed in the fires of adversity and overcome challenges.

I took a class in pottery one year in high school. I was always amazed at how much the pottery changed after it was fired in the kiln. We would paint glazes on the outside of the pottery. The pots always looked dull and plain before we put them in the oven, but after they had been fired for several hours they came out with blazing colors and depths of texture that completely changed the pottery. The same is true for our character traits. As youth and as untried and untested adults, we often look plain and seem dull of spiritual qualities. But something miraculous happens to every person who is tried in the fires of life, their true character traits and talents come to the surface.

Finally, there is one more point I want to make. Like the fable of the tortoise and the hare, it is the slow and steady that wins the race. It is those who are quietly faithful *every day* who are the true servants of God.

> I observed that "the race was not to the swift, nor the battle to the strong," neither riches to men of wisdom. . . . I could place my hand upon many in this congregation, who will win the race, though they are not very swift, for outward appearance, and they make no great pretensions; they are found continually attending to their own business. They do not appear to be great warriors, or as if they were likely to win the battle. But what is their true character? They have faith today, they are filled with faith, their words are few, but they are full of integrity. You will find them tomorrow as they were yesterday, or are today. Visit them when you will, or under what circumstances, and you find them unalterably the same; and finally when you have spent your life with them, you will find that their lives throughout have been well spent, full of faith, hope, charity, and good works, as far as they have had the ability. These are the ones who will win the race, conquer in the battle, and obtain the peace and righteousness of eternity. (Discourses of Brigham Young, p. 230)

# Becoming a Great Missionary

# Two
## Starting Out Right

After you receive your mission call, it's important that you start out right. Hopefully, you have already had one or two experiences in sharing your testimony with nonmembers. Some, especially those living in the mission field, have had lots of opportunities to split with the missionaries and participate in teaching a discussion prior to leaving on their own missions. After receiving your mission call, it is time to consolidate all that you have learned from your parents, your teachers, and your own study of the gospel. When you go into the Missionary Training Center, they do not teach you the gospel—you should already know that. They teach you how to teach the gospel in an effective manner. When you are in the mission field, even though you will learn more about God and how the Spirit works than you ever thought possible, that knowledge comes as a result of the work you have been called to do. You are not sent out to learn. You are sent out to teach. But as every teacher knows, the teacher always learns more than those whom he teaches.

## Becoming a Great Missionary

## Preparing Missionaries *Before* They Go

As we have already discussed, it is important for all missionaries to be prepared *before* they ever leave on their mission. By the time young men find themselves in the Missionary Training Center, it is too late to *prepare* to go on a mission! This preparation *must* start when they are children, by loving parents who desire to fulfill their obligation to teach their children the doctrines of the Kingdom of God,[1] and the steps they should take to lead a faithful and productive life.

> *I am asking for missionaries who have been carefully indoctrinated and trained through the family and the organizations of the Church, and who come to the mission with great desire. I am asking for better interviews, more searching interviews, more sympathetic and understanding interviews, but especially that we train prospective missionaries much better, much earlier, and much longer so that each anticipates his mission with great joy. (Spencer W. Kimball,* Regional Representatives Seminar, *April 4, 1974)*

One major purpose of this book is to give parents, prospective missionaries, and priesthood leaders a better understanding of what kind of person makes a great missionary. As Spencer W. Kimball once put it: We don't want any more "scrubs" in the mission field! We want prepared, fully qualified, and worthy missionaries to serve in the Army of the Lord!

> *When I ask for more missionaries, I am not asking for more scrubs or mentally disturbed missionaries, or more testimony-barren missionaries, or more immoral missionaries. I am asking that we start earlier and train our missionaries better in every*

---

[1] Doctrine and Covenants 68:25.

*branch and every ward in the world. (Spencer W. Kimball,*
Regional Representatives Seminar, *April 4, 1974)*

## *Homesickness*

One of the problems that arises right at the start is homesickness. Many missionaries are away from home for the first time, experiencing this feeling of homesickness for the first time, which can be powerful and debilitating. It will distract them from what they have to learn in a short time and, most importantly, it will make them lose their focus—they will forget why they came in the first place.

The best solution to this problem is to make sure that the missionary has been away from home before. Send him away to school or somewhere where he has to physically live away from home. Send him to an out-of-state relative and let him work for six months or some other meaningful length of time. The most important thing is to send him *away from home* where he will be *on his own.* Then when he begins to have problems with homesickness, he can learn to deal with these feelings in an atmosphere that is not as stressful.

I was fortunate to have four sons go on full-time missions. Three seemed to have no problem with homesickness. One left home at 17 to join the Marines, another had lived in another state going to college, and one had not been away from home for any length of time but had always had an independent spirit and so had no problem saying "so long" to his family. However, there was one who did have trouble. He was sensitive, kind, introverted, and shy and had seldom been away from home for any length of time. Fortunately, we had always strongly believed in the importance of making our children independent and able to stand on their own two feet. So, as soon as we could, we arranged to send him away to

## Becoming a Great Missionary

school. The school was less than two hours away, and he easily could have driven to school every day, but we knew how important it was to have our children feel as though they were "on their own." So despite the extra cost, we made him live at school in the dorms. It was clearly going to be a struggle. We dropped him off on Saturday morning with all of his stuff, and he drove home the very next day. For some time he came home every weekend, but each time we would gently try to convince him to stay at school and find things to do and people to do them with. It was a struggle for a month or so just to get him to stay at school, but slowly, over time, he began to feel confident about being away from home and on his own. Not long afterward, he received his mission call. How grateful we were to have had the insight to send him away from home! When he got to the Missionary Training Center, he could smile with knowing understanding at all his fellow missionaries who were struggling with homesickness. While they fought with their feelings and lived day-to-day trying to get thoughts of home out of their heads, he was able to focus and get down to the business of learning to be a missionary. It made all the difference.

## The Missionary Training Center

After entering the Missionary Training Center, and after all the tears have been shed and the goodbyes have been said, it is time to focus. I wonder how many of you have ever truly focused on something all consuming, something life changing. As a convert to the gospel, I had already been through that powerful process and understood how much energy and concentration it takes. The Missionary Training Center is the Church's boot camp. It is a pressure cooker where they force-feed you the Spirit of God until it seeps out of every pore of your body. It is a time machine where you will process a year's worth of learning in one month and learn not only a language but also a lifestyle in two months. Is it hard? Yes, it is one of the most difficult things you will ever do. But so what? Are you a man or a mouse? You are a man and it is time to stand up, pull your shoulders back, and bear the weight that comes with being a man. You think the Marines are tough? Well, God is looking for the few good men among the few good men. God expects you to "choose the right" and wants you to "put your shoulder to the wheel;" you are "Christian soldiers marching as to war" and "are all enlisted 'til the conflict is o'er." It is time to say, "O Babylon, O Babylon, we bid thee farewell." It is time "to seek out the righteous where-e'er they may be."

It is time to focus. It is time to take seriously a serious call. It is time to leave behind the slap and tickle of the locker room, the loud laughter of high school and college friends, and the safe haven of parents and home. It is time to be men of God and that always starts with obedience.

1. *Obey the rules.*

The Missionary Training Center has rules and they are there for a reason. If you break them, you only hurt yourself. The great men and women who are called to run this "boot camp" have confidence and power beyond your understanding. They have seen slackers come and go, and they will be there long after the slackers have squandered the opportunity of a lifetime. It is called commitment. It is called will power. It is called having, perhaps for the first time in your life, the determination to do what is right because it is right. And as you do so, your spiritual muscles will gain strength (you have to run and not be weary!), the power of your intellect will be expanded (you have to learn all those discussions!), and, most importantly, the conduit of your eternal soul will connect with the powers of heaven (you will be teaching *adults* how to live correctly!) and the dews of eternal knowledge will fall upon you and fill you with confidence and peace.

   *2. Set some goals.*

I have never been one to set goals. In many cases I feel it is pretentious and a waste of time. But I did set goals on my mission: a few small goals and one big goal. I was fortunate to attain all of them before I came home. Now is the time to set those goals. Everyone is different and there is no way I could possibly presume to tell you what goals you should set. But I do know you need to set them! Let me share mine with you for what it's worth.

My goals were set after my mission call and before entering the Missionary Training Center. During that time, I was visiting a friend in Provo, and we had gone to the temple grounds to talk. He was a returned missionary whom I respected, and I wanted to gather as much information from him as I could. Most of what he told me I do not remember, but one thing stuck in my mind. He told me of a missionary who had become so sensitive to the Spirit of God that he was able to know where he should go to find people to teach. He was able to kneel in prayer and receive direct revelation as to where to go and what to do! It captured my imagination and I began to think about what kind of missionary I wanted to become. What did I want to accomplish during those two years? After much thought and prayer, I came up with these four goals (yes, only four!) that I wanted to accomplish on my mission:

   A.  Learn the discussions within one month (i.e., I would be able to "pass off" my discussions within one month of being on my mission). I completed this goal a couple of days ahead of schedule.

B. Slowly begin to get up earlier and earlier until I was able to start my day at 5:00 a.m. As a teenager, I worked during the summers putting shingles on roofs. During hot weather, it was best to get up early, while it was still cool, and then quit when it got too hot to work. I enjoyed getting up early and had read that one of the prophets said that getting up early was conducive to receiving insight and revelation, so I decided to set that as a goal. Unfortunately, I had gotten out of the habit of getting up early. In addition, missionary work was much more tiring than I would have ever believed. However, I was able to accomplish this goal after about three months.

C. I would become a "real" missionary by six months. This goal is a little harder to define. I had in my mind a "picture" of what I thought a missionary should be, and I wanted to be that missionary after six months. In my mind, a missionary knew all the discussions so well that he could be distracted by an idea or concept, or problem brought up by the investigator (which often happens when teaching) and be able to deal with that issue and come right back to the discussion without missing a beat. A real missionary knows his scriptures well enough to answer most questions asked by those he is teaching without fumbling or hesitation. A real missionary is a professional, prepared and ready for anything. I also met this goal. God even sent me a sign to let me know that I was, in fact, the kind of missionary I wanted to be: at six months I was called to be a senior, training companion.

D. I wanted to be led directly by the Spirit of the Lord to those who were ready, as my friend in Provo had described. I was able to reach this goal after being on my mission one year. I will talk more about obtaining this marvelous goal later.

Three of my goals were very simple and reachable, but the last made me stretch, and, to tell the truth, I always had doubts about obtaining it. You also need to make sure that most of your goals are

# Becoming a Great Missionary

simple and obtainable, or you will set yourself up for two years of disappointment. But you also need to set one or more so high that they seem unreachable and then let God and time sort them out.

## The Mission Home

The first stop for most missionaries once they arrive in the mission field is the mission home. This is where the mission president and his family live and is often where the mission office is located. The mission home is the "eye of the hurricane" of the mission. Once you have left the Missionary Training Center, there are things you can do to start off on the right foot. Here are a few:

*1. Start at once, don't wait.*

Most missionaries are sent from the Missionary Training Center with the admonition to teach someone on the way to the mission home. Let me suggest that you do just that. If you're going to be a missionary, then be a missionary! Why wait? You have to start some time! Many will have already tasted the joy of teaching the gospel before they leave on their missions. There is fear—there is almost always fear—but faith overcomes fear. So use the faith you have brought with you and open your mouth and teach! Even if you try several times only to get shut down, you will have the confidence that comes from just getting started. The hardest part of every journey is that first step. Take your first step on your way to the mission field and you will be way ahead of the curve.

I was fortunate, twice. On the plane to Pennsylvania, I sat next to a lady whom I approached about the gospel. We ended up talking for about 30 minutes, and I was able to get her name and address to send to the missionaries who served her area. After arriving at the mission home, and after all the pre-interviews with the mission president were over, the new missionaries were asked if anyone wanted to go out and tract that night. I was the only one who raised his hand, so I went out with one of the assistants and tracted for about an hour or so. God opened a door that night and we taught a first discussion. While all the others were back at the mission home unpacking and resting from the long flight from Utah, I was in a stranger's home teaching the gospel. It was just one of the many things that made a difference.

2.   *Be open and honest in the interview.*

The one person who will have the most impact on you throughout your mission will be the mission president. It is he who chooses the areas in which you will work, the companions you will have, and the leadership positions you will hold. If he does not have a full understanding of who you are and what you are like, it will adversely affect your whole mission. He will base all his decisions on what he knows about you. If you have misled him about anything, or if you have refused to disclose an important aspect of your life or personality, then every decision he makes about you will be based upon a lie. The path you end up taking will not be the path you should have taken. Instead of matching you with companions who will build your character, or meet your needs, you will end up with companions who are at odds with you. Instead of sending you to areas that were prepared just for you, you will be sent to areas unprepared for you. Instead of calling you to leadership positions that enhance your natural talents, you will be called to positions that go against the grain. In the end, your fear of telling the truth, or of sharing problems, or even of sharing your goals and desires, will put road blocks in your path and leave you struggling your whole mission. If this does happen, it won't be the mission president's fault—it will be yours!

## Becoming a Great Missionary

On the other hand, if you are always open and honest with the mission president about everything—your problems, your fears, your goals, your hopes and desires—you will be giving to him one of the most important keys to your own success: knowledge. Knowledge is power and if your mission president knows you— really knows you—then he can use the priesthood authority he has been given to receive revelation directly for you—about where you should serve, with whom you should serve, and what callings you should have. Then God will truly be in charge of your mission, and everything you can be, and should be, as a missionary will be fulfilled.

## Learning the Scriptures

An important part of everyone's preparation for becoming a great missionary is to learn the scriptures, but there is a key to learning the scriptures properly and preparing oneself to use them in the work of God: ***God cannot draw from an empty well.***

Joseph Smith taught, and the scriptures clearly confirm, that God did not create the universe from nothing. Even God cannot create something out of nothing! All spirit and matter is as eternal as God himself and has always existed.[2] God did not *create* the universe, he *organized* it out of material that already existed. In other words, our Father in heaven is a God, not a magician. Using the very same concept, we can understand that God cannot draw from an empty well. Each of us has a well of talents and abilities that God will draw upon while we are in His service. However, if we lack the knowledge and talent to do a specific task, God cannot magically transform us into something we are not. For example, if you have

---

[2] D&C 93:33.

never read the scriptures, God cannot help you "bring them to mind" when you are teaching the discussions. In order for the Spirit of God to work within you and help you while teaching the Gospel, you must do your part by filling the well of your mind with the word of God.

*1. Read the Standard Works all the way through.*

The very first thing every missionary must do is to read the scriptures from beginning to end. All of them. From beginning to end. Read them like a novel instead of schoolwork or study. Start with Genesis 1:1 and read. Don't skip the dry parts; read it all from beginning to end. Then read the New Testament, the Book of Mormon, the Doctrine and Covenants, and the Pearl of Great Price. Read them all from beginning to end without stopping.

Then, and only then, should you begin your own personal study of the scriptures, which for every person is different because we all learn differently. Some people study by topic, some study concepts or themes. It really doesn't matter; it is up to you. However, the reason for reading the standard works from beginning to end is so you can fill up your well for the Lord. By reading all of the scriptures at least once, all the way through, you will fill the well of your mind with the words of God. Then if God chooses to inspire you, or if you need to call on God to help you teach a certain principle, God has something to draw on. *God cannot bring to your remembrance something you have not read!* Once you have filled your well with the word of God, when necessity requires it God can bring to your mind a remembrance of the specific scripture that you need.

> *But the Comforter, which is the Holy Ghost, whom the Father will send in my name, he shall teach you all things, and bring all things to your remembrance, whatsoever I have said unto you.* (John 14:26)

**37**

## Becoming a Great Missionary

*2.   Write it down.*

Whenever you receive an insight or inspiration concerning a doctrine or concept, write it down.[3] Preferably, write it in the margins of your scriptures or on paper or cards that you keep with your scriptures because you will need and use them again and again. There is nothing so frustrating as to be in a discussion and to forget that perfect scripture or principle that backs up what you are teaching. By *always* writing down this information, you will always be prepared. By the end of my mission, I had elaborate notes on every subject imaginable, and as I taught a discussion and sensed a person's specific need or the specific concept that would touch his soul, I could quickly turn to that scripture and hammer home the truth.

*3.   Scriptural helps.*

These instructions on how to enhance your study of the scriptures come from Howard W. Hunter.

♦   **Look for definitions of unfamiliar words or phrases.** Sometimes the scriptures use a particular word or phrase and then defines it.

♦   **Ask questions of the text.** Ask such questions as who, what . . . when, and where . . . How does this scripture apply to me right now?

♦   **Study antecedents and meanings.** Insert the antecedent (the word or phrase replaced by a pronoun) for its pronoun. For example: "And inasmuch as thy [Nephi's] brethren [Laman and Lemuel] shall rebel against thee [Nephi], they [Laman and Lemuel] shall be cut off from the presence of the Lord." (1 Nephi 2:21)

---

[3] ". . . for neglecting to write these things when God had revealed them, not esteeming them of sufficient worth, the Spirit may withdraw, and God may be angry . . ." (*Teachings of the Prophet Joseph Smith*, p. 73).

♦ **Substitute your own name.** Substitute your own name for that of the person being addressed.

♦ **Memorize.** Memorize the content and location of verses of scripture.

♦ **Recognize patterns.** The scriptures contain numerous patterns that illustrate and explain such principles as prayer (see Enos 1), faith and testimony (see Alma 32:27–43), judging (see Moroni 7:15–18), and revelation (see D&C 6; 8; 9).

♦ **Study author annotations.** Those who wrote the scriptures sometimes left the "story line" and inserted explanatory comments.

♦ **Mark scriptures.** Marking scriptures helps you remember where certain scriptures are located, arrange scriptures into related groups, follow certain topics, and so on. Ways to mark scriptures include underlining, outlining, shading, circling, and numbering.

♦ **Add notes to scriptures.** In the margins of your scriptures, write such things as cross references, references to stories or personal experiences applicable to certain verses and concepts, lists or short summaries of what is taught, or short quotes from modern prophets.

♦ **Use the study aids in the scriptures.** The LDS edition of the scriptures include such study aids as descriptive chapter headings, section introductions, footnotes and other explanatory notes, excerpts from the Joseph Smith Translation of the Bible (JST), Topical Guide, Bible Dictionary, gazetteer and maps, pronouncing guide for the Book of Mormon, and index. (Howard W. Hunter, *Missionary Preparation*, Religion 130 Institute Manual, p. 51)

## Write in Your Journal Every Day

You will experience unique events and spiritual highlights almost every day. I promise that there will be too many to remember so write them down in your journal. I'm sure this has been, or will be, drummed into you. So, just some words of advice:

*1. Keep it simple.*

When I returned from my mission, I put my journal on the shelf and it stayed there for some time. Then, when I found interest again in reading about the events of that time in my life, I was very disappointed with what I had written. Much of my journal had been written about my personal feelings of inadequacy or the spiritual struggles I was going through, instead of the specific events that had happened and the names of the specific people I had met or taught. As I read the journal, I remembered those struggles but since I had long ago moved on, and overcome, I was much more interested in remembering the events that happened and the people I had met. In this I was greatly disappointed. I had spent far too much time in introspection and not enough time on the simple day-to-day activities that had occurred and descriptions of the people I had met.

So, be simple and straightforward when writing in your journal. Spend your time writing specifically about what you did and who you saw rather than feelings about yourself and the personal struggles you were going through. Make sure you have a proper balance. Years from now you will be glad you did.

*2. Keep mementos.*

Every area to which you're assigned will provide you opportunities to acquire mementos that one day will become treasures. Be careful with letters, gifts, newspaper articles, pictures, etc. Send them home so they are not lost and after your mission take time to put them together in a scrapbook (or make them part of your journal). A picture says a thousand words. Sometimes it is easier to take a picture than it is to write about an event. Your mission is important

**40**

and it will have a profound affect upon the rest of your life. Take the time to document it!

## Keep the Mission Rules

Obedience is the first law of heaven. It is the key that unlocks every blessing available to the sons of God on earth. As this is true in life, it is doubly true while serving the Lord on a mission! God expects us to become perfect. This almost numbs the mind when we contemplate the magnitude of work and effort that goes with that injunction, but we *can* contemplate *one* principle or *one* law or commandment at a time. And as we create good habits, we become perfect in a few things. One of the best places to start is with your white missionary handbook and the rules contained therein. No matter how silly they may seem at times, those rules are there for a reason. They have been tried and proven to work over many years and carry with them great blessings.

> *When we use the term perfection, it applies to man in his present condition, as well as to heavenly beings. We are now, or may be, as perfect in our sphere as God and angels are in theirs, but the greatest intelligence in existence can continually ascend to greater heights of perfection.* (Discourses of Brigham Young, p. 89)

I promise you that the more perfectly you live the mission rules, the faster you will progress as a missionary, the more blessings you will receive, and the more power you will obtain to achieve the goals you have set. Miracles are the result of the power of faith and your faith will be nurtured and watered every time you obey. Faith comes a drop at a time (the dews from heaven), but when your glass is full you will have the power of the universe in your grasp! Many missionaries fail to obtain this power because it comes so slowly. It takes patience. It takes developing good habits and living the mission rules *every day.*

## Going the Extra Mile

President Hugh W. Pinnock used to talk about going the extra mile every day. He hammered it into us because it is while on the extra mile that miracles occur, as the priesthood flexes its muscles in the work of the Lord. Going the extra mile humbles us, which, in turn, makes us sensitive to the Spirit of the Lord, which, in turn, opens our minds and hearts to the possibilities of eternity. Let me give you a couple of examples of going the extra mile.

### 1. *Living the mission rules.*

If you remember, one of the goals I had for my mission was to get up every day at 5:00 a.m. The mission rules required missionaries to get up at 6:30 a.m., be out on the street at 9:30 a.m., and end work at 9:30 p.m. Was my goal out of line? Was it breaking the mission rules? No, I was attempting to go the extra mile and I had permission to do so. Getting up earlier had a purpose: it gave me 90 minutes more each day of personal study. Add this time to the other study time during the day and a missionary could spend up to four hours every day studying the scriptures in preparation for teaching God's children. That is over 20 extra hours per week. That works out to 2000 hours over the course of a mission! In this way, you will always be prepared for those you meet that day, and you will always have the answers to the questions people throw at you. Your personal well will be full to overflowing and God will be able to draw upon it without fear of it going dry.

*2. Working.*

Work is the lifeblood of a mission. The mission rules I served under required me to be working from 9:30 a.m. to 9:30 p.m. Most missionaries thought this was a starting and ending time for their work, but they were wrong! It should have been the starting and ending time for *teaching.* Instead of leaving the apartment at 9:30 a.m., we would leave at 9:00 a.m., so we would be knocking at the first door or teaching our first discussion at 9:30 a.m. At the end of the day, we would be knocking on our last door or teaching our last discussion at 9:30 p.m. That let us teach an additional 7 to 10 hours per week. That came to almost 1,000 hours over the course of my mission. Anyone can see, in a practical way, how that additional 1,000 hours would bring increased success. All by going the extra mile.

> President Ezra Taft Benson said, "One of the greatest secrets of missionary work is work. If a missionary works, he will get the Spirit; if he gets the Spirit, he will teach by the Spirit, he will touch the hearts of the people; and he will be happy. There will be no homesickness, no worrying about families, for all time and talents and interests are centered on the work of the ministry. That's the secret—work, work, work. There is no satisfactory substitute, especially in missionary work." (James E. Faust, Conference Report, *April 6, 1996*)

# The Purpose of Missionary Work: *To Warn*

One thing you need to remember as you prepare for your mission and as you read through this book is that the primary purpose of missionary work is to *warn* people about the second coming of Jesus Christ! It is to *warn* and to teach. What people do with the knowledge you give them is totally up to them. What did the Lord say?

# Becoming a Great Missionary

> *Hearken, O ye people of my church, saith the voice of him who*
> *dwells on high, and whose eyes are upon all men; yea, verily I*
> *say: Hearken ye people from afar; and ye that are upon the*
> *islands of the sea, listen together. For verily the voice of the*
> *Lord is unto all men, and there is none to escape; and there is*
> *no eye that shall not see, neither ear that shall not hear,*
> *neither heart that shall not be penetrated. And the rebellious*
> *shall be pierced with much sorrow; for their iniquities shall be*
> *spoken upon the housetops, and their secret acts shall be*
> *revealed. And the* voice of warning *shall be unto all people,*
> *by the mouths of my disciples, whom I have chosen in these last*
> *days. And they shall go forth and none shall stay them, for I*
> *the Lord have commanded them. (*D&C 1:1–5, *emphasis added)*

The simple truth is that every man, woman, and child has the
divine *right* to hear the gospel message and choose for themselves
whether or not to live it. As servants of God, we have the obligation
to *warn* and to teach but everything else is out of our hands.

> *The Gospel must be preached to the world, that the wicked may*
> *be left without excuse. It is necessary that all have the privilege*
> *of receiving or rejecting eternal truth that they may be prepared*
> *to be saved, or be prepared to be damned. (*Discourses of
> Brigham Young, *p. 319)*

What do God's servants do? They *warn*, they testify, they tell
people to repent. Does it matter whether or not the people listen?
NO. Does it matter whether or not people act upon what they hear?
NO. That is totally up to them; it is on their shoulders; it is their responsibility. Your responsibility is to *warn*. Your responsibility is to
lift up your voice and give people the *opportunity* to hear. That is all.
Everything else is gravy. How great will be your *joy* if you bring people to the Lord. But does it say you are condemned if you don't

have success? NO. That is not how it works. You are to serve your God, no matter where you are called, no matter how difficult the task, regardless of the success or failure you might achieve. If you teach a lot, good. If you baptize, even better. *But do your duty!* Do not whine, do not complain, and certainly do not shirk the responsibility given you by the Lord. Go and serve with all your might, mind, and strength and leave the rest up to the Lord.

> *Now, you cannot be responsible for whether or not those you teach will accept your testimony and join the Church. Do not feel that you must obtain a quota of baptisms to be successful. An old saying teaches that you can count the number of seeds in a single apple, but you can't count the number of apples in a single seed. The harvest is the Lord's. Your responsibility is to thrust in the sickle. (James E. Faust,* Conference Report, *April 6, 1996)*

## Seek and Cultivate the Gifts of the Spirit

As you progress in your ability to teach the gospel, it is totally appropriate to seek and develop gifts of the Spirit to help you in your work. In fact, it is your duty to learn what your personal talents and gifts are and to develop them to the best of your ability.[4]

> *Is it proper to seek for spiritual gifts? Should we plead with the Lord for the gift of prophecy, or of revelation, or of tongues? Is it fitting and right to pray for the soul-sanctifying privilege of seeing the face of the Lord Jesus while we yet dwell as mortals in a sin-filled world? Does the Lord expect us to desire and seek for*

---

[4] "Salvation cannot come without revelation; it is in vain for anyone to minister without it. No man is a minister of Jesus Christ without being a Prophet. No man can be a minister of Jesus Christ except he has the testimony of Jesus; and this is the spirit of prophecy." (*Teachings of the Prophet Joseph Smith,* p. 160).

"No man can receive the Holy Ghost without receiving revelations. The Holy Ghost is a revelator." (*Teachings of the Prophet Joseph Smith,* p. 328).

*spiritual experiences, or do the divine proprieties call for us
simply to love the Lord and keep his commandments, knowing
that if and when he deems it proper he will grant special gifts
and privileges to us?*

*Are we not commanded: Ask and ye shall receive; seek and ye
shall find; knock and it shall be opened? Why, then, should we
smother a desire to heal the sick or raise the dead or commune
with friends beyond the veil?*

*Also by way of answer to the queries at hand, we might with
propriety reason along this line: If spiritual gifts are interwoven
with and form part of the very gospel of salvation itself can we
enjoy the fullness of that gospel without possessing the gifts that
are part of it? If gifts and miracles shall—inevitably, always,
and everlastingly—follow those who believe how can we be true
believers without them? And if we are to seek the gospel, if we
are to hunger and thirst after righteousness, if our whole souls
must cry out for the goodness of God and his everlasting
association how can we exempt ourselves from seeking the gifts
of the Spirit that come from and prepare us for his presence?*

*"Ye are commanded in all things to ask of God, who giveth
liberally," the Holy word acclaims. Note the Lord's language:
We are commanded to seek the gifts of the Spirit; if we do not
do so, we are not walking in that course which is pleasing to
Him whose gifts they are.* (Bruce R. McConkie, A New
Witness for the Articles of Faith, p. 369)

Do not confuse the righteous desire to seek and obtain spiritual
gifts with "sign seeking." God wants and expects us to develop the
gifts of the Spirit for the purpose of spreading the gospel. If done
with an eye single to the glory of God, it is not only our right as
children of God, it is our duty as servants of God to use every
means at our disposal to push the work of God forward.

*To seek the gifts of the Spirit through faith, humility, and devotion
to righteousness is not to be confused with sign-seeking. The saints
are commanded to "covet earnestly the best gifts."* (1 Corinthians
12:31). *But implicit in this exhortation is the presumption that
those so seeking will do so in the way the Lord has ordained. For
instance, the gift of testimony is obtained through a course of desire,
study, prayer, and practice. Indeed, whenever a person abides the
law entitling him to receive a gift, that gift is then freely bestowed
upon him." (Bruce R. McConkie,* Mormon Doctrine, *p. 715).*

# Becoming a Great Missionary

# Three Companions

After the mission president and your relationship with him, the thing that will affect your mission the most will be your relationship with your companion. A good companion will push and inspire you to greater heights, while a bad companion can and will drag you down into a mire of slothful servitude. This is one of the reasons unprepared missionaries should not be sent out—they become a burden to their companions. Let's talk a little about good companions and bad companions and the difference between them.

## Section I: Bad Companions

Almost all missionaries will experience at least one companion with whom they do not get along. This is normal. But having a companion with whom you do not get along is not the same as having a bad companion! Part of being on a mission is learning how to get along with a stranger, even one who is very different from you. The fact that your companion is different (e.g., thinks differently, believes differently, acts differently) does not mean that your companion is bad. It just means that your companion is different. These differences are there so you can learn and develop into a more tolerant person. You may even be surprised to find that many of your differences will diminish over time. You will begin to accept and even adopt some of your companion's characteristics, and he, in turn, will take on some of yours. If you think about it, if you were to be paired with a companion who thought and acted exactly like you, what could you possibly learn? All of your faults, and we all have faults, would be magnified, and you would never have the opportunity to see how someone else lives, how someone else believes, how someone else relates to their God. You would remain shallow and small instead of growing into a well-adjusted, well-rounded, multi-faceted adult.

> *Judge not, that ye be not judged. Let no man judge his fellow being, unless he knows he has the mind of Christ within him. We ought to reflect seriously upon this point; how often it is said—"Such a person has done wrong, and he cannot be a Saint, or he would not do so." How do you know? We hear some swear and lie; they trample upon the rights of their neighbor, break the Sabbath by staying away from meeting, riding about the city, hunting horses and cattle, or working in the canyons. Do not judge such persons, for you do not know the design of the Lord concerning them; therefore, do not say they are not Saints. What shall we do with them? Bear with them. The brethren and sisters from the old countries frequently place great confidence in the American elders who have been their pastors, but some trifling thing occurs that does not appear right to them, and they say in a moment, "That Elder is not a Latter-day Saint." Judge no man. A person who would say another is not a Latter-day Saint, for some trifling affair in human life proves that he does not possess the Spirit of God. Think of this, brethren and sisters; write it down, that you may*

*refresh your memories with it; carry it with you and look at it
often. If I judge my brethren and sisters, unless I judge them by
the revelations of Jesus Christ, I have not the Spirit of Christ; if
I had, I should judge no man.* (Discourses of Brigham
Young, pp. 277–278)

So if a bad companion is not just someone who is different
from you, or one with whom you don't get along perfectly, then
what is a bad companion?

## How to become a bad companion

### 1. Refuse to work.

Perhaps the most identifiable characteristic of a bad companion
is his refusal to work. Instead of getting up and going out to tract or
visit members or go to discussions, he sleeps in and finds endless
excuses for not going to work. These actions prevent the work of
the Lord from going forward, and it prevents his companion from
going to work also. So, whatever negative karma is brought about by
one companion's failure to act properly is automatically doubled because of the effect on his companion.

### 2. Break the mission rules.

The second thing a bad companion does is consistently break the
mission rules. He stays up late, sleeps in late, watches TV, plays video
and board games, and participates in numerous activities that waste
time. A bad companion wastes his own mission with trivial pursuits
and, at the same time, places his companion in a purgatory of frustration as he tries to determine how best to spend his time in a productive way while being unable to go out to do the work to which he has
dedicated two years of his life. At its worst, this behavior leads to sin
and all the additional consequences associated with sin.

### 3. Bad beyond belief.

Occasionally you will have a missionary who goes beyond bad judgment. He leaves the mission, goes to the beach, dates, and generally wreaks havoc within his area. Unfortunately, this type of missionary can only be created with help. No missionary could get away with *serious* actions without the help and aid of his companion. In fact, this scenario is usually the result of two bad companions being put together (two dark stars collide!). Very seldom will stern admonitions from the mission president, changes in areas or companions, or any other form of punishment work to correct the problem. This type of missionary should be sent home.

## How to create a bad companion

### 1. Refuse to compromise.

Since almost all of your companions will be different from you, it will be natural for you to clash over day-to-day things: what area to work, what specific schedule to keep, what food to eat, etc. All such things are both normal and petty. All such things should be compromised and resolved so that both companions give a little and get a little. Bad companions can be created if *you* refuse to compromise, insist that your way is the only way, or try to browbeat or force issues to go *your* way. Arguing over such *petty* things is immature. You are on a mission to serve the Lord. All minor differences are simply a distraction and not worth your time and effort.

### 2. Be a Know-It-All.

Some elders come on their missions with large egos and great self-confidence, while others come out shy, introverted, and/or lacking in confidence. It is easy for the former type of elder to totally overpower the latter. One can constantly dominate, thereby leading the other to feel inadequate. One can feel a false sense of power while the other feels a false sense of humility that usually leads to depression. You can create a bad companion by not treating your companion as your equal.

Another form of this know-it-all attitude is believing that everyone must be the same—as though the gospel is a Jell-O mold and in order to live it correctly you must look and act a certain way. If our companion doesn't match the picture we have in our minds, we assume there must be something wrong with him. This is just false doctrine. God accepts all kinds of people into his kingdom, large and small, fat and skinny, black and white, introverts and extroverts, shy and bold, etc. The bottom line is that your companion can annoy you as much as he wants, but as long as he obeys the commandments and fulfills all the requirements God has set, he will get to heaven just as quickly as you.

> *It floods my heart with sorrow to see so many elders of Israel who wish everybody to come to their standard and be measured by their measure. Every man must be just so long, to fit their iron bedstead, or be cut off to the right length; if too short, he must be stretched, to fill the requirement. If they see an erring brother or sister, whose course does not comport with their particular ideas of things, they conclude at once that he or she cannot be a Saint, and withdraw their fellowship, concluding that, if they are in the path of truth, others must have precisely their weight and dimensions. The ignorance I see, in this particular, among this great people is lamentable. (*Discourses of Brigham Young, *p. 279)*

## 3. *Develop bad habits.*

Bad habits are like a cold; those close to you almost always get it too. If you permit yourself to live and develop bad habits, those habits will eventually infect your companion. The best way to create a bad companion is to be a bad companion.

# Becoming a Great Missionary

## The legacy of bad missionaries among the members

Bad missionaries affect everyone. We have discussed the effect of bad missionaries on their companions. It is appropriate to mention the other people they affect. Missionaries live and die according to the help they receive from the members of the ward or branch in which they work. If they are bad examples to the members, if they prove unworthy of the trust the members place in them, they will leave a negative legacy with long-lasting effects. For months, perhaps for years, the members will refuse to give referrals, refuse to go on splits, refuse to feed or help the servants of the Lord in any way—and for good reason! Their faith and trust has been destroyed by the action of unfaithful missionaries, unaware of the ripple effect of their acts. For this reason, missionaries should take care to set a good example at all times!

## What to do with a bad companion

Now that we have described what a bad companion is, it is time to talk about what to do with a bad companion. This is very difficult. First of all, you need to determine that the problems you are having with your companion are not just the normal differences that occur between companions. It must go beyond these differences and be to the point of being a detriment to the work. It is not enough just to have differences–a bad companion doesn't just complain or have strange habits, he must refuse to work or inhibit the work. Then something must be done.

### 1. Don't be afraid to tell.

One of the biggest problems that a mission president confronts is lack of information. We discussed how important it is to be truthful in your first interview with your mission president; being truthful about what is happening within your companionship is just as important. How can you expect the mission president to correct the problems that are occurring in the mission if he knows nothing of them? It is not only the right thing to tell the mission president about problems that are occurring, it is your priesthood duty! What is most important, our näive beliefs about "not telling" on someone or making certain the work of the Lord goes forward? If you know things about your companion or someone else in your district or zone that is hampering the work of the Lord, it is your duty to tell your mission president about it. He is the only one who can really deal with a bad missionary. Work with your mission president and lay the burden on him. He can also help you discern whether the problems you are having are things *you should* be working out between yourselves or whether they go beyond your responsibility. Differences of opinion should be worked out between yourselves, but where a missionary is willfully breaking the mission rules and causing havoc in his area or district, your duty is to inform your mission president of the situation. It is the mission president's responsibility to deal with these situations (poor guy!).

You are not part of a prison system where evildoers agree not to snitch on each other. You are part of the Lord's Army where truth is the banner and personal integrity is the flagpole. When I was on my mission, I had no problems, qualms, or hesitancy in talking to the president about what was going on in my life or anyone else's that made a difference in my mission life. I had made a commitment to serve the Lord. That meant that the Lord's work came first. It came before my own ego and problems, and it certainly came before any missionary who was not working toward the same goals as I. In any situation it is good to ask yourself: What is the worst that can happen? As I saw it, by my talking to the mission president the following things could take place: (1) I would be able to correct problems in my life that were standing in the way of my perfection as a Saint and my abilities as a missionary; (2) my companion would be forced to confront his own weaknesses and have the choice to reflect and change or choose to continue on the path he was following, and (3) others in the district would be confronted with the same choice—change and become better or continue to disobey and become hardened in a path that would not magnify.

Now is the time, and your mission is the place, to learn once and for all to choose between good and evil and to stand by your choice. Hiding behind a false sense of brotherhood by not wanting to tell about the improper actions of others is a sign that you are weak in this area. After all, where do you draw the line? What if the others were swimming or dating or leaving their mission—would any of these actions prompt you to tell on them? Yet all of these actions are damaging both to the missionary himself and to the work of the Lord in his area and the entire mission. Small indiscretions lead to larger and larger ones. Better to tell immediately, and get the problem corrected, than to let it go until it reaches a larger transgression.

Let me say it very clearly: You should not feel guilty about telling your mission president about things happening to you or your companion, nor should you hide the fact that you are going to speak to the mission president about something. Honesty and integrity go in both directions. You cannot hide what you or your companion is doing from the mission president any more than you should hide from your companion your intent to discuss the matter with the mission president. *Everything* should be up front and above board. No lies, no secrecy, no hidden agendas. If you feel guilty about performing this priesthood duty, it simply means that you have an incorrect understanding of your responsibilities as a missionary and priesthood holder. It also means you have an incorrect understanding of how the Kingdom of God works. The time will come when all things will be known about people. Every act performed, every mistake, every good deed will be made known. If this "uncovering" is a bad thing, why will God make us all go through this process? It is because it is actually good. When everything is known, it forces ourselves and others to face reality. It will force everyone to accept the judgments of God as just, because they will be self-evident to everyone. The reasons this kind of truth is considered bad "in the world" are that (1) people want to hide their sins, and (2) we cannot fully understand someone's actions unless we know all of the thoughts and events that led up to them—which only God can do. But the priesthood can bridge this world/heaven gap with the power of the Holy Ghost. We can both tell and hear the full truth because the Holy Ghost will help us put it in the proper perspective and understand what must be done. So, do what is right and what is good—and let the consequences follow.

Whatever you do, do not feel guilty about helping your mission president correct a bad situation. If anything, you should be happy that you were able to help correct a situation that was impeding the work of the Lord. The time will come when you will look for opportunities to cleanse the Lord's church. Angels will come to reap the earth and gather the wheat unto the Lord and burn the chaff. They will not second-guess their actions in cleansing the earth prior to the coming of the Lord. You should not second-guess the actions taken to cleanse the mission and push forward the work. Your only concern should be to keep yourself clean and above reproach and to work with all your heart in bringing to pass the Kingdom of God on earth. If your mind and eye are single to His glory, you never have to worry about the outcome.

> *God forbid that there should be any of us so unwisely indulgent,*
> *so thoughtless and so shallow in our affection for our children*
> *that we dare not check them in a wayward course, in*
> *wrong-doing and in their foolish love for the things of the*
> *world more than for the things of righteousness, for fear of*
> *offending them. (Joseph F. Smith,* Gospel Doctrine, p. 286)

One of the things you will learn is that there are times when you need to speak up about things that are wrong. As you grow spiritually, you will understand that there are times you must confront people and force them to deal with their problems. There is a reason the scriptures talk about "reproving betimes with sharpness,"[1] because as priesthood holders and spiritual leaders we are *supposed* to do this in order to correct and build the character of those whom we serve. You will have to do this with your investigators. You will need to show them where they have to change and repent. When done with love and the Spirit, there are few things more powerful or influential in a person's life than properly and lovingly correcting them and helping them to change.

*2.   Stop the problem before it starts.*

The real solution to the problem begins at home. Bad missionaries should never have been sent in the first place. It begins with parents who should be sensitive to the real needs and abilities of their children. It begins with realizing that when the Prophet says that every young man should go on a mission, he is just giving a general principle by which the Church should be guided—he doesn't really mean *every* young man should go on a mission. God forbid! It

---

[1] Doctrine and Covenants 121:43.

should be realized by parents and others that for those who are un-prepared to go on a full-time mission there are other ways for young men to serve in the Church

### 3. *Really, stop the problem before it starts!*

The second line of defense is priesthood leaders. They need to be open and honest with the young man and his parents about the wisdom of *not* sending a young man out on a mission who is unprepared or incapable of fulfilling one.

### 4. *Attitude is everything.*

When all else seems to have failed and you seem to be stuck with a companion whom you dislike, don't get along with, or who won't work as hard as you would like him to, the only thing you have left is your own attitude. Gaining a new, broader perspective can change your attitude about your situation, which, in turn, will change everything. This is hard for some to understand because most people can see the faults in others much easier than they see faults in themselves. It is natural to judge others based upon our own perspective of a situation (what other perspective do we have?). But what if *how* we look at things is wrong? What if we do not, or cannot, see the whole picture? What we need is called a paradigm shift—a shift in how we perceive things.

Psychologists use the concept of paradigm to explain how we trap ourselves into thinking "inside the box." We are raised with a certain set of beliefs, a certain way of looking at things. Right or wrong, these beliefs shape the way we see the world and color all our problems in a certain light. If we can learn to see "outside the box," we will be able to see and understand the truth more clearly. Let me tell you a story to illustrate.

## Becoming a Great Missionary

One day a woman was sitting in an airport waiting to board her plane. It was going to be a while, so she went to a small shop across the aisle and bought a bag of cookies. As she read her book, she began eating the cookies, which had been placed on the seat next to her. Suddenly, the man in the next seat reached over, took a cookie, and began eating it! The woman was shocked at the effrontery of this man—eating her cookies without even asking. Frustrated, but not wanting to be confrontational, she simply continued to read and eat her cookies. To her surprise and consternation, every time she took a cookie, the man next to her took one also. Each time she became more and more angry. Finally, there was *one* cookie left. She saw the man take it, break it in half, and eat "his" half of the cookie. This was the last straw! She was just about to give him a piece of her mind when the call came to board the plane. She decided that it just wasn't worth getting into a fight, so she boarded the plane.

Once she was on the plane, she just couldn't get what had happened out of her mind. That man had been so rude! And he hadn't even thanked her! To get her mind off this disturbing event, she opened her carry-on bag to get her book. To her surprise, there was the bag of cookies she had bought!

See how your perception of the man sitting next to this woman changes! All I had to do was add *one fact* to the story and *everything* changed. Suddenly this rude man became almost a Saint—sharing all of his cookies, even the very last one, with a stranger. All because one small bit of information was added. This is what is known as a "paradigm shift." It is the ability to change one's perspective of a situation by simply gaining more information.

Let me give you a couple of personal examples of how this paradigm shift happened to me—how by gaining a broader perspective of things my entire attitude about a situation was changed. The *event* or the *person* never changed at all, the only thing that changed was how I looked at things.

While serving as ward mission leader in Connecticut, a situation developed that drove me crazy. We were beginning to gain great success in our area. I had developed a program of working with the missionaries which was unique and very successful. As new missionaries came into our area, I trained them in how I wanted them to do things. Sometimes the new missionaries would fight a little about doing things my way, but after they saw how well things worked and how much success they themselves obtained, they fell in line. Everything ran like a well-oiled machine. There was only one problem. As time went on, the mission president began to transfer the missionaries in my area every few months. I would just get a missionary trained and he would transfer him! It became *very* frustrating. Finally, I confronted the mission president about this problem. I asked him (or should I say accused him) why he transferred "my" missionaries so quickly! What was he thinking? Then he explained, and his explanation changed everything. He said that my area had the most successful missionary program in the entire mission. He knew that I not only worked hand-in-hand with the missionaries but that I actually *trained* the missionaries! Because of this, he wanted to move as many missionaries through my area as possible so they could be trained in the way I did things. He said that as missionaries trained in my area were transferred to other areas of the mission, they took with them everything they learned and ended up increasing the success of every area of the mission!

## Becoming a Great Missionary

Instantly, this information from the mission president changed my whole perspective. His constant transferring of missionaries in my area was no longer a problem—it was a blessing! All of the frustration I felt was suddenly changed into feelings of excitement and joy. Where I had been dreading every change that took place, I began to look forward to the challenge of teaching every new missionary. Think about it; not one thing had actually changed, but my whole attitude about the situation was now completely different. With a simple change of attitude, frustration turned to excitement and challenge, hardship turned to great joy and accomplishment.

Another example of this happened with my eternal companion. For years after we were married my wife had a trait that drove me crazy—she would procrastinate. If she got an assignment or needed to do something, she would almost always put it off until the last minute. Instead of getting things done in a timely manner (as I would have done), she always seemed to be in a mad rush to get things done the day it was needed. She *always* made it on time and it was *always* done very well. It was just the mad dash at the end that drove me crazy. As most husbands do, I put up with this "character flaw" in my wife as I assume she did with me. Then one day everything changed.

As the wife of a ward mission leader, my wife was involved in almost all of my activities, including dinners for the missionaries. One day my wife got a call from the Relief Society president. The zone leaders had just called her and there had been a mix-up. They were holding a zone conference in our ward building the very next day and needed the building opened and dinner prepared for over 40 missionaries! The Relief Society president was having an anxiety attack and called my wife for help. My companion calmly said she would take care of it—and she did. To my utter amazement, she dashed around (as she usually did) and by the next day had everything prepared. It was great. The zone conference was held, everything went off without a hitch, and you would have thought that she had been planning and preparing for a week when, in fact, she had done it all in less than a day!

Suddenly my wife's "character flaw" had become a great asset. Her weakness had become strength. I could see how this same ability in my wife could be used in many crisis situations. Where others would give up in dismay or be intimidated by time or material constraints, my wife would calmly get things done.

This must be what the scriptures mean when they say that God will make our weaknesses strengths.[2] God does not take away our weaknesses. He *changes* them so that we can use them for good instead of ill. I never again judged my wife for things I thought were weaknesses. Instead, I learned to see beyond the immediate problem, to look for a broader perspective, and wait until I had *all* the information I needed to see things clearly. After a while, I was able to do this with my children as well. As parents, we know all too well what faults and weaknesses our children have (we live with them every day) and, as a result, we tend to judge them in a negative way because we assume that the problems we see are weaknesses that have to be corrected. Sometimes, no matter how hard we try, our children continue to have problems in the same areas, but I have learned not to rush to judgment about these things. In almost every case, what was once a weakness (in my eyes) turned into strength as they got older. Then, over time, I was able to develop the same

---

[2] Ether 12:27.

objective outlook to other people in the ward and the neighborhood and at work. As soon as I would begin to think ill of someone because of some perceived problem or weakness, I would stop and force myself to think "outside the box" concerning this person. Was this *really* a problem, or was I misjudging the situation due to a lack of information and perspective? My whole world has changed as a result of fully understanding this process. You can do the same.

## Section II: Good Companions

There is nothing more exciting and marvelous than working with a good companion. Much like a marriage, a good companionship will not just double the spiritual power of each but will magnify their power many times over. A united, loving, and hard-working companionship will excel in almost everything they do. And best of all, they will discover the true joy of serving the Lord with all their heart, mind, and soul.

### How to become a good companion

*1. Live the mission rules.*

Here we are again. Back to rule number one: Live the mission rules as perfectly as possible. It is the door to every success. By living the mission rules you will receive great blessings, you will become an example for your companion, and you will begin to inspire everyone around you.

*2. Work very hard.*

Nothing of value comes easily. There is an eternal reason that God commanded men to earn bread by the sweat of their brow. Work develops character. Work develops good habits that will last a lifetime. Work makes men out of boys. Want to grow up? Want to become a real man? Want to prepare yourself to become a husband

and father? Then learn to work hard, very hard, and nothing on this earth, or in eternity, will be beyond your reach.

### 3. *Be good beyond belief.*

Go the extra mile whenever asked. Be the Boy Scout: always prepared, doing a good turn daily, always at the right place at the right time. Know your stuff. There is nothing more impressive than an elder who knows the discussions backward and forward and who can teach any discussion, in any order, and can jump back and forth, in and out, without missing a beat, who can be asked a question, turn immediately to the appropriate scriptures, and carry on an intelligent conversation concerning a difficult gospel principle, and then, when it's time, turn right back to the prepared discussion without missing a beat and without the investigator knowing it wasn't all part of the standard discussion anyway.

A good missionary is just that, good. He is kind and thoughtful to his companion. Over time, he actually begins to spend more time thinking of others than himself. He spends time on his knees praying for those whom he is teaching and to find those to teach. He develops the habit of choosing to do good every day.

Finally, a good missionary is a pawn in the hand of the Lord. This is a marvelous principle taught to me by President Pinnock. The mission field is like a chess game. The mission president is fighting a war against the Evil One, each having a set of people they use against the other. Each person, on either side, has various talents and abilities, each one different, each one important. As the "chess game" is played, each side uses every tool they have, every stratagem, in order to win the day. The mission president uses his missionaries. As he looks over the mission and sees through inspiration the requirements of the battle he is fighting, he then looks over

## Becoming a Great Missionary

the missionaries with whom he has to work and places them as wisely as he can to make sure the work of the Lord goes forward and he wins the battles being fought.

Now everyone who has played chess, or knows anything about the game, knows how important every chess piece is. Even the loss of one pawn can easily change the outcome of the entire game. Think of the consequences for the game if the mission president has unprepared missionaries. What happens if all he has are pawns—no queen that can move any direction, no bishop that can dart across the board to protect positions, no knight that can jump over obstacles to attack the enemy? He would be at the mercy of the enemy and would quickly lose every battle. But what would happen if all his missionaries were prepared? Instead of one queen, he has many; instead of two bishops and two knights, he has many! He could take the battle to the enemy and crush him! No position would go unfilled, no assignment would go uncompleted, no battle would find him unprepared or without the proper men to throw against the enemy.

A good missionary is well rounded and qualified to fill *any* position within the mission. He can be a walking elder or an assistant to the president or anything in between. He has prepared himself to be a true servant of God by being able to fill any calling that is presented to him. At that point, it is up to the Lord to decide how best to use him. In the game of chess, like life, people with different talents are needed at different points in time. A queen cannot jump over other men and a knight cannot move in any direction. Only a castle can protect the king by switching places with him. What happens if a mission president needs a knight and does not have one? He does the best he can, often losing the battle because he does not have the right man for the job. However, if he has an army of men who can fill *any* position, he is truly blessed, because no matter what situation arises, no matter what crisis the Evil One throws at him, he has men who can fill the need. A good missionary should be able to play any part, fill any position, in the chess game of life. Does this mean that a great missionary will always become a zone leader or assistant to the president? If you have those thoughts, read this section again. A great missionary is *capable* of filling any position, but that does not mean he will! That is for God to decide.

This is an easy principle to see, even within the ward where I now live. When we know a new bishop is going to be called, I look at the men within the ward and know there are *many* worthy and capable priesthood holders, any one of whom could fill the position of bishop with honor. That does not mean that all of them will be called. God will look at the needs of the ward and choose the specific man who can best fill those needs at the time. Just because one is chosen to a specific calling does not mean others are unworthy. That is the beauty of the gospel plan. Once we become true servants of God, able to fill *any* calling, we truly become equal before God and each other. Then we can relax our petty differences and jealousies and rely on God to choose who is best. If called, we serve faithfully. If another is called, we are not angry or disappointed because we have our own job to do, our own calling to fill to the best of our ability. We don't have time to waste on feelings of inadequacy or guilt. We simply move ahead with the job at hand and magnify the calling we do have to the best of our ability. A just God has promised us that the rewards will be the same.

And do not think to justify someone being chosen instead of you by backbiting or making excuses. That is not how God works.

## Becoming a Great Missionary

That is not how the battle is fought. Let me give you a couple of examples.

When I served as a high priest group leader in Connecticut, I chose my counselors. Either one of the counselors could easily have been chosen the leader in my place, but God chose me. My counselors served me faithfully and well, and I always tried to honor them for the work they did for the quorum. Several years later, a change occurred in the ward that reversed our callings. Suddenly my second counselor was bishop and I was his executive secretary! Should I have whined and moaned that I should have been made bishop? How silly. I was honored to have been chosen to fill and fulfill the calling I had been given under this great man.

When we lived in Cleveland, I served as the Melchizedek Priesthood leader. Due to the few priesthood brethren in the ward, I was called to preside over *both* the high priests and the elders. In addition, I acted as a surrogate second counselor to the bishop, who had only one counselor at the time. Just a few years later, after moving to Utah, I was called to close the building at night. Each night, my daughter and I went to the ward building and made sure that all the windows and doors were closed and locked. That was my only calling! For an entire year! Now I could have cried and whined about how this was too menial a job for someone as great and stupendous as myself, but that would have been silly. In fact, it turned out to be one of the most memorable and fun callings I have ever had because I was able to do it with my daughter. A short time later, I was called to one of the greatest callings in the Church–teaching the Gospel Doctrine class. Several years later, I was called to clean the building—literally clean it! I was called to be in charge of cleaning the building every Saturday (my children called me "Janitor Bob"). Now I could have cried and moaned about being called to such a menial position, but that would have been silly. After two years of filling that call, I was called to serve a part-time service mission teaching literacy, job skills, and English as a Second Language at the state penitentiary. This is just how the Church works! We must be willing and prepared to serve anywhere at any time!

Once you become a true servant of God, able to fill *any* calling or position in the Church and kingdom, then we all become equal. Then it is up to God, in His great wisdom, to see within our souls and choose what is right for us. We can lay aside our egos and trust that God will do what is best for us. We experience the peace of God because we no longer worry about "getting to the top" of the ecclesiastical ladder. We are at peace with ourselves, knowing that we are ready when and if He calls, and self-confident enough to know that if God does *not* call us to some high and holy calling that we will still be blessed, still receive the same reward that all worthy servants receive—the Celestial Kingdom of God.[3]

## How to create a good companion

### 1. Be a good example.

Good companions can be developed. It starts with being a good example. As we noted earlier , companions rub off on each other, both for good and ill. If you are a good missionary, living the mission rules, studying the scriptures every day, and working hard every day then your good habits, talents, and abilities will rub off on your companion. You cannot browbeat your companion into becoming better. Remember, we have all learned by experience that

---

[3] Matthew 20:1–16.

# Becoming a Great Missionary

"unrighteous dominion" does not work, and that if you try, it will be you who loses the power of God, not those you are trying to change! So use your example, your kindness, and yes, even your love towards your companion, to create changes in him.

> *Each of us is an individual with unique strengths and talents, different from any other person in the world. Each of us has weaknesses. In a harmonious companionship, there is teamwork—where one is weak, the other is strong. As a boy I learned to drive a team of horses. If one horse was balky, the other could not pull the load alone. So it is in a missionary companionship. Each must pull his share of the load.* (James E. Faust, Conference Report, *April 1996)*

## 2. *Take the time to train.*

Believe it or not, the most important calling in a mission is not assistant to the president but senior companion and trainer to a new missionary. If you set a good example for a new missionary and start him out with good habits, you have not just affected your companion but everyone he in turn contacts and teaches! It is a domino effect that can actually have eternal consequences. If you do nothing of worth on your mission except train one young man to become a great missionary, your reward will be assured. We all share in the success of others. The very first convert I taught was a friend who listened to me before I even left on my mission. He eventually went on a mission himself and had great success, baptizing many. I shared in that success! I was a part of every baptism he had, because I had helped place him on the right path. There was a family in Connecticut that my wife and I helped bring into the Church and then helped to prepare for the temple. In the process we became lifelong friends. He has "achieved" many wonderful things within the Church: He was called to be a bishop after being a member for only four years and has since served in the stake presidency. My wife and I share in everything that family does, in every success they experience, because of the part we shared in bringing them into the gospel. The same is true for senior companions. They can and will share in the success of every missionary they properly train and prepare to become great! Isn't God's eternal plan wonderful![4]

*3. Do splits, splits, and more splits.*

As a leader, one of the most effective tools in training and developing the missionaries in your care is to visit and split with them as often as possible. This provides teaching moments that can come in no other way. I remember how exciting it was for me to split with my district and zone leaders (and even the assistants on occasion). I admired them and learned from them and cherished the time I spent watching them. I watched how they did door approaches, studied their teaching techniques, and listened and learned from their comments and suggestions. Just as we have learned through long experience that example is the best teacher (follow me!), you have to place yourself in a position to be an example, and the only way to do that, the only way to become a one-on-one example to other missionaries, is to go on splits as often as possible.

*4. Share the rewards.*

When success does come your way, and it will, make sure you share the rewards. Make sure you treat your companion as an equal in everything you do. From door approaches to baptisms, make sure you share and share alike. If one missionary companion does everything, makes every decision, always gives the blessings while the other always pours the oil, and always gets to baptize, then the example and training will never be complete. You must seek to give

---

[4] D&C 18:15.

your companion opportunities to grow and serve and expand in ways he has not experienced before. You must think of him before yourself, knowing that blessings will come to you as well. There is no better time than your mission to learn that it is better to give than receive. As Christ himself admonished, you cannot know whether a doctrine is true until you test it for yourself.[5]

## *The legacy of good missionaries among the members*

A pair of good missionaries can have a profound effect on the lives of the members of the Church in their area, a much greater and longer-lasting effect than the devastation that is left behind by bad missionaries. Good missionaries energize the membership and remind them of the excitement that can be felt when learning gospel principles, and the power of the Spirit that is available to servants of the Lord. Good missionaries are an example to weak members, a support to overworked priesthood leaders, and a source of spiritual influence that can flood a ward or branch with light and power. Never underestimate the wonderful influence a pair of good missionaries can have on members of the Church.

## Principles of Power

Here are a few general principles that you can apply to developing a good working relationship with your companion.

### *1. Learn from every companion.*

No matter how bad you think your companion is, you can learn from him. Do not waste time grousing about the habits of your companion; spend time trying to learn from him. My first companion had a reputation of wasting time. I thought I was doomed to a

---

[5] John 7:17.

life of wasted time and unfruitful work. For a while, I spent time complaining to myself about what we did and where we went and why we weren't working harder. But, after a while, I wised up and began looking for the good things in my companion. After all, my mission president (who I *knew* was inspired of God) had chosen us to be together. When my attitude changed, I began to see the good things my companion brought with him. Even now, years later, I thank the Lord for pairing me with this wonderful young man. He had been a Catholic, a convert, and as such had no fear about going to Catholic churches and talking to priests. At first I thought he was crazy, or that he just wanted to "Bible bash" with members of his old faith. How foolish I was! The next thing I knew, we were teaching in Catholic high schools, in Catholic Sunday Schools, and in Catholic seminaries, sharing our view of the gospel to whole groups of interested Catholics. Wow! (We will cover the specific ways to do this in the chapter on teaching.) Never underestimate what you can and will learn from your companion.

   *2.   Recognize that time is a precious commodity.*

My third companion and I discovered the real joy behind missionary work—the secret not only to success but also to experiencing joy in missionary work. It was something President Pinnock talked about a lot, but I had not experienced it until being paired with this elder. That secret is hard work. There is a natural progression that occurs when working hard—it is the desire and ability to learn and develop time management. When you are working as hard as you should, there is never enough time to do everything. Time becomes a precious commodity. My new companion and I not only had the fortune to get along, we also shared a burning desire to work hard. We learned to constantly look for ways to use our time more wisely.

## Becoming a Great Missionary

For example, we had always washed our clothes at a member's home. It saved us money and gave us the opportunity to spend time relaxing in a comfortable place. But since there was only one washer and dryer, it took up most of our day. We decided we could save time by doing our laundry at a laundromat where we could wash and dry all of our clothes at once. We used the time there to write letters and study, enabling us to get back to work more quickly. The harder we worked, the more success we obtained, the more excited we got, and the harder we worked. Time became more and more precious to us. There just wasn't enough time in the day. Whenever we could find better ways to use our time wisely, we rejoiced. The members noticed our hard work and dedication, and, even though a pair of bad missionaries had devastated the area just a short time before, the members began to respond. We began to get member splits again, which greatly increased our teaching potential. Each week, our joy and our numbers climbed until we were right on the edge of breaking the mission record in the number of discussions taught in one week. We had learned to work hard and to work smart, making sure to account for every minute of our time.

Another example of how precious time became to us was a wonderful directive that came from President Pinnock. He told us that we had been called to teach, not to be taught, so if we did not have any investigators at Church we were to use the time during Sunday School to work (this was before the Church went to a three-hour block). We thought this was a wonderful idea, especially since at the time we were working in a city. We would go to priesthood meeting in the morning and during Sunday School go out into the streets around the church and tract. President Pinnock taught us a powerful lesson, which led to even greater success.

### 3. *Learn to enjoy the work.*

In my second area of labor, I ran into an elder who completely changed my attitude about missionary work. From the time I had been converted, I was a zealot and an overly serious and sober person. Sometimes I took my calling too seriously and feared letting my guard down even a little. Suddenly I ran into a missionary who was almost the complete opposite. Elder B was happy-go-lucky, outgoing, funny, a practical joker, and didn't seem to take anything seriously. In fact, at my first introduction to Elder B, he played a practical joke on me. He and his companion were working in the same city as I. I was going to be training a new missionary and my new companion had arrived in my assigned area well before I arrived. By the time I got to my area, the three of them had already set me up with this practical joke. They convinced my new companion to pretend that he was deaf and mute. They sucked me in so easily! I was devastated at the challenge this presented and fretted and worried until they finally gave up and started laughing. However, I did not take it well. I was such a sober and somber missionary, I could find nothing funny about what they had done. Elder B continued to work on me as time went on and, after a while, I began to see his point of view. There was no need to be so serious all of the time. The gospel is meant to be enjoyed! Remember, man is that he might have joy! Having *fun* on your mission is not a sin. It was watching Elder B work that convinced me. Having a sense of humor and having fun did not negatively affect his missionary work at all! In fact, it seemed to help. Making missionary work *fun* made us forget our tired bodies and buoyed up our tired spirits. There was a time to be serious and Elder B was wise enough to know when that time was. But there was nothing wrong with having fun and finding joy in the mundane between times, while tracting or getting to and from an area. By the time I transferred again, I was having fun! I will always be grateful to Elder B for teaching me to enjoy life and not take myself too seriously.

## Having Fun on your Missions

Missions are not all serious. Sometimes we have to unstring our bows and just have fun. This can take the form of recreation, or music, or, at times, just being silly. Now I warn you that some of the things I am going to talk about may not be appropriate for missionaries . . . but the fact is we did them, had a lot of fun doing them, and they have become some of the stories I am asked to tell over and over again. So batten down the hatches, and here we go.

### 1. *Foreigner for a day.*

One of the silly things we did to break up the mundane routine of tracting was to talk with different accents. My favorite was acting like I was from Texas. "Howdy ma'am, mah name is Elder Clawson, and we here are coming ta ya to talk about awr church. Can we come in an set a spell?" Of course we would only do these door approaches on people we knew we would never get in—or so we thought. One day, I did get in while speaking with my Texan drawl. Then we had to give a discussion! Worst of all, what was I going to do during the prayer? The woman must have thought angels were in the room, because as I said the prayer my accent totally disappeared (I could not bring myself to blaspheme *that* much) and after I was done, it miraculously reappeared again! Needless to say, getting in this door cured me of my "foreign accent" door approaches.

### 2. *Practical jokes.*

I was never one to pull practical jokes on people. In fact, when I had one pulled on me (my new companion pretended to be deaf and mute), I did not think it was funny. However, after I transferred to the Nauvoo Visitors Center and the summer season was over, my companion and I had way too much time on our hands. On our P-day, we were able to get hold of some firecrackers. It was an accident waiting to happen. One of the missionaries in our group was nicknamed Betty Crocker because he was such a great cook. We all looked forward to eating his food. One day, a mischievous design came into our minds. We decided to sabotage his next cake. We sneaked into their house and taped firecrackers to the heating coil of their stove. The plan worked perfectly. "Betty Crocker" had just put a cake in the oven and turned it on. A minute or two later, BANG! The oven door blew open and the cake flew across the kitchen. It hit the wall with a splatter! We were never invited to eat there again, to our great disappointment.

Not one of us is perfect. All of us do and say stupid things. The point of these stories is not to encourage you to go wild on your missions—far from it. It is to help you recognize that it is okay to have *fun* on your mission. Missions are very serious business. So serious, in fact, that it takes a lot out of us keeping up the image and example. There have to be times when we unstring our bows or they will break. There has to be a way to learn to have *fun* on your mission, or it may become an endless drudgery of tracting, work, and unending pressure to perform. This is not how life was meant to be. Man is that he might have *joy*. A mission is not supposed to be "enduring to the end." It is supposed to be service to others that brings joy and happiness to those we serve, and to ourselves as well. President Pinnock *often* said to me: Lighten up! Don't take life so seriously! *Enjoy* this life and all the blessings that it can, and will, bring. God is not a tyrant or taskmaster who is just waiting to punish you for any minor infraction that might occur. He is a loving God who knows your weaknesses and strengths and knows that a large part of life is learning to enjoy life itself.

## What to do about those "other" missionaries

Occasionally you will be in an area where there is more than one set of missionaries serving together. There is nothing wrong with this; in fact, this can sometimes greatly enhance and help the work of the Lord go forward. However, it does lead to the possibility of increased tension and problems. So what do you do if you see those "other" missionaries acting up, behaving badly, or dealing with the members improperly? I turn again to the wisdom of President Pinnock:

> *You cannot be concerned about rapport between different missionaries laboring in the same branch or ward. Your only concern is the rapport that you and your companion have with the members and your investigators and the Savior.*

This is great advice! You need to concentrate your efforts and focus your energies. If you are concerned with what everybody else is doing (or not doing), you will lose sight of what *you* should be doing. Don't lose your focus! Concentrate on your own responsibilities and what you can control. Let the Lord and the mission president handle the rest.

# Four
## Living in a New World

### Section I: Finding a Place to Live

One of the most important aspects of missionary work is finding a proper place to live. Most missionaries live in low-end apartments that just barely fit their needs. They do this because of cost concerns, not because they choose to live in a slum. In some countries, this same type of apartment would be considered first class. What it comes down to is a judgment call. But if you are the one responsible for picking a place for the missionaries to live, remember that it is a far-reaching decision. Very few missionaries will take the time to move to another apartment, no matter how bad it is. They will simply endure it and be grateful when they get transferred. However, if you happen to get stuck with a terrible place to live, it is entirely appropriate to take time to find a better place. It's like filling up your mission car with gas—it has nothing to do with missionary work, but it is still necessary. Even though finding a good place to live takes time away from doing the work of the Lord, it is necessary and worthwhile.

### The Leopard house

My district leader and I were given the assignment to find a new apartment and we blew it—my name was forever placed next to stories of the "leopard house." Finding an apartment in our price range was tough. Most of them were one-room studio apartments with hardly enough room for beds, let alone other furniture. Finally, we came across a small cottage for rent. It was rather drafty, but its big selling point was the wallpaper: it had leopard skin wallpaper. Tired of looking, we decided to take it. Little did we know the disaster that awaited future missionaries because of our decision. When we moved in the weather was warm, so the drafty house did not bother us. But by the time I got another companion (and another district leader), it had gotten cold and the drafts were getting to us. We always sat with our feet on the chairs or the table because the floor was so cold our feet would freeze (in fact, there was an open space between the floor and the walls—you could actually see outside while lying on the floor!). We had electric heat, which was very expensive, so we could not turn the heat up enough to really get warm, just enough to keep the pipes from freezing. I could also talk about the mice that lived in our attic, but I think you get the picture; this was not an appropriate place for missionaries to live. Finally, I was transferred, but the legend of the leopard house followed me for years afterward.

## The dishwasher

While the rest of the district lived in semi-slum conditions, one pair of missionaries decided to really live it up. They got an apartment in a nice building with a dishwasher. Even though it was more out of jealousy than anything else, we all gave these two missionaries hours of teasing and grief over the comfort and style in which they were living. Sometimes too much of a good thing is just that—too much.

## *Cleanliness is next to godliness*

It should go without saying that a good missionary should keep his living quarters clean. The adage that cleanliness is next to godliness is true for a reason. If you live in filthy conditions, your spirit will soon follow suit. No one expects missionaries to be Martha Stewart, but common sense has to rule and missionaries, on their P-day, need to take time to clean.

However, a note to leaders at large and a continuation of the theme that missionaries should be treated as adults. Missionaries should not be required to endure apartment inspections unless absolutely necessary, and then it should be by their district leader only. Would a bishop "inspect" one of the member's home and rate it for cleanliness? I don't think so, because they are adults and expected to clean their own home. Is it necessary sometimes? Actually it is. I know of a bishop who had members come to him complaining about a family in the ward. People refused to sit by them because they smelled and home teachers refused to visit them because their home was so filthy that it smelled and had animal feces everywhere. The bishop took it upon himself to "inspect" their home and give them some counsel. It was everything people said it was, and more. Under the purview of "living the Word of Wisdom," he wisely instructed them to clean up their home and themselves so that they would be acceptable to the members of the ward and society in general. Of course they were offended, but it was the right thing to do. So, there are times when even adults need to be counseled on their personal habits and living conditions, but it is the exception to the rule. For most people, and most missionaries, this part of their life should be left up to them. President Pinnock was approached a number of times concerning this and every time that I know of he refused to inspect missionary apartments. He refused to treat his missionaries like children. None of the missionaries I came in contact with had a problem in this area.

## Section II: Transportation

Part of every missionary's responsibility is learning how to manage transportation. Whether you are in an area where you walk or use public transportation, or are in a bike area, or have the privilege of using a car, it is important to know how to get where you are going in a safe and efficient manner.

### *Walking areas*

The best area I had on my mission was a walking area in Altoona, Pennsylvania. We either walked or took the bus to get around the city. Time management is very important when living in a walking area. If you miss the bus, you miss your appointment. If you misjudge how long it takes you to walk, you will be late. Being realistic about the time it takes to get places and being organized enough to be on time makes all of the difference.

Take the time to get a good map of the area along with current information about bus and train times and have them with you if necessary. Take time to note how long it takes you to go places so that if you have to go there again, or somewhere near there, you will have accurate knowledge concerning travel time. These are little things that may make a big difference to the work of the Lord. If you are constantly late for appointments, or miss them due to your mismanagement of time and scheduling, you may lose investigators. Considering how hard it is to get investigators in the first place, you do not want to do anything that will discourage their interest.

## Bike areas

Whenever possible, get a bike that has fenders and a basket. The basket is simply a convenience for packing books and stuff, but the fenders are a necessity. If any of you have ridden bikes in the rain, you know what I mean; water from the bike's wheels will cover your front and back with dirt and road grime.

Safety is another factor in bike areas. Most walking areas, and even most car areas, don't have nearly as many accidents as bike areas. People riding bikes often think they have more control than they really do, and they seem to forget they have *no protection* in the event of an accident. There are rude people in cars that will drive you off the road, throw things at you, and cause you all sorts of problems. Just be an aware and defensive rider.

## Cars

There are two problems with cars that missionaries are seldom taught. One is keeping track of miles, the other is simple maintenance of vehicles. Many missionaries don't know the simple things to do to keep their car running.

Missionaries with cars usually have rules about how many miles they can drive each month. This is a good rule to prevent obvious abuse of cars and teaches missionaries to manage their time wisely. In the same way you learn to control and manage your day while in a walking or biking area, you should also plan your day when you have a car. Instead of making appointments in completely different areas, try to arrange your appointments to conserve your miles. When you're running low on your miles, call your ward mission leader and tell him you will *definitely* needs splits for the week. That way, you can use the cars of those with whom you split and save your miles for when you absolutely need them. This can be a real

## Becoming a Great Missionary

icebreaker with people who might not otherwise split with the missionaries. It gives those members who are somewhat timid about teaching the gospel the opportunity to serve the missionaries by simply "going along for the ride."

Make sure to do the simple things with your car. Whenever you fill your car with gas, check the oil, the washer fluid level, and the tire pressure. If the car begins to have problems, take care of them immediately. If you don't, it will end up costing a great deal more money. I was foolish enough to postpone a problem too long. It was winter in Pittsburgh and, as we were coming home from an appointment, we hit an icy hill. The car slid and hit a curb, resulting in a bent wheel. We had an appointment the next day so rather than get the problem fixed we drove the car. By the time we did take it in to get fixed, we not only had to get a new wheel, but, by driving the car, we made it necessary to replace the tire also. It was a foolish mistake that I did not make again.

## Section III: Preparation Day

All missions have a day set aside for personal preparation; a day (or partial day) when missionaries don't have to work. On this day you can do laundry, write letters home, listen to music, play sports and exercise, go sightseeing, etc. Some missions have tried to make this just another work day by giving missionaries enough time to do their necessary washing but not enough time to "play." Often this does not produce the desired result because all missionaries need time off! Let me start with instruction from the Prophet Joseph Smith:

Joseph Smith told a simple story of a hunter and his bow to members of the Church who criticized him about his "undignified" roughhousing with the boys. He told them that a hunter could not keep his bow strung at all times or it would lose its spring. He said that, in like manner, a prophet could not always act as such because he would become ineffective if he did so.[1]

The same is true for missionaries. They cannot be on-call at all times or they will lose the Spirit, lose their "edge," and become ineffective. Just as every child looks forward to recess, and every adult looks forward to the weekend, every missionary on earth looks forward to P-day—the day he can let his hair down, relax, and just rest. It is important that missionaries take time for themselves—to listen to music, to play sports, and to exercise. This time is precious medicine that *must* be taken weekly. I remember with great joy the basketball games we played with other missionaries, with members, with gang members, etc; beating my district leader in tennis week after week. Personally I enjoyed classical music, but my companions enjoyed all kinds of music from country to reggae. No hard rock, no bad words or music that was inappropriate, just good music to uplift the soul and gladden the heart. We went sightseeing and even went to movies (G-rated of course). It made life full and prepared us for the hard work ahead.

> *Recreation is an essential and vital part of the gospel of salvation—a gospel which makes provision for every need of man, both temporal and spiritual. After a person has performed his assigned or appointed labors—both in making a living and in service on the Lord's errand—it is edifying, relaxing, and proper to enjoy the diversion of wholesome recreation. (Bruce McConkie,* Mormon Doctrine, *p. 622)*

Once again, we return to the theme of treating missionaries like adults. Taking away a missionary's free time under the misguided

---

[1] William Allred, *Recollections,* p. 471.

idea that they need to work harder, or under the assumption they will not use their personal time wisely, is shortsighted and will end up doing more harm than good. If even the Prophet of the Lord needs time to relax and "unstring his bow," surely the same privilege should be, must be, given to all of the Lord's servants.

## *What should you do on preparation day?*

There is sometimes confusion among missionaries about appropriate activities on P-days. Since the list is much too long and varied to write, you should let the Spirit guide you in this matter. As for President Pinnock, he permitted us to do *anything* that was appropriate and safe. We played non-contact sports of all kinds: basketball, softball, touch football, tennis, etc.; everything but swimming. We played any music we wanted except hard rock and music with inappropriate lyrics. We went anywhere we wanted: museums, movies (G-rated), sightseeing, ball games, etc. We were considered adults and were expected to act appropriately. If a missionary did something wrong, the mission president would deal with that one missionary on a case-by-case basis rather than punish all missionaries for the actions of the one or a few.

## *P-day isn't only on P-day*

Even though there is one day set aside for relaxation, that doesn't mean there aren't times during the work day you can take time to relax or see the sights of the country. Often you will never have another opportunity to see and experience the sights, monuments, and other strange and wonderful things of the mission you are in. This is not cheating or backsliding but an appropriate and a wonderful blessing that comes from going on a mission. Obviously it isn't right to spend all of your time sightseeing, but if the time is right and the opportunity is there, then do it. Let me give you a couple of examples.

When I transferred to Pittsburgh, I found there was total miscommunication between the assistants and the missionaries. I arrived, but it was going to be several hours before my companion got there. The zone leaders and I were stuck in the city of Pittsburgh, so we decided to spend the otherwise wasted time sightseeing. We came across their new convention center that was holding the Ice Follies. I went to the ticket window, told them who we were, and asked them if we could get in for free. Sure enough, since we were "ministers," they let us in and we watched a wonderful show. After it was over, we went back to the bus station and got my companion. It was not P-day. We did not ask the mission president for permission. But there was nothing wrong with what we did. It enhanced our lives, gave us a needed break, and did not in any way detract from the work in which we were engaged.

When I was in Scranton as a zone leader, we were required to spend a lot of time driving to different areas of the zone. While driving, we would often come across monuments or sights we would never have the opportunity to see again. One day we were driving past the site of the Anthracite King, the largest steam shovel in the world, so we took time to see it. It wasn't all day; it wasn't even an hour. It was just a few minutes to drive down the road to see a shovel so big that the operator worked on the 30th floor! It had two large tracks and walked a little like a duck, one foot at a time. It simply walked backwards as it slowly dug up the earth. It was wonderful. Did we feel guilty? No. Was it wrong? No. It was totally appropriate for the time, place, and circumstance.

## Section IV: Food

Believe it or not, food will be a big part of your mission. Preparing your own food for the first time is a real trick-or-treat experience: you either learn to cook relatively well or you will suffer the consequences on a daily basis. In addition, many of the experiences you will have with both members and investigators will involve food.

### *Cooking for yourself*

Don't be afraid to think big with the food you eat. What I mean is that most missionaries think of food on a day-to-day basis rather than a weekly or even a monthly basis. Learn to use your freezer and to fix meals that can be used over several days. For example, we would purchase a large amount of ground beef and form it into hamburger patties using some kind of mold about the size of bread (such as a plastic cover, a cup, or a bowl). Make them thinner than normal, so they will cook quickly and then freeze them using foil or freezer paper to separate the meat. Then for dinner, all you need to do is peel off a couple of frozen patties, cook them in a pan for a few minutes, and you are all set. The meat will last weeks longer in the freezer.

Another thing we would do is cook a whole chicken or turkey. We could then use it for dinner and sandwiches for a few days. Since we usually got up by 5:00 a.m., there was plenty of time to cook a full turkey *before* leaving for the day at 9:00 a.m.

Anyway, you get the picture. We began to develop better ways to cook meals as a result of our time management program—thinking of anything that would save us time doing the mundane things so we could spend that time on other, more productive things.

## *Be willing to eat almost anything*

Part of being a missionary is trying to become a part of the country or area to which you are sent. Part of learning about that country or area is learning to eat the same food they eat, no matter how strange it may be. This is part of good manners. It is part of becoming one with those whom you seek to teach. God has promised that he will protect us, as long as we use wisdom in what we do and eat. Use wisdom in what you eat but do not be so fearful that you end up offending people. Let me tell you a story.

One day my companion and I were tracting about dinnertime in a very poor section of town. It was a rural area and homes were more like shacks than real houses. We knocked on the door of one particularly poor home and were invited in. Inside was a wonderful family of four. The home was clean and the family loving, but they were dirt poor. They invited us to dinner. We knew we had to accept in spite of our reservations of burdening them with extra mouths to feed. But we also were well aware of the great blessings that would come to this family through this sacrifice. So we accepted and sat down to . . . dinner? We were given a plate that had three things on it, only one of which we even had a clue what it was. There were two small piles of green stuff that looked a little like spinach and a piece of bread. When we asked what the food was, they acted a little embarrassed and said, "weeds." They had gone into the backyard and picked several kinds of weeds, such as dandelions, to have as their meal. We swallowed hard and said we looked forward to sharing their meal with them. To our surprise, it was quite good! The mother had cooked out any sour taste and had seasoned it so that it was not just edible—it was good. We thanked them for the meal, reminded them of our next appointment, and left. I learned a great lesson that day. I learned not to judge people by their living conditions. I learned that food that some people would not eat, others have to eat, and even like to eat. Like many other similar lessons, I learned not to judge people or situations before I had a full understanding.

## *Learn some manners*

One of the surprising things about many missionaries, including myself, is their lack of simple manners. From remembering to say "please" and "thank you" to simple table manners, some missionaries need help.

One woman in my first area took it upon herself to teach the missionaries good manners. This dear sister had a beautiful home and often invited the missionaries to dinner. This dinner served two purposes: it fed hungry missionaries and it also taught them table manners. She would set out a full, formal setting of china, silver, and crystal with all the accompanying spoons, forks, knives, plates, etc. One of a hundred missionaries had the slightest clue which fork or spoon to start with; napkins in the laps, no arms or elbows on the table, no reaching across the table, etc. This was formal, formal, formal, and we all loved it! Many missionaries learned more about table manners from one dinner with this sister than they had all their life from their own mothers. I was no exception.

You see, before my mission I was not what you would call the most cultured of people. In fact, I vividly remember one meal I was invited to just before leaving on my mission. The second counselor in the bishopric had invited me to Sunday dinner with his family. They had set a very formal table, and I thought I had done pretty well trying to follow everyone else during dinner (I would use the same utensil everyone else was using, etc.). Then it happened. Before I even realized it, I made a fool of myself in front of this entire family. You see, the food had been so good that I didn't want to waste any of it, so I began to lick my plate! I had picked up the plate and begun to lick it clean when I suddenly felt I was being watched. As I slowly peered over the top of the plate, I could see that everyone at the table was staring at me! I immediately put the plate back on the table mumbling something about how good the food was. To this day, I am grateful I had this sister in my first area.

# Becoming a Great Missionary

# Five
## Developing Into Men

*I*n a way, this chapter is written as much to the priesthood leaders as it is to the missionaries. Priesthood leaders have so much influence and power over the development of those in their charge that they must learn to use that influence wisely. Although most missionaries are teenagers, and are seen as "just boys," they *must* be treated as men. People will live up to what you expect of them. If you treat them as boys, they will continue to act like boys. If you treat them as men, I promise you, they will begin to act like men.

*Do not create unnecessary rules*

President Pinnock was a master at teaching boys to become men. He gave us strict rules about important things but always gave us the freedom to choose about other things. It wasn't until I was transferred to the Nauvoo mission that I learned what a truly great teacher and leader President Pinnock was. Missionaries from five or six missions had been sent to Nauvoo to work at the Visitors' Center during the summer season. Thus, I had the opportunity to hear how other missions were being run. I was surprised to learn that the rules

# Becoming a Great Missionary

and conditions placed upon the missionaries by their mission presidents varied greatly from one mission to another. Many mission presidents placed upon their missionaries unrealistic rules and expectations that demoralized them and ended up detracting from the work.

Here are just a few examples:

- *All* missionaries were to wear dark blue. Blue suits with blue ties and black socks and shoes. No other color was permitted in the entire mission. Not even different ties were permitted! If elders came out with brown suits, or black suits, or pin-striped suits, they had to send them back and find dark blue suits. (I've seen the Prophet of the Lord wear something other than a blue suit, and even a colorful tie!)

- No matter how hot it got, the missionaries were not permitted to take off their suit coats. Even in the middle of summer, and this was a mission in a southern state, they had to wear their full suit with jacket whenever they were out of their apartments. (I've seen the Prophet of the Lord take off his jacket during the priesthood session of General Conference when it was too hot!)

- The missionaries could not listen to any kind of music—none—not even uplifting music or the Tabernacle Choir.

- The missionaries were not permitted to study while eating.

- Missionaries were not allowed to sleep in on P-day, and instead of getting a full day off (until 6:00 p.m.) they had to work.

- They were not allowed to play basketball or other sports with the other missionaries in their district.

- Every missionary had to comb his hair in exactly the same way.

- Missionaries could call home just once a year, and then for only 15 minutes.

♦ No missionary could have the color yellow in his tie.

The list could go on and on, but you get the picture. They are simply arbitrary rules drawn up by mission presidents. I'm sure they seemed like the right thing to do at the time. Perhaps the mission president wanted to show how "unified" they were by all wearing the same color suit. Perhaps one was having a problem with missionaries listening to inappropriate music, so he decided to ban all music. Some, such as everyone wearing the same hair style, I can't come up with a reason for their creation. But this I am sure of: No matter how innocent and pure the intent, the effect of these rules can be devastating within a mission.

Almost all young men have self-esteem problems. This lack of self-confidence makes them feel inadequate, awkward, and unworthy to receive blessings from the Lord. *Any* problem that arises, any minor sin or infraction, will lead these young men to feel unworthy of God's love and blessings and therefore unworthy of the natural success and joy that should come with serving the Lord. By creating rules and regulations that are unnecessary, you place undue burdens upon the shoulders of these young men. No one is perfect. No one can live every day without making a few mistakes, sleeping in late, forgetting an appointment, etc. By placing these additional rules upon the missionaries, no matter how well intentioned, you will end up causing unnecessary problems.

> *For through the law is the knowledge of sin. Because the law worketh wrath: for where no law is, there is no transgression.*
> (Romans 3:20; 4:15)

What is the final result of these innocent rules? The result is that missionaries will break them. Not because they are willful, but because they are weak, because they are human. Then, when they

## Becoming a Great Missionary

kneel before their Heavenly Father at night to ask for His help and guidance, they are hindered from obtaining what they seek. For as they begin to ask of God, they remember: "I broke a mission rule today, therefore I am unworthy to ask God for a blessing," and they are stopped from doing the most important thing they can do while on their mission: communicate with their God. I testify to you that this is exactly what happens and how it happens.

But what about those who break the mission rules? How does a mission president control problems that occur within his mission? He does what President Pinnock did—handle it on a case-by-case basis. It is wrong to punish *every* missionary for the actions of a few. It is wrong to place additional rules upon missionaries because of their youth. What do I mean? It's simple. Do unto others what you would have them do to you. Would you ask an adult priesthood holder living within your mission to obey this rule? Would you be willing to live this rule yourself? I cannot imagine priesthood leaders going to the elders quorum president and asking him to stop listening to music, or going to the Relief Society president and telling her she cannot read her scriptures while she eats. Mission presidents would not think to place on the senior missionaries, or *any* adult for that matter, all too many of the rules they place on the young missionaries. Remember, if you want these missionaries to act as adults, you must treat them as adults!

We have been taught this lesson so many times and yet it never seems to stick: teach people what to do and then let them govern themselves!

> *When asked how he governed so many people, the Prophet Joseph Smith answered, "I teach them correct principles, and*

*they govern themselves." (George Q. Cannon,* Life of Joseph
Smith the Prophet, *p. 529)*

This is simple in theory but much more difficult in practice. In
practice, it means that we have to *trust* people to behave appropriately. We have to *trust* these young missionaries to act like adults.
We have to *trust* God that He will protect them and guide them
when we cannot. Does anyone really believe that someone who is
breaking the mission rules will suddenly reform because he has *more*
rules to follow? Does anyone truly believe that by adding more rules
all of their problems with missionaries will be solved? It is the oldest
story of all: The difference between a shepherd and a sheepherder.

A shepherd *leads* his flock. A sheepherder *drives* his flock. A
leader who adds more rules and burdens upon the backs of missionaries is simply using those rules as a stick in an effort to drive the
missionaries the direction he wants them to go. A real leader *teaches,*
uplifts, and motivates his missionaries to greater and greater obedience. He does not need a stick to drive them, he uses his love,
knowledge, and testimony to teach them correct principles, and,
when done correctly, they willingly follow him.

Do not be the sheepherder who drives his sheep only to scatter
them further. Be like the good shepherd whom the flock loves and
respects so much they willingly follow.

### Permit them to make the tough decisions

President Pinnock never made a decision or did anything else
that took responsibility away from the missionary. Again, he treated
us as adults. Only in the case of *serious* problems, such as moral
transgression, would he get personally involved. Here are a couple
of examples of how he dealt with problems that arose:

## Becoming a Great Missionary

### 1. *Going to court.*

While working in and around Philadelphia we ran into the police quite often. Many of the townships had laws against soliciting, especially at night. We were stopped by the police many times and told not to come back to an area. We did our best to be considerate of people, but the work had to go on. So, one day it finally happened. We were stopped by the police, given a citation, and commanded to stop all proselyting in the area under penalty of jail. We were told to come to court to defend ourselves at a certain place and time. Not knowing what to do, we called President Pinnock. We called, feeling scared and unsure of ourselves (whether we had done something wrong or not) and unsure of what President Pinnock would say. Would he be mad at us? His response was surprising, uplifting, and literally changed our lives. First of all, and perhaps most importantly, he assured us that we had done nothing wrong. We had been doing our duty, just as we were supposed to. Second of all, he placed the burden back on *our* shoulders by telling us that we would have to go to court ourselves and take care of the problem. And lastly, he gave us confidence by assuring us that we could do this, that he *trusted* us to do the right thing, and that he knew it would turn out all right. He finished by asking us to report back what happened and how it went.

We had gone from timid young missionaries, afraid we had done something wrong, afraid we would get yelled at, afraid even to call our mission president, to becoming confident servants of God. We took upon ourselves the responsibility for our actions; taking actions to solve our own problems and suddenly having the confidence that we would prevail. And we did prevail! After talking with President Pinnock, we prayed and then sat down to discuss what we should do to resolve the situation in which we found ourselves. We decided that the first thing we needed to do was to find a copy of the specific law or ordinance with which we were charged and read it. We went down to the courthouse and obtained a copy of the law. Upon reading it, we discovered that the law with which we were charged was for soliciting—for *selling* things door to door. But we weren't selling anything! A few days later my companion and I appeared in court. The judge was on the bench and the police officer who gave us the summons was also there. After introducing the case, the judge looked at us and asked us what we had to say. I stood and told him that the ordinance with which we were charged had to do with selling goods, and that we had not sold anything, nor had we ever sold things door-to-door. We were simply talking to people about our Church. The judge then turned to the police officer and asked him if he had anything to say. He looked sheepish and a little embarrassed as he stood and said, "No, your honor." The judge admonished us to behave and not cause problems, then dismissed the case! As you can imagine, we floated out of that courtroom. We felt so good, so excited, and so wonderful about the whole experience! From that day forward, we became more self-confident, more willing to solve our own problems, more willing to take on greater responsibility, more like real men. And it was all because our mission president had trusted us and shown confidence in us.

2.  *Casting out Satan.*

I was serving in Scranton, Pennsylvania as a zone leader. We had been having problems with Satan. I don't mean depression and sin, I mean real confrontations with Satan! Both my companion and I had been physically attacked by evil demons. We even had a coven of witches seeking to harm us and thwart the work we were doing.

## Becoming a Great Missionary

Once again, we felt like we were out of our league. So we called President Pinnock—with similar results. He listened to the situation, stated he was confident we could handle things ourselves, and then gave us "back-up" in case what we did failed. He told us that if we could not rid the area of evil spirits, he would call an Apostle of the Lord to do it! Wow! Once again, we were lifted up by our wonderful mission president, who gave us confidence to solve our own problems and comfort to know that if we made mistakes, or failed in what we decided to do, we would not be condemned for trying. Further, we would be sent help if needed. I cannot explain how powerful a lesson this was to learn—how much this affected my life and the lives of my companions. We were set on a path of responsibility and self-confidence that continues even today. How easy it would have been for him to say, "I'll take care of it," which would have really meant, "You are too young and stupid to work this out for yourself. I will do it for you so you don't screw it up." Instead of treating us like children (as our parents may have treated us), he treated us like men—like *equals*. I will be forever grateful to him for it.

### *Real men get things done*

One of the frustrations you learn in life is that people do not do what they say they will. They promise you everything and, if you believe them, you end up with nothing. The Savior understood this weakness in men. He talked about two sons—one who *promised* to do what his father wanted and the other who didn't. But one son actually *did* what his father wanted. One son let his actions speak louder than words.[1] The Savior talked about a foolish man who "talked" about building a tower but failed to plan properly and was laughed at when he could not finish the project that became a white

---

[1] Matthew 21:28–31.

elephant to those who lived in the neighborhood.[2] The Savior understood that *real men*, men of God, do what they say they will. They do not promise to do something without first thinking it through and planning it in their minds, so they are confident they will be able to live up to their word.

*Real men* are simple in speech. They do not need flowery words to convince people of the truth. They say things simply and directly and then let their actions and the truth of their words stand for themselves.[3]

*Real men* are results oriented—they don't care about the pomp and fanfare that comes with life; they care about *results*. They care about actually getting things done. As President Pinnock used to say:

> Always remember that a "results-oriented" person is the one who gets the job done. Concentrate on results, results, results.

*Real men* don't just talk, they do. Remember the famous saying of the Prophet Spencer W. Kimball: "Just do it!" He, too, understood this simple principle. Enough meetings. Enough planning. Enough talking. Now, *just do it!*

Continuing on his teachings about serving and doing what needs to be done to carry the work forward, President Pinnock often talked about the dedication we need to have in the service of God:

> Total dedication becomes one of the great steps an individual takes in his attempt to serve the Savior. Periodically we hear that someone "does the right thing for the wrong reason . . ." and that might be true. But never forget it is better to do the

[2] Luke 14:28–30.
[3] Matthew 5:33–37.

> *right thing for the wrong reason than not to do the right thing at all.*

To the Savior, few things were more offensive than those who talked but did nothing. Even if you end up making a mistake, or just foul things up, you will be looked upon in a much better light than those who do nothing. At least by acting and making mistakes, we are learning that if we do not act, for better or worse, nothing will happen at all!

### The worst-case scenario

What happens if you find yourself with a mission president you do not like or cannot get along with? Perhaps one who seems to create arbitrary rules that you find hard to accept and live? What do you do? The answer is to be obedient to the best of your ability. God will always bless obedience, even if it seems to make little sense at the time. Remember what happened to Adam after leaving the Garden of Eden? He was commanded to sacrifice animals to God but was not told why. I don't know about you, but that would have frustrated me to no end! I would want to know *why* something was being done before I would spend the time and effort to do it! But Adam, in spite of whatever reservations he may have had as to why he was being asked to do this thing, was obedient. He trusted God and believed that if God asked him to do something there must be a good reason for it! So, he obeyed. It was only later that the importance of what he had been asked to do was revealed to him.

> *And Adam and Eve, his wife, called upon the name of the Lord, and they heard the voice of the Lord from the way toward the Garden of Eden, speaking unto them, and they saw him not; for they were shut out from his presence.*

*And he gave unto them commandments, that they should worship the Lord their God, and should offer the firstlings of their flocks, for an offering unto the Lord. And Adam was obedient unto the commandments of the Lord.*

*And after many days an angel of the Lord appeared unto Adam, saying: Why dost thou offer sacrifices unto the Lord? And Adam said unto him: I know not, save the Lord commanded me.*

*And then the angel spake, saying: This thing is a similitude of the sacrifice of the Only Begotten of the Father, which is full of grace and truth.*

*Wherefore, thou shalt do all that thou doest in the name of the Son, and thou shalt repent and call upon God in the name of the Son forevermore.* (Moses 5:4–8)

As a reward for Adam's obedience, both he and Eve received a witness of the truth, and a promise that they would live again in God's presence.

*And in that day the Holy Ghost fell upon Adam, which beareth record of the Father and the Son, saying: I am the Only Begotten of the Father from the beginning, henceforth and forever, that as thou hast fallen thou mayest be redeemed, and all mankind, even as many as will.*

*And in that day Adam blessed God and was filled, and began to prophesy concerning all the families of the earth, saying: Blessed be the name of God, for because of my transgression my eyes are opened, and in this life I shall have joy, and again in the flesh I shall see God.*

*And Eve, his wife, heard all these things and was glad, saying: Were it not for our transgression we never should have had seed, and never should have known good and evil, and the joy of our redemption, and the eternal life which God giveth unto all the obedient.*

*And Adam and Eve blessed the name of God, and they made all things known unto their sons and their daughters.* (Moses 5:9–12)

As difficult as it sometimes is to obey the directions given us by those placed in authority over us, we must learn to obey. When you get into a position of leadership, remember what you learned and how you felt when others might have used unrighteous dominion and make sure not to repeat it! Learning to follow and obey is an important part of learning how to become a good leader. If you do not know what it takes to be a good follower, you will never learn what it takes to be a good leader. So, after all is said and done, learn to obey. Put your ego and your poor attitude in your pocket and humble yourself! Besides, it will be good medicine for your soul.

# Six
## Tracting

*M* ost missionaries hate tracting. Great missionaries find it fun. The reason? Great missionaries have the confidence to know they will get in doors and teach. Most missionaries spend most of their time tracting. There are a number of reasons for this. Europe, the United States, Canada, and many other areas around the world have been taught and re-taught by the missionaries for many, many years. In a way, the field has already been reaped and now missionaries are just gleaning the fields.[1] In some areas of the world, the Church is very young and does not have the membership to produce the referrals required to keep missionaries busy. And, of course, there are the areas that have been devastated by bad missionaries. Whatever the reason, most missionaries spend a great deal of time walking and knocking on doors. Let's look at how to do this in a positive and effective way.

## Door Approaches

*1. Keep it simple.*

The first of the basics is the door approach. It won't take long

---

[1] Deuteronomy 24:19–22; Ruth 2:2-23.

for you to understand that it is not what you say that will get you in the door; it is the Spirit of God you carry that touches people and gets them to let you in. There is no need to create some elaborate door approach to "wow" them, or convince them, or coerce them. It is the Spirit that gets you in. So, work on your aura. Yes, your aura. This is one of the first principles I learned while being converted to the gospel. Righteous people carry the Spirit of God with them (an aura) that you can feel and see.

I remember the exact moment I learned this principle. I was sitting in a friend's apartment in Park City, Utah. It was night and there was a candle lit in the room. I had been reading the Sermon on the Mount and the parable of the candle[2] came to my mind. A candle should not be hidden under a bushel but put on a candlestick to give light to all who are in the house. And just as the light of a candle shines, *our light*, the Spirit of God within us, can shine before men. I remember that night, closing my eyes and trying to picture the Spirit of God within me, trying to *expand* the light of my spirit to extend outside my body. Even then I felt it was possible. Now, I *know* it is possible.

When you go to a door, instead of fretting about what you will say (for it shall be given you what ye shall speak[3]), spend your time preparing your spirit and mentally *pushing* your spirit outward, so others can feel it. It may feel awkward at first, like a child taking his first steps, but over time you will actually be able to influence others through the presence and the power of your spirit.

*2. Change your approach often.*
There is nothing more mundane, boring, and damaging than to

---

[2] Matthew 5:14–16.
[3] Matthew 10:19–20.

use the same door approach time after time. It dulls the mind and the spirit during a time when you should be the most focused. Even worse, it limits what the Lord can do (remember the lesson of the well?). Every person you meet will have different needs, wants, and desires. Every person is looking for answers to different questions. So why not use that knowledge by expanding what you say at the door? Ask a probing question, or make a statement containing a gospel principle:

♦ Do you know that there are prophets on the earth today?

♦ Are you happy? Would you like to be?

♦ Do you know where you go after death?

♦ Do you know we lived before being born on this earth?

♦ We represent a church that has the largest women's organization in the world.

♦ Are you interested in your ancestors?

♦ We believe the family is the most important thing on earth; do you feel the same?

♦ Faith in God has the power to heal and cleanse. You can have this power in your life!

♦ Do you know that little children who die automatically go to heaven?

♦ We are servants of Jesus Christ who hold the Priesthood of God. May we leave a blessing upon your home and family?

♦ Would you like to learn about the Second Coming of Jesus Christ?

♦ Some people believe that the end of the world is near. Would you like to learn how to prepare for it?

Well, I think you get the point. By constantly changing what you say at the door, you will not only keep yourself energized but will provide the Lord with a deep well to draw upon. Think of it: if you only have one door approach and the next door you knock on has just had a death in the family, they will just say they are too busy right now. But if you have a full repertoire of things to say, the Lord can *inspire* you to say just the right thing. Then, instead of just saying something dull and without feeling, you will come to this same door and say: Did you know that death is not the end but all men will live forever because of the sacrifice of Jesus Christ? You might touch their spirit and catch them at the right moment to teach them an eternal principle.

3. *Don't be afraid to experiment.*

One of the silly things we tried while I was learning to have fun on my mission was to sing a song as a door approach. Yes, sing! Now, I am not a great singer but we gave it a try. It went something like this:

> "Hi, we are elders from the Church of Jesus Christ of Latter-day Saints. We have a special message we are sharing with people today. Could we come in?"
>
> "I'm sorry, I'm just not interested."
>
> "I understand, but before we go, could we sing a song for you?"
>
> Suddenly interested, and perhaps with a roll of her eyes, she says, "Yes."
>
> "There is beauty all around, when there's love at home . . ."

By the time we were through the first verse, she had tears in her eyes. When we were done, she invited us in. The song had given us the time to touch her with the Spirit (remember, it is the Spirit who gets you in the door!). Sometimes people would laugh, and sometimes, when we were particularly off tune, we would laugh, too. But no matter whether we got in the door or not, they remembered the Mormon missionaries and the sweet (and sometimes funny) Spirit they carried with them. The next time the missionaries stop by, they will get in.

Singing is just one of many different things you can try at doors. After all, what have you got to lose? It will keep the time from becoming tedious, it will expand your talents and abilities, and it will provide the Lord a wide array of possibilities with which to inspire you when the right time comes.

### Get to know the neighborhood

The best thing to do when arriving in a new area is to get to know the neighborhood. Take time to walk around and find the areas of local interest—gathering points for people to talk or play or congregate for any reason. Just as you prepared the well of your mind by reading the scriptures, learning the discussions, and learning many door approaches, you must learn about your area so the Lord can inspire you as to where you should begin your work. You can use this information in many ways. Don't be afraid and don't reject any group of people, no matter how strange they may seem at the time. Let me give you a few examples:

### 1. Meet the local gangs.

In most areas of this country there are street gangs that roam a specific territory within a city. Don't be afraid of them; get to know them. Most, no matter how hardened, have a soft spot for people they know are there to help them or their families. Priests, medical personnel, and missionaries are usually safe.

One Saturday, shortly after arriving in one area, we came across a gang playing basketball on the local playground. Most people would have walked on the other side of the street. We decided to

## Becoming a Great Missionary

introduce ourselves. We walked up and told them who we were and why we were in their neighborhood. They gave us the typical sass and backtalk you would expect from ruffians. Undeterred, I told them we loved to play basketball and that our day off was on Monday. If they were around, I said, we would like to play a pick-up game with them. They laughed and chided the stupid "morons," but they also said yes. That next Monday about noon (it being the middle of the summer with school out), we went to the playground and started playing basketball. It wasn't long before a few gang members showed up and we started playing. It was rough, but acceptable. Of course when the swearing and cursing started we had a problem. What to do? If we refused to play because of their abusive words, we would offend them and lose a valuable contact. If we let it go without saying anything, we would lose their respect. So we somehow had to meet them halfway. We decided to simply give back in a lighthearted and humorous way, mimicking the way they treated us. Just as they chided us for being Mormons and goody two shoes, we began to chide them over their foul language. We told them it hurt our ears and how our mothers never let us play with boys like them, etc., all in an atmosphere of fun and teasing. At first, they did not know how to react—just as we did not know how to react to them. But over time, a few weeks perhaps, their swearing slowly disappeared. They began to treat us with respect and even protected us. One night we were coming home late and noticed someone following us. At first, we got nervous, but then noticed it was one of the gang members with whom we played every Monday. As we finally neared our apartment, I saw him tip his head and disappear. I suddenly realized he had been following to protect us. Not only had their respect for us grown, but my respect for them grew also. We never did teach them any discussions, but I have no doubt that we had a positive effect on their lives.

*2. Pray in public.*

Make certain that everyone knows who and what you are, at all times. Although usually very awkward, we decided to pray before eating, wherever we happened to be. If we were in a public restaurant, we would simply bow our heads and pray silently to ourselves for a few moments. One day we happened to be in Burger King, and, as usual, we bowed our heads in silent prayer before eating our food. Nothing big or showy, just something we did every day. But this day someone took notice. As we were walking out of the restaurant, a woman stopped us, asked us who we were, and thanked us for being such good examples to those around us. It reminded us again how one never knows how our actions and examples will affect other people.

*3. Stop at every door.*

One of the mistakes most missionaries make is to assume that one type of person will not be interested in the gospel.

"Let's skip this house, nobody lives here." When I was in Pennsylvania, we found people living in the most horrid conditions imaginable. Poor people living in homes with no lights or power, who gathered coal from the roadsides to heat their homes in the winter; homes with no windows or with boarded-up doors; street people with nothing to live for. Remember what Peter said when he came across the beggar at the temple:

> *Silver and gold have I none, but such as I have give I thee.*
> (Acts 3:6)

We did not seek out the poor, nor did we seek out the wealthy. We set a plan, mapped it out, and then went where the Lord led us.

## Becoming a Great Missionary

While tracting in an area, who are we to judge who is worthy to hear the gospel we bring? Though you may not be able to help them with their physical conditions, you can bring the peace of God into their lives by letting them know someone cares. People's lives change dramatically from year to year. My family once spent several months living in a tent at a campground because we had no other place to go. A few months later, we were living in a house. I wonder how the missionaries would have judged us had they knocked on our tent door?

"She's too old," or "He's too young." We taught people as young as eight years old and as old as 100, on their deathbed (of course, getting permission of the parents of those under 18 years old). Again, who are we to judge?

"She smokes," "He's a drunk," "She's a prostitute," "He's a convict," "They are drug dealers," "They are living together in sin," etc. The list could go on and on about types of people whom I have seen other missionaries decline to teach because of judgments they have made about the person, their lifestyle, or their living conditions. Who are you to judge?! You are sent to call sinners to repentance! You are sent to show them a better way of life! If you pass by those who *need* the gospel the most, then why are you on a mission? While on my mission, I taught all of the above people, without judgment or fear, but with a hope in my heart that I could better their lives. I did this because I had been a sinner. I had done what they had done–just a few years before I had been where they were. God did not judge me; He forgave me. I could do no less for them.

"We can't teach him, he's a priest!" Do not be deceived by the powerful mask most ministers and priests wear. They have to wear them for the congregations they teach. Remember, if they don't have the fullness of the gospel, they just don't understand. They are as lost as those whom they teach. Most will not listen out of pride. But many will at least talk and some will listen. When you are tracting a street and come across a church, go inside and introduce yourselves. I have heard priests openly confess that they don't believe in God, ministers who refuse to believe in the literal resurrection of Christ, and pastors who see their calling only as a job, a career with a pension. I am telling you the truth when I say that most ministers of other churches I have met, behind the arrogance and pomp of their positions, are just as confused about God as their congregations. Do not pass up the opportunity, the duty, to call upon these men and women and teach them the gospel.

One more time: Don't judge people! You are not on a mission to judge or condemn. You are there to teach. Remember that conversion to the gospel is not a one-time event; it is a process that takes a long time. Those you will baptize listened and accepted because they have been prepared for many years. Through the spirit of the Lord, other missionaries, other members, even other churches and ministers, have been preparing them, softening their hearts, so they are finally ready to hear the full gospel and accept it. When you teach a family only one discussion and can't go back, or when you talk at the door but can't get in, or when you just talk to people on the street, *always leave a good impression.* This cannot be stressed enough. No matter how rude people are to you, no matter how long a day you have had, do not be rude or ill tempered to the people you meet. I promise you that something you have said will touch them—maybe not enough to let the missionaries in now, but perhaps next time, or the next. Do not judge people! You do not know their hearts or what is happening in their lives to cause them to reject you. And because you don't know, you should give them the benefit of the doubt; you should have *compassion* on them and bless them in spite of their negative attitudes. *Always leave a good impression.*

**113**

# Becoming a Great Missionary

*Mapping out a plan*

    *1.  Get a physical map of the area.*

After you have gotten to know the area for which you are responsible, the next thing to do is to get a map of your specific area. You can get these at most stores or gas stations. However, if you have trouble finding one showing all of the streets in your area, try going to a real estate office. I promise you will find one there. Then buy a couple of highlighters to mark your map. There are two reasons for this, the first being rather pragmatic. You do not want to re-tract an area you just worked. By marking the streets you have tracted, you will be able to prevent problems and embarrassment. The second reason is much more profound. A map will permit you to develop a plan of action for teaching. Remember, this area is your responsibility. Every person within that area is under your care. Sometimes that can be overwhelming. For example, in my first area in Philadelphia we had over one million people! One million people we were responsible to reach, warn, and teach. But like eating an elephant, one need only eat one bite at a time. By getting a map and creating a plan of attack one can begin to eat that elephant, street by street, until the entire area has been reached. This is no different than the prophetic plan of Prophet Spencer W. Kimball when he explained, for the first time, how the Church would take the gospel to the whole world. He took a map of the world, made a plan, and showed, step by step, how it would be done.

    *2.  Enlist the help of angels.*

Mapping out a plan may seem ridiculous to some, a waste of time and effort, something to which an accountant or obsessive-compulsive person might resort. But how wrong they would be. The fact is that mapping an area is absolutely necessary in obtaining help from the angels of God! Make no mistake, you have not been sent on your mission alone! You have the angels of God standing by to help.[4] But in order to obtain their help, you need to know how the process works. How do you, an elder holding the Priesthood of God, turn the key that permits angels to intercede in the works of men? Remember, God has given men free will and will not interfere with that eternal principle except under very specific conditions.

God has directed us to ask in order to receive. This is not to make things inconvenient but because God has placed laws by which things work. One of those laws is agency. God will not interfere with the free will of men. Whether they choose good or bad, God permits them to choose and suffer the consequences of their actions. That being the case, how do we receive help from God? By asking. When we ask God for help, it is our *free will* that He intercede on our behalf. It is our *choice* that God help us. And one of the ways God helps is to send His angels. So, when we kneel and ask for help from God, it *automatically* turns the keys of power to permit angels to help us in our work. It is a simple process, but a necessary one. If you don't ask, you will not receive.

So how does the map come in? It has to do with how angels work and having a realistic view of how God works. God is not a magician. He works miracles using the natural laws of the universe. Sometimes the help God is sending you takes time. Let me give you an example.

◆◆◆

A man and his family are going on a trip to California. They are all very excited as they load the car for the trip. The father is a righteous man and so the Spirit begins to whisper in his ear to check the

---

[4] D&C 84:88; 103:20.

spare tire. But, like most of us, the hectic pace of packing, and kids, and the excitement of the trip prevents the message from getting through (although when he gets into trouble later he will remember that small whisper and be angry with himself for not listening). This family is destined to have big problems because of that spare tire! But they do something right. Before they leave, they take the time to say a prayer and ask for the Lord's help in getting to their destination safely. They take the time to turn the key. As a result, the Lord sends his angels before them.

The angels immediately see the problem. The spare tire is flat and one of the tires on the car is ready to blow. The family will be stuck somewhere, the vacation ruined. So the angels fan out ahead of this family to find a solution to the problem. Finally, they find it. There is a farmer who has a field just about where this family will run into trouble. If only they can persuade this farmer to work his field today! Fortunately, the farmer and his wife had prayer that morning and as he starts into the fields with his tractor, almost as an afterthought, he decides to go to the south field instead of the west field. He doesn't know why, but has learned long ago not to fight these quiet inspirations. As the family drives toward their destination, their left rear tire suddenly blows out. A few minutes later, they find the spare is flat also. What are they to do? Just as a feeling of desperation is about to set in, they hear a voice coming from the field next to the road: "Need some help?" There is the farmer. He gives the whole family a hayride back to the farmhouse, and while the kids play with the animals the farmer fills the spare tire with air. Then they all get a hayride back to their car. Because of their prayer and the help of angels sent before them, a serious problem is turned into a wonderful, unforgettable adventure. New friends are formed who will become a regular part of their family trip from then on, and this family is blessed, literally beyond their understanding.

*But behold, I say unto you that ye must pray always, and not faint; that ye must not perform any thing unto the Lord save in the first place ye shall pray unto the Father in the name of Christ, that he will consecrate thy performance unto thee, that thy performance may be for the welfare of thy soul.* (2 Nephi 32:9)

This is not new doctrine. It is taught from the very first discussion:

*If any of you lack wisdom, let him ask of God, who giveth to all men liberally, and upbraideth not; and it shall be given him.* (James 1:5)

But there is one more thing to understand. One more principle to make it all work correctly. You cannot change or waver in your actions or it will not work.

*But let him ask in faith, nothing wavering. For he that wavereth is like a wave of the sea driven with the wind and tossed. For let not that man think that he shall receive anything of the Lord.* (James 1:6)

He that asks in faith gets everything, but he that wavers, or changes, gets nothing. Why? Because of how it all works. Let's go back to our example:

The family has done almost everything right, and due to the prayer with which they began the angels of God have been sent out before them so everything will turn out all right. But then something happens. The father changes his plans. Halfway there, the father decides to change direction and take a different route to California. His willful change of plans, his wavering, places the whole family in jeopardy. By taking a different route than they had planned, they find themselves with a flat tire on a lonely road with no help in sight. Instead of having an exciting adventure, they have their vacation ruined. But where is their help? Their help is where it is supposed to be; with the farmer and his family on the other road. And their angels are probably a little frustrated . . . after all, they spent all of that time preparing the way before this family only to have it all for naught due to the wavering of the father.

Those who ask in faith get everything because their path is prepared before them by the angels of God. Those who continually waver and change their plans get nothing because God and his angels have no clue what they are doing or where they are going.

So now, we go back to the map. By working out a *plan*, you tell God ahead of time what you will be doing and where you will be going. In response to your prayers, the angels are sent before you, following your plan, and preparing the people whom you will meet. If you follow a logical pattern in tracting, street by street in progression, God can send his angels ahead of you to prepare the people you will meet. They will touch the minds and hearts of the people in your path before you even get there! But, like the family described above, if you continually change your plans, God will not know what you are doing and will hold his angels back from wasting their time.

I cannot begin to tell you how many times I saw the work of angels as we tracted the streets of our areas. We would catch people home, just at the right time. People fell ill or got better; their cars broke down or got fixed; people changed their plans or had their plans changed by others—just at the right time and in the right way for us to meet them. I cannot tell you how many times we heard, "You're lucky you caught me, I'm never home at this time."

I testify to you that this works. If you get a map, lay out a plan of attack so that the Lord and His angels know what you are going to do, and then ask for God's help, I promise that the path will be prepared before you, and you will find success in ways you have never dreamed.

### Tracting is fun

I know this sounds crazy, but it is true. When you get home from your mission and begin to tell stories about the crazy and fun things that happened to you, 90 percent of the best stories will have happened while tracting. It is while tracting that strange things happen. You meet crazy people and, at times, miracles happen. Let me give you a few stories of my own to give you a feel for what I mean.

One of the great opportunities you have while tracting is meeting famous people, or at least *they* think they are famous! On my mission I met all of the following:

♦  Adam and Eve: Adam was an 80-year-old man who had been reincarnated. As soon as he was able to get Eve (the lady who lived next door) to move in with him, they were going to be taken to populate a new planet.

♦  Christ: Actually, I met quite a few "Christs" while on my mission. Most had been reincarnated and were just waiting for people to realize who they really were.

# Becoming a Great Missionary

- ♦ Mary: One young woman was convinced she was Mary, reincarnated, of course (which always puzzled me, since no Christian I know believes in reincarnation, yet all of these people claimed to be Christians).

- ♦ Prophet of Mary: One young woman claimed to be Mary's prophet. Mary would appear to her while she was having an epileptic fit. She became attracted to my companion and me for a while and followed us around.

Well, you get the picture.

## *Tracting is dangerous*

The other memorable set of events that will happen to most missionaries while tracting comes in the form of physical abuse. Yes, I'm sorry to say it's true. I don't say this to scare you, but there are times when people just can't take life anymore and take it out on you. They will release their dogs on you, physically throw you out, or try to run you over. Very seldom does this become serious, but you have to be aware of the dangers. Here are a few examples.

One day during the summer, we were tracting at a door. The door was open with just the screen door closed, but we could see inside. We rang the doorbell and I could see a large man get up off the couch. Suddenly he began swearing and cursing and ran full throttle at the door. We could tell he had totally lost control, and we immediately turned to run; too late. He came bursting right through the screen door, caught me, and catapulted me into the front yard. Before I knew it, I was head over teacup rolling on the grass! He stood on the porch and continued to curse us as we ran up the street.

My children's favorite story is the one about the Weed-Wacker. It is a great lesson about always leaving with a good impression. We had just started to tract a new area. There was a man outside doing yardwork. We approached him and he rejected us. For some stupid reason, I gave him some flip remark that offended him. It didn't happen often, and I was sorry as soon as I said it, but it was too late. He yelled and threatened us if we ever came back. Several months later, we tracted the same area again. I had forgotten about the incident but this man hadn't forgotten! He was in his yard with a Weed-Wacker. As we started up the driveway, he saw us, started cursing, and came at us with the Weed-Wacker in hand! We turned and ran for our lives, as we could hear the buzz of the Weed-Wacker just behind. Just as we were sure we would be "wacked" to death, the man ran out of electrical cord and had to stop chasing. We escaped a harrowing fate, and I learned a good lesson about mouthing off to people.

Not all situations that arise are dangerous, but a great missionary must always be prepared for the unexpected. I was on splits with another missionary in Philadelphia. We were working the assigned area when my companion suddenly told me he had to go to the bathroom. Okay, no big deal. We couldn't go back to the apartment but there was probably a gas station in the neighborhood (we had taken the bus to this area). As we began to walk back the way we came, he became more and more urgent. I finally told him I would knock on a couple of doors and ask to use their bathroom (the action of last resort, usually too embarrassing). Just as I was about to knock, my companion told me he just couldn't wait anymore and ran around the side of the house and into the bushes. I yelled at him, "You can't do that!" He slowly walked out from behind the bushes with an embarrassed look on his face. My poor companion had come down with the flu and had developed a case of diarrhea that just happened to catch him at the wrong time. When we finally got back to the apartment, we had to put him in the shower, clothes and all! So, just a word of advice about being prepared . . . when you go into an area to work, decide ahead of time where the local bathroom facilities are.

One door we came to almost led to tragedy. Just after an older man opened the door, his eyes rolled back in his head and he fell backward, hitting the floor with a crash. Then he didn't move. We opened the screen door to see if he was dead. We found he was still breathing and, after a few moments, he revived and got up. He told us that he had just gotten up too fast and fainted. It was a very scary few moments.

Most of the time missions are just hard work and fun, but occasionally they can be deadly. Not long after I came out on my mission, three missionaries in my district were murdered. Four missionaries were together in a car, out on splits, when a driver came up from behind and began to harass them. At a traffic light he got out, came up to their car, and began to kick the car and curse them. It was one against four and they could easily have overpowered the guy, but they did not want trouble so they just drove off. But the man continued to follow them. When they got to a four-lane highway and speeds picked up, the man rammed into the back of their car, forcing it into oncoming traffic. Three of the four missionaries were killed with only the driver escaping alive and unhurt. This resulted in a murder trial.

This is, of course, the worst-case scenario for any missionary and his family, but it has to be understood that there is *always* the possibility that God will call us home. Remember, it is God who has control, and it is God who will decide to call us home if it is His will. Shortly after this accident, I had the opportunity to talk to the surviving elder. He had been devastated by the event and wondered why it had happened. He questioned why he had been the only one saved; why, why, why? Then one night, God in His infinite mercy and love gave him an answer. That night the three deceased missionaries visited this elder. They had not changed at all! They were laughing and joking and teasing the elder about staying behind when they were having so much fun on the other side. They told him they had been called to serve their mission on the other side. He was told that he was not to be sad or depressed because they were happy and excited about where they were and what they were doing. They did not know why he had been left behind, but they assured him it was all part of God's plan. Then they said goodbye to their friend and left. It is my understanding that these three elders also appeared to my mission president with a similar message.

So, yes, a mission can be dangerous. Yes, missionaries are occasionally killed or die while on their missions. But God is in control. You will not be taken unless it is God's specific will that it be so. Remember the angels? They are there to protect as well as help. Every mission has stories about elders escaping danger in miraculous ways. Sometimes these are just mission legends but some are actually true! Be aware of the danger and be prudent and wise in your actions and decisions. Let your faith take away any fear you may have, because, in reality, whether you will die on your mission is not the issue—after all, we all die sometime—what is at issue is how you live! Be faithful and true and you need have no fear. And then, even if you die, you will find joy in the presence of God. So go forward with faith, not fear, and experience joy while working in the fields of the Lord.

## Going the Extra Mile

We have talked about going the extra mile and how important it is while doing missionary work. Let me give you a specific example of how this works. In fact, this story shows how I learned that going the extra mile really is the key to success.

My companion and I decided to start working harder and smarter. We found ways to cut out wasted time and work longer. As our understanding of how to work harder and smarter progressed, we pushed ourselves, and each other, until we felt very good about the direction in which we were heading. The success we began to have proved to us that what we were doing was working.

One day we had been out tracting without getting in to a home all day. It was dinnertime and we were tired, hungry, and frustrated. We had one more street to finish an area and then we would be moving to a completely new area that evening. As we stood at the bottom of the street, we debated whether or not to finish or just go home and eat. We finally decided we had made a commitment to "go the extra mile" and needed to finish what we had started. With great sighs of resignation, we started up that last street without success. On the next-to-the-last door before the street was done and we could go home, we found a golden young family with two small children. They had become frustrated with their church and had turned to God for help. They had been praying for several days for the Lord to send them an answer as to what church to join; then we knocked on their door. They told us straight out that we were an answer to their prayers, that they had been waiting for us. We could see the joy in their faces as we entered their home. We could feel the power of the Spirit as we began to teach them the first discussion. Do you think we felt hungry or tired or frustrated any longer? No way! All of this was swept away in a moment, and we were left with feelings of great joy and a peace of Spirit that lasted for weeks.

As we walked home, we pondered the decision we had made. What if we had decided to quit? What if we had just gone home because we were too tired or hungry? What if? We both decided then and there that we would never again even debate "going the extra mile." It would simply become part of our standard missionary workfare. We learned a great lesson that day and never, ever forgot it.

# Becoming a Great Missionary

# Seven
## Finding People to Teach

This chapter will suggest a number of ways to find people to teach the gospel. The real key to finding people to teach is to think about teaching everyone. Most missionaries walk down the street, passing by many opportunities to teach simply because they have a limited view of where they can find people. They walk by churches, schools, businesses, malls, and parks, unaware of the great teaching opportunities they are choosing to ignore.

All missionaries know how to tract; all you have to do is walk down the street. So I will concentrate on some of the other, lesser-known opportunities you will have to share the gospel.

## Using Local Newspapers

The first thing a missionary should do upon being transferred to a new area is to go to the local paper and ask them to publish a story about you. Sound fantastic? It is, and it is very easy to get them to do. The key is to go prepared with everything they need. You will need a picture of yourself (you can get a picture taken at almost any mall at one of those instant photo booths). Then write a short biography: where you are from, how long you will be serving in the area, why you are here, etc. It doesn't need to be very long, just a couple of paragraphs.

You might wonder *why* a newspaper would do this for you. The reason is they have a newspaper to sell, and it is their job to find something, anything, to put into their paper. If they can get a story by someone coming in and giving them information, instead of having to send a reporter out to find stories, they are very happy! If you do the work for them (get the picture, write the story, etc.), they are usually more than willing to accommodate you.

When you have the picture and information, go to the newspaper and ask for the reporter assigned to religion (almost all newspapers have someone responsible for this area). After getting to this reporter, tell him that you have been transferred into the area and ask to have an article in the paper about you and why you are serving in the area. Also, tell him you have a picture, a short article, and are willing to provide even more information if necessary. I was never once denied this request! I had my name and picture in almost every paper in every area of my mission.

The immediate effect of this is immeasurable. You won't believe how many doors this will open for you. As you knock on doors, people will recognize you from the article and the feeling of familiarity will allow them to let you in. Some who would normally be afraid to open their doors to strangers will let you in because they read about you in the paper. And, if nothing else, people will read about the work of the Lord being conducted in the area.

In addition to using *any* transfer as an excuse to get a missionary's name and picture in the paper, you can use any number of other things as a reason: zone, regional, and General conferences and any other special activities that you or the local ward may be doing, such as open houses or a change in the bishopric.

## Teaching in Schools

The next area to look at is local high schools: religious schools (like a Catholic high school), private high schools, and public high schools. Go to the main office and ask if they have any classes in world religions or ask for the history teacher. If they have a world religions class, you have a perfect reason to approach the teacher of that class and offer your services to teach them about the Church. If all they have is a history class, you can approach the teacher to talk about Brigham Young, the pioneers, and the westward movement in the late 1800s. Since it is a history class, you can teach them *why* the Mormons left the United States and moved west: religious persecution. And what is it about our Church that caused this persecution? A perfect opening for telling them about Joseph Smith, the First Vision, and that we believe in modern-day prophets.

Why would these teachers allow you into their classes to teach? Because teaching is hard work and if they have a "visiting professor" who will teach their classes for them, they will jump at the chance. Let me give you a couple of examples of when we taught in schools.

*1.  Teaching in Catholic high schools.*

My first companion had been a Catholic before being converted to the Church. As a result of the background, he wasn't afraid to approach and talk to the priests who ran the local Catholic high school. They had a world religions class and said they would be willing to let us come and talk about our church. At first we thought this would be just one class. Little did we know; it turned out that they held this class all seven periods. We taught the Joseph Smith story in every class and then answered questions from the students. They liked it so much we were invited back the next day. Other teachers got wind of what we were doing and asked us if we would teach their classes as well. Think of it. Seven classes of potential investigators, a captive audience of 20–30 students in each class. That is over 200 people we were able to teach about the gospel at one time! We were not afraid to be bold. When asked questions, we answered honestly. When asked about the priesthood, we told them that we believed that the authority once held by the Apostles was lost due to the wickedness of the popes and priests and therefore had to be restored. When the priest running the class challenged us on this point, we asked him straight out if he denied there were wicked popes, and he could not deny it!

As you might imagine, our teaching caused some furor in the classes and at the homes of the students when their parents found out. For weeks and months afterward, we would run into the homes of these students and were almost always invited in. The students wanted to talk to us because they were interested in what we had said, or the parents wanted to talk to us to find out what we had been teaching in their kids' school. In either case, we got in doors as a result of teaching in schools, and we were able to touch them with the Spirit of God.

*2. Teaching in public high schools.*
Once we found success teaching in a few Catholic high schools, we decided to try our hand at the public high schools. After all, what did we have to lose? To our surprise and delight, they almost always said yes! The first public high school we taught ended up having a riot in the lunchroom over our visit.

## Finding People to Teach

We began teaching the Joseph Smith story and answering questions as usual. Their questions were a little different, because they were mostly Protestants, but we had no problem handling them. Of course, polygamy and the blacks not being able to hold the priesthood always came up, but we never seemed to have any difficulty answering their questions. At lunchtime, we were invited into the teachers' lounge. It was here that the most interesting discussion began. Several of the teachers were Protestants and several others were Catholics, so there began a rousing debate about religion. At one point, the issue of authority came up. I decided to stir the fire a little and said, "There are only two religions that can possibly be true: either the Catholic Church is true or the Mormon Church is true. The reason has to do with authority. Either the true authority from God has stayed upon the earth from the time of the ancient Apostles, as the Catholics claim, or they lost their authority through wickedness and it had to be restored in the last days, as we claim. The Protestants have no authority no matter which way you look at it. If the Catholic Church is true then the Protestants have lost all authority by breaking away from the true church. If the Catholics lost their authority, as we claim, then the Protestants, who broke off from the Catholic Church, still have no authority!" Well, after a long moment of silence, this really got the debate going between them as to whether or not anybody had any authority from God. It was wonderful.

Sometime during the conversation, we started hearing a ruckus in the lunchroom. Chairs were being thrown about and a food fight had started. As we followed the teachers into the lunchroom to see what was going on, we could not believe what we were seeing! There was a full-blown riot going on between two groups of students. After the teachers got things settled down and asked what caused the trouble, it became clear that the students from our morning classes had been debating the things we had taught. They began arguing about their own personal religions and soon the debate turned into a fight. It was great!

As before, after we had taught in a high school we scheduled our days to tract in that school district, so we would be knocking on the same doors as the students we had been teaching. And, as before, we found great results.

### 3. *Teaching in colleges.*

Although I never had the opportunity to teach at a college or religious seminary, I have no doubt that the experience would be the same. Teachers are interested in bringing in outside help to teach their classes. It means they do not have to prepare a class themselves, and it gives the class a more objective feeling. So do not be intimidated by people who claim to know everything. The fact is that *we have the truth*, not them, and the truth will stand up against anything thrown at it. Look for opportunities, be unafraid to ask (all they can do is say no), and then teach them the truth. Don't change it or sugar coat it; lay it out for them. You will be surprised how many people respond to the simple truth.

### 4. *Teaching a seminary in Connecticut.*

While serving as ward mission leader in Connecticut, I taught the missionaries about contacting churches where they tract. One day while tracting, they came to one of the largest and most prestigious seminaries in the country. It is here that people from all over the country come to learn how to become priests (in order to become a priest or a minister a person has to go to college and get a formal degree). The missionaries went to the main office, offered their services, and the seminary jumped at the chance. As it turned out, the bishop of our ward (who was a college professor with a Doctorate in music) went with the missionaries. As usual, it turned out to be a wonderful experience.

## Teaching at Other Churches

Once we had a taste of teaching large groups of people, we began to look for other groups we might teach. To our surprise, we found we could arrange to teach whole congregations of people right in their own churches! Once again, it was as simple as "ask and ye shall receive." The process is simple. As you tract in an area and come across a local church, do *not* just pass by this opportunity to teach! Knock on the door and introduce yourselves as the local representatives of The Church of Jesus Christ of Latter-day Saints. Tell them you will be serving in the area and wanted to stop by and meet the priest (or minister, or whatever). Most will invite you in and give you an opportunity to tell them more about who you are and why you are there. Although the success rate for teaching is very low in this case, all it takes is one or two to create a marvelous teaching opportunity. At the very least, you may be able to teach the priest or minister himself (it has been known to happen). Remember, they are just as lost as their congregation when it comes to knowing the truth. Cardinal rule #1: *Never assume they will not be interested!* Always leave it up to them to say no to your request; do not deny them the opportunity to hear because you are intimidated or afraid. Be bold, knowing that you have the truth on your side. I had at least three opportunities to teach in other churches during my mission.

*1. Teaching in Sunday School.*

The first opportunity to teach in another church came when we talked a minister into letting us teach his Sunday School about our church. This was a Congregational church. Many of the Protestant churches have very loose doctrine; in other words, they do not have a strict set of beliefs. Their beliefs seem to change each time they get a new minister. This is doubly true of Unitarian churches and the like. They are much more open to listening to others' points of view. When you are talking to the minister, you will get a feel for how interested he is in what you are saying. If he shows interest, ask if his Sunday School class or his congregation might be interested. Most of the time they will say no. But sometimes, enough times, they say yes. This was just a one-hour class with a few members of the congregation. We were not invited back.

*2. Teaching an entire Catholic church.*

The next opportunity came while on a split with one of the missionaries in my district. I had been talking to him about my experiences teaching in schools and churches when we just happened to tract by a Catholic church. Of course, it was suddenly put up or shut up time for me! So we knocked on the parish door and the priest let us in. We decided to talk to him about the Family Home Evening program of the Church. He got very excited and wanted to know more. We gave him the literature we had and went through in detail how the program works. He asked if we would be willing to come to his church on Sunday to talk to his whole congregation about Family Home Evening–on the condition that we did not talk about the Church or our doctrine. We quickly agreed to his terms. That next Sunday, we arrived at the Catholic church and were escorted by the priest to the front pew of the church. Of course, all eyes were upon us with our nametags and "missionary uniforms." They held their standard mass with everyone but us taking communion. Then the priest stood, introduced us, and explained why we were there. He then gave us the floor.

We introduced ourselves, gave a rough outline of the Family Home Evening program, and then launched into a specific outline of what is done on Monday nights:

1. We always begin with a prayer. This not only brings the family closer to God but also binds them closer to each other.

2. Then we sing a song together. For example: "There is Beauty All Around." Then the two of us, standing in front of the whole congregation, sang all three verses of this song! We didn't sound too bad since we sang that song quite often as part of door approaches and lessons.

3. We then teach a short lesson. This opportunity is usually passed around so that every member of the family gets a chance to share their thoughts and feelings about what they believe.

4. Sometimes there is time set aside to schedule the week's activities. Families are so busy these days that our activities often come into conflict. By taking time to ask each member of the family what they will be doing that week, schedules can be arranged or rearranged so that nothing of importance is missed. In addition, the attention paid to children and what they are doing makes them feel important.

5. There is some kind of activity, a game of some kind. Sometimes the whole evening is just an activity that was chosen, like a movie, going sledding, or going to a museum. Once again, it is important that each member of the family gets to participate and is allowed to choose what activity will be done.

6. We end with a song and a prayer.

## Becoming a Great Missionary

After we finished, we thanked them for listening, encouraged them to set aside time each week with their family, and thanked the priest for the opportunity to share. As we were about to sit, several members of the congregation shouted questions to us: "What else do you believe?" "Why are you *really* here?" Some of the questions were directed at the priest: "How could you let someone from another faith come into our church?" We responded to the first couple of questions by explaining we had promised the priest that we would not talk about our doctrine; we were there simply to talk about the Family Home Evening program. Now there began to be more people asking about our church. We again said we had promised not to. Then even more people began to shout, this time directed at the priest. He looked at us and told us to go ahead and answer some questions. Once we had the priest's permission, we began to answer their questions as honestly as we could. Why were we here? We were in this area talking to people about our Church and about the Family Home Evening program, which we felt would be useful for people of all religions. What is the difference between our Church and theirs? We believe that some time during the dark ages, the Catholic church lost the authority of God and much of the original doctrine of the church was changed, which brought about the Protestant reformation. We believe God restored His true church again in the last days through the Prophet Joseph Smith. What about polygamy? We do not teach or practice polygamy any more. What else is different about your religion? We believe in what we call the Word of Wisdom. It is a health law that forbids us to drink alcohol, coffee, or tea, or to use tobacco products or illicit drugs. Can you use hospitals? Yes. We are permitted to use doctors and hospitals and drugs of any kind as long as they are prescribed by a doctor and are for our *benefit*. These questions and short answers lasted for another half hour or so. Then the priest stood and said that, due to the time, he had to close the meeting, but he invited us to stay after the meeting and join them during their coffee hour.

After the priest closed the meeting, we were led into their reception room, or coffee room, where the congregation meets to talk after church. We stood for another hour and answered more questions. We kept it all very positive. We let them know that we believed all churches had truth, and if they lived that truth they would be rewarded. We told them we did *not* believe *only* Mormons go to heaven, or they would go to hell for being a Catholic (which are both *true* by the way). We knew we had an obligation to the priest who had been kind enough to let us teach his congregation. If we had been argumentative in any way, or said anything that would offend them, they would later take it out on the priest. This did not mean we did not stand up for the truth. It meant we were sensitive to the situation and refused to be drawn into any kind of debate as to who was right or wrong. We simply told them what we believed and let it go at that. No "we're right" and "you're wrong." Just showing them that our beliefs were different, and in what ways they were different.

The elders then spent the next few weeks tracting the area around this church and found great success getting in doors and teaching those who had been at that Sunday service and those who had heard about it by word of mouth.

3.  *Teaching a whole congregation at the Church of Christ.*
Another opportunity came when we tracted out the head of the Sunday School for the Church of Christ, a large Protestant church. We met this woman for the first time at her home and she invited us in. She found what we taught fascinating and wanted us to teach

## Becoming a Great Missionary

her Sunday School, especially about premortal existence. We gave her our phone number. She said she would arrange a meeting, if she could. We began to lose hope, but a few weeks later she called and asked if we could come on a Wednesday night to teach her class. Of course, we agreed. We decided to teach the Plan of Salvation lesson because it contained the concept of premortal life.

When we got to the church, we were shocked to see so many people! Almost the whole congregation was there. We were introduced to the pastor of the church, who was not at all happy about what was going on, and, to our surprise, left the building after being introduced to us. This meant we were left totally alone with almost his entire congregation. We showed the film "Man's Search for Happiness" and then taught them the discussion we had prepared. Following that, we answered questions. In all, we taught for about two hours.

The next few weeks and months were very busy for us. *Many* of those whom we had taught called and asked us to come and teach their family. And, of course, we made sure we tracted the entire area around this church, getting in many doors of those who had been there or heard about the lesson we had given.

## Teaching at Malls, College Campuses, Parks, and Other Gathering Places

One of the opportunities available in almost every area are places where large groups of people gather; malls, public parks, college campuses, public squares—*any place* where large groups of people gather. There are several things you can do at these places, depending upon the location and physical surroundings.

*1. Information booths.*

Probably the most useful tool, and the easiest to arrange, is a simple information booth about the Church. This can be built in about an hour with the help of members of the ward and takes just a few minutes to set up at the location. Take three pieces of 4' x 8' plywood, hinge them together lengthwise, cover them with some kind of cloth (secured with thumbtacks), and you have a background upon which to hang pictures and other information. Add a table and two chairs and you're all set. Take with you lots of pamphlets, books, flyers, and any other information you can obtain.

To get permission to set up a booth in a mall or a college, all you have to do is ask! They will usually approve the request as long as they control where and when you set up your booth. If they do say no, it may be a bad time so ask if there is a better time or some other place you can set up your booth. *Don't assume anything, ask!* Once you get permission, set up the booth and wait for people to come to you! Make sure you have referral forms for people to fill out (so you can go to their homes and teach) and plenty of things to give away. This type of information booth can be used anywhere you receive permission to set it up. Don't be afraid to try new places. If it doesn't work—so what? Try something else.

*2. Public speaking.*

One of the least-used methods of spreading the gospel is public speaking. This was *very* common in pioneer days but has unfortunately gone out of use. However, this is a good way to bring attention to your presence in the city and to reach people you may never be able to teach any other way. It is simply this: stand on a corner, or in a park, or at some other public place, and begin to preach the gospel. It is sometimes difficult to find the courage to do this, but it is effective. Just turn your normal discussions into sermons (there is very little give-and-take during this kind of missionary work, except for the occasional heckler). Missionaries talk for hours one-on-one with investigators; this is really no different. You can even offer yourself the questions investigators might ask: "Many people ask, where did we come from? Our religion teaches . . ." "Are you happy? Do you know how to obtain real joy in your life? Our religion teaches us that true peace and happiness can only come from Jesus Christ. Let me tell you about our Savior. . . ." Well, you get the picture. You must be bold and prepared for anything, but in the end you will have both fun and success.

In most places you will need permission to do this. You might need to go to City Hall and get a permit. At the very least, it is appropriate to *ask* if you need a permit. Normally these permits do not cost anything, or are minor in cost. Get a soapbox (or some other platform so you are above the crowd) and go to it! Make sure you continue to "preach" for several weeks in a row, at the same time and place each week (like every Saturday at noon). Over time, you will begin to acquire a following. People will come to hear you because they will know when and where you will be.

While one companion is talking, the other can be handing out tracts, getting the names of those there, and obtaining referrals to go to people's homes to give formal lessons. If this doesn't work, try another location or another time. Lunchtime is a great time to do this, as people are taking a break from work and have nothing better to do. Always be *thinking* of new things and ways to find people to teach.

3. *Street contacting.*

If you live in or near a busy city, street contacting is another way to meet a lot of people. This involves stopping people as they pass on the street and asking them if they would be interested in information about the Church. Make sure you have a *lot* of pamphlets to hand out; you will need them.

Just make certain you are not obnoxious, which sometimes happens after working a long day with little success. You may hand out a lot of information, but few people will stop to talk with you. This is no reason to get angry or short with people. Try to enjoy the time for what it is—another way to get information about the Church into the hands of people.

4. *Business contacting.*

For those missionaries who have real courage, try business contacting. President Pinnock, a very successful businessman himself, developed this idea. One of the main goals of any missionary is to find and teach men and fathers. During the day, this is very difficult as most men are at work. So why not go where the men are? Remember, I talked about not passing by *any* opportunity to teach. *Never* assume that something won't work, or that people will say no, until you ask them. Business contacting works! If you are tracting in an area and pass by a business or shop of any kind, go in and ask for the owner or manager. Don't talk to the employees, since it is inappropriate to talk to them while they are working. However, the owner's time is usually his own, as he does not have to answer to anyone but himself. So if he chooses to spend time to talk with you, it is okay. Make sure to tell him you will only take up a few minutes of his time. You may even want to specify an exact time, like 10 minutes. Then make sure that you stick within that time frame! Go in, introduce yourselves, explain why you are there, and that you don't want to take up a lot of his time now but would like to set up a time later, perhaps at his home, to talk about the gospel. If he says no, be gracious and leave. If he is interested and wants to talk, make sure you still recognize the time frame you set up at the start! When it comes to the time you agreed to leave, remind him of your promise to take up only 10 minutes of his time. If he then asks you to stay longer, you may, but only *after* you have notified him that you are keeping your word about the original time agreement. When you reach that time cutoff, if he wants to end the conversation make sure you do so! It is more important to keep your promise than to go on with any discussion you might be having. At this point all you can do, all you should do, is try to set up a return appointment.

Some missionaries got carried away with this form of contacting and ran into trouble. One missionary was so full of zeal that when he was told the president of the company was busy, he strode past the secretary anyway and right into the man's office. It turned out they were having a board meeting! Figuring he had committed himself, he walked to the front of the conference table and began giving his introduction. He was then hastily ushered out of the office. Funny story, but in reality it was totally inappropriate. I'm sure the next time any of the men seated at that conference table comes across a Mormon missionary, they will think twice about listening.

## Service Projects

We were not allowed to do service projects on my mission unless it was on our P-day. Fortunately, this has changed and service to the community is now an integral part of missions. Missionaries can now spend part of their time every week doing community service. This is a great tool for contacting potential investigators. Even if you never find anyone to teach, the goodwill that it generates for the Church is beyond price. *Every* missionary should spend some time doing service work. When things are slow, what better way to spend your time than helping others? Here are just a few things you can do.

1.  *Inner city food kitchens.*

Every city has homeless shelters. Every homeless shelter needs help. Offer your time once a week for an hour or two to help in the kitchen or serve food or clean up. Always wear your nametag so people know who you are. You will feel good about the service, obtain invaluable public relations for the Church, and be helping people at the same time.

2.  *Hospitals.*

One of the best places to spend a little time each week is at hospitals, talking to people, offering them comfort, and giving blessings. People are usually very open and honest when they are facing death or serious illness. They *want* to know about life after death, about why we are here on earth, and about forgiveness of sins. This is where the rubber meets the road for many people. You can provide answers for them and help them heal through the power of the priesthood you hold.

We were able to participate in two miraculous healings in a hospital setting, both with the same nonmember woman. This older woman was the mother of one of our investigators. The daughter had asked us to visit her mother, who was in critical condition and expected to die. We went to the hospital and gave her a blessing. She was healed completely and three days later went home from the hospital. We began to teach the mother as a result of the blessing.

## Becoming a Great Missionary

Many people in the hospital heard about the blessing we had given this woman and how quickly she was healed, so they all wanted blessings from the Mormon missionaries. It started with the woman who was sharing the same hospital room with the woman whom we healed. "Could I get one of those special blessings, too?" she asked. We took time to get a little information about her and to tell her about us and how blessings work. "Are you a Christian? Do you believe in Jesus Christ?" we asked. "Our blessings work best upon those who have faith in Jesus Christ. He is the one who will grant to you the blessing to be healed, if it is His will that you be healed. Do you understand this? Do you believe in Jesus Christ?" Even though we took the time to teach people about Jesus Christ, and how the Church and blessings work, we *never* turned down anyone who asked, even if they were a little unsure about their faith.

A short while later, the woman we had healed got sick again because the hospital had given her the wrong dosage of blood-thinning medicine. They had given her so much medicine that she was beginning to bleed internally. Suddenly she was back in the hospital, in intensive care. When we went to give her another blessing, we found her engulfed in an oxygen tent, awake, but at death's door. The doctors told us they expected her to die at any time, certainly before morning. Access to this woman was difficult—we could each use only one hand as we reached inside the oxygen tent. My companion anointed her head with oil (he placed the oil in his right hand then reached in and placed his hand on her head). Then I sealed the anointing (standing on either side of the bed, we both reached our right hands in and placed them upon her head). The Spirit was *very strong*, and I was able to promise her a complete recovery. In fact, I told her that she would be healed as a sign to her that the gospel she was being taught by us was true. She made a complete recovery and two days later returned home.

Of course our names were now well known throughout the hospital and many people asked us for blessings. We did everything we could to accommodate those who asked.

3.   *General service projects.*

All missionaries become aware of the needs of the people they meet. Many need help of some kind. Using wisdom and with the understanding that the most important thing you have to do is teach, you can serve both members and nonmembers alike in any number of ways. If there is any question in your mind about whether the service is appropriate or not, all it takes is a call to your priesthood leader or mission president. Your first calling is to teach the gospel. If you have a conflict between teaching and service, you should teach. But usually you will be able to find the time to do both.

# Becoming a Great Missionary

# Eight
## Working With Members

This chapter gives missionaries ideas on how to work with the members of the wards in their area in order to increase their ability to find and teach more people. It also gives members a better understanding of their role in helping the full-time missionaries. Understanding this relationship is an important step in learning how to become a great missionary. Just as a good missionary teaches one person at a time while a great missionary teaches many, a great missionary will also learn how to expand his abilities by using the labor of the local members. One person can only do so much in a day, but if you learn how to motivate the members to do missionary work you will be able to attain ten times, even a hundred times the success previously achieved. Like most of the other ideas presented, the process is very simple but takes courage and perseverance to make it work.

### Working with the Ward Mission Leader

The primary contact for missionaries in most wards will be the ward mission leader. This is a man who is called specifically to coordinate the missionary work of the ward. He is the one who meets each week with the missionaries, coordinates splits with the members, solves any problems members might have with the missionaries, etc. He is also the bishop's eyes and ears, and reports weekly to the bishop and the Priesthood Executive Committee (PEC) on everything that is going on including any baptisms coming up and any needs the missionaries or new members might have. He works with the elders quorum president to arrange home teachers for new members and makes certain they follow up with additional instruction and lessons for new members. He also meets with the Relief Society president, the Young Men's president, the Young Women's president, and the Primary president, depending upon the makeup of the families being taught. If you have a good ward mission leader, he will make your life easy. If you have no ward mission leader, or a disinterested one, you will struggle much harder to get the cooperation of members.

1. *A good ward mission leader* will meet with the missionaries every week to review the progress of investigators so the bishop and other leaders can prepare to receive the new members when they are baptized.

As ward mission leader, I always met with the missionaries *prior* to the weekly PEC meeting. This was important so I could give them up-to-date information about those who were progressing towards baptism. It also permitted me to tell them which investigators were coming to Church that week so they could seek them out and introduce themselves.

2. *A good ward mission leader* will arrange splits whenever the missionaries need them. In a perfect world, it is the ward mission leader who will arrange splits for the missionaries;

they should not have to do this themselves. However, if the missionaries wait until the last minute it does become their problem. The missionaries should be organized enough to inform the ward mission leader during the Sunday meeting how many splits they need for the upcoming week.

As ward mission leader, I always spent Sunday afternoon calling the members of the ward to arrange splits for the week. As the work in the area grew, this sometimes entailed getting eight or more members lined up to split with the missionaries every night. We had eight missionaries in our area at one time and by working through one person (the ward mission leader) we avoided the confusion that would come with four sets of elders calling the members for splits.

3. *A good ward mission leader* works with the bishop to assign fellowshipping families to each of your investigators.

All investigators, once they have taken two or three discussions, should have a fellowshipping family assigned. Most of the time this comes about naturally, as the result of arranging splits with the missionaries. Once members meet a family that is being taught, they will be touched by the Spirit and want to continue the relationship they have developed with that family. If this doesn't work out, an active family in the ward should be asked to participate in the remaining discussions so the investigators know someone when they come to Church.

4. *A good ward mission leader* works with the elders quorum president to insure new members have home teachers ready and waiting to start after they are baptized.

This is just a matter of giving the elders quorum president up-to-date information so there is no lag time between baptism and the assignment of home teachers. If the ward mission leader is doing his job, the elders quorum president will have plenty of warning and will have time to select the home teachers who will be assigned when the investigator has a date for baptism. The home teachers can then attend the baptism and begin home teaching visits immediately thereafter.

5. *A good ward mission leader* coordinates with the stake missionaries (a) splits with the full time missionaries, and (b) new member discussions in coordination with the home teachers.

Most stake missionaries, and some senior missionaries, have little or no leadership without the ward mission leader. Stake missionaries can be invaluable as they assist the full-time missionaries in their work and as they help new members assimilate into the Church. The ward mission leader is responsible for seeing that stake and senior missionaries are busy with rewarding work and experiences. I learned how important this part of the calling is the hard way. As they were about to go home, one senior missionary couple took me aside and gave me some well-placed criticism about the lack of effort I had made on their behalf. For some reason, I had never considered that I was responsible for the senior missionaries too! It seems foolish to me now, since the ward mission leader is responsible for *all* missionary work in the ward! From that time on, I paid special attention to the stake and senior missionaries in my ward, making certain they had a positive and fruitful time while serving.

6. *A good ward mission leader* works with the Relief Society president if there are district or zone conferences to be held in the ward building, for access to the building and the provision of food.

One of the joys that came with the calling of ward mission leader was being able to attend district and zone conferences when I had the chance to get away from work. The Relief Society president and my wife would work together to make sure the missionaries had enough to eat and that the building was ready for them. I remember one Christmas when the zone had a combination zone conference and Christmas party. My wife and I arranged to prepare a full Christmas dinner for some 50 missionaries with presents for each missionary (something silly and inexpensive like a toy car or some other "stocking stuffer"). I remember this party well because it was the night we accidentally left one of our children behind! We had brought two cars because my wife had come early to prepare and serve the food. As we left and all of the kids ran for a car, somehow one of our children was missed! We drove all the way home thinking the child was in the other car. When we got home and realized our mistake, my wife and I drove hurriedly back to the church (it had been about an hour since leaving the church—this was the mission field remember, no church building within two blocks of home!). It was dark and cold and we had all kinds of thoughts running through our heads.

When we got to the church, there was no one outside but all the missionaries were still in the building. When we went inside, I witnessed a never-to-be-forgotten scene: There was our small son sitting on an elder's lap with several other elders surrounding him, playing with toys and trucks and having a good old time! Our son was having so much fun he didn't want to go home. God bless the missionaries.

7.  *A good ward mission leader* sees that the missionaries have a place to go on all holidays: Thanksgiving, Christmas, New

## Becoming a Great Missionary

Year's Day, Easter, Mother's Day, Father's Day, etc. No missionary should be without a place to go!

Perhaps the greatest joy my family had while I served as ward mission leader was providing a place for the missionaries to go during the holidays. If all else failed, they were always welcome at our home. My entire family has a favorite memory of the elders getting up very early in the morning so they could be with us when we opened presents on Christmas morning (and share that personal family experience with them). We told the children they could not come downstairs until the elders came. As soon as the elders arrived, we "let the hounds loose" and the children ran for the presents under the tree. Of course we had arranged for each elder to receive a small gift (if I remember right, we gave them each a small "transformer," a toy that changed from a car into a monster of some kind). The children didn't mind at all; in fact, they loved it. I will always remember one very large BYU football player (an offensive lineman) helping my 4-year-old daughter dress her new dolls, as he sat cross-legged on the floor with her. Or another elder far away from home and family who spent all morning helping one son put together a bicycle while my wife and I made breakfast. These are cherished moments that many families miss because they don't want the missionaries to "interfere" with their family time. How foolish are people who think that! Missionaries are God's servants, manning the front lines of a war that started before we were ever born. Anything we can do to make their lives better is not enough.

The best ward mission leader I worked with on my mission was in Altoona, the area in which we had so much success, so I don't think it was a coincidence! He was the first member we met as he picked us up at the bus station and took us to our apartment. He arranged for rides to church, meals, and splits—almost anything our hearts desired. He counseled us when we came upon unusual circumstances and prayed for us, and with us, in our work. He had been a member about a year and had been saving money to drive to Salt Lake City in order to go to the temple and have his family sealed (the Washington Temple was just being built). Even though they had almost no money, they saved everything, sold everything, and drove to Salt Lake City. I arranged to have my family meet them there to help them through the maze of finding a place to stay, getting their temple garments, arranging to get to the temple, etc. When they got back, you could actually see a change in them. They practically glowed with joy and the Spirit of God! We all redoubled our work and felt the joy of seeing our work produce fruit.

The worst ward mission leader we worked with was a young man who had just gotten married. He was so preoccupied with work and family that he had little time for the missionaries. When the holidays came, we had nowhere to go. We ate Thanksgiving dinner in our apartment, and stayed in our apartment all Christmas day. The highlight of Christmas that year was receiving permission from President Pinnock to watch some of the football games. This was important to me because the University of Utah was in a bowl game that year, which they won. I had gone to the University of Utah, and my family was good friends with the running back who was named MVP for the game. It was a very lonely Christmas for my companion and me, so President Pinnock's permission to watch this game meant a lot.

For those of you who do not have a ward mission leader, you will have to work with the members directly. Sometimes this will mean meeting directly with the bishop to arrange help and assistance in your work.

## Becoming a Great Missionary

## Working with the Bishop

For missionaries, the most important person in the ward, next to the ward mission leader, is the bishop. The commitment of the bishop towards missionary work will have a profound effect upon the missionary work in the ward. If the bishop is committed to helping the missionaries, the work will be easy and will progress quickly. If the bishop does not have time for missionary work, it will invariably suffer.

*1.  Ineffective bishops and branch presidents.*

It doesn't happen often, but occasionally you will have to deal with a bishop or priesthood leader who seems to actually hinder the work. These are difficult situations to deal with. One bishop I worked with told me that it was too hard to bring new members into the Church. It was his opinion that it was better to let people die, pass on to the Spirit world, and hear the gospel there! It was obvious that this poor bishop not only did not understand the doctrine of the Church in which he was a leader, but was so burdened by his responsibilities he looked with dread upon any baptism because it just meant another person for whom he was responsible. This is one of the reasons the Church took the responsibility to interview new members out of the hands of bishops. If it were up to some of them, we would not have any new members.

Another ineffective bishop (actually he was a branch president) with whom I worked was a relatively new member himself who carried a large chip on his shoulder. He led a branch that had a history of serious problems. The legend was that the branch had been cursed. Yes, actually cursed by the stake president when the branch refused to sustain the stake presidency's choice for the new branch president. I don't know if the story was really true, but it seemed to be true because of how this branch president and the members acted. I remember one Sunday he got up to talk to the branch about paying tithing. Unfortunately, we had investigators that day because he started to question the members' faith and faithfulness. "You think you're saved? You're not saved!" We shrunk down in our seats, wishing we could hide and wondering what our poor investigators thought.

Your best hope in working with bishops like these is to find ways to help them in their work. Most of the time these bishops are just overburdened with the calling and lack understanding of how to perform their responsibilities properly. By finding ways to help such a bishop in his calling, you will endear yourself to him and find him more willing to help you. What you should *not* do is add to his burden or condemn him in any way for his lack of experience. This will only add to his stress and make things more difficult. How do you help a bishop? There are several ways:

◆ Inspire the members to work harder and fulfill their callings.

◆ Help members fill their callings by offering your services on Sundays to give talks, teach Sunday School, or prepare and pass the Sacrament.

◆ Help reactivate inactive members.

◆ Find new ways to help the bishop in his calling.

2. *Effective bishops and branch presidents.*

Getting the bishop on board with the missionary program is one of the best ways to get the whole congregation to participate in missionary work. One of the best bishops I had the privilege to work with was the bishop when I was first called as ward mission leader. We worked hand in hand to bring many people into the Church. There were a number of things he did as bishop that greatly influenced the entire congregation to become missionaries.

# Becoming a Great Missionary

A. *Make sure the ward mission leader does his calling.* One of the things that happens within a bishopric is that priorities are set. Sometimes this can be very subtle, yet have very lasting effects. This bishop in Connecticut made sure that everyone knew missionary work was his highest priority. During PEC, he made sure that I, as ward mission leader, would "return and report" what was happening with the missionaries. He did not just want a brief report concentrating only on the people who were ready for baptism; he wanted a full report on every investigator. He wanted specific suggestions from me about what he could do to help every investigator (assign fellowshipping families, meet each investigator, organize member-missionary work, etc.). He then gave out assignments to other members of the PEC to insure I got the help I needed.

B. *Lead by example.* This bishop not only made sure we were all doing our job and working hard, he insisted upon splitting with the missionaries himself at least once a month. He wanted to be in the thick of things as much as possible. Whenever we started a new missionary program, he was the first one to volunteer. For example, when we started the mini-mission program in the ward, he assigned himself to be the first one to go. He actually "released" himself from his duties as bishop for one month to concentrate on missionary work (he simply assigned his counselors to take on his work while he was gone). He continued this example time after time. He was truly a shepherd. He did not simply assign and coerce other members of the ward to do missionary work (as a sheepherder would do). He led by personal example—and everyone willingly followed.

C. *Give the missionaries time.* Bishops should make sure to give the missionaries time, every week if necessary, to talk about the work being done in the ward, to tell their success stories, allow new members to testify of their conversions, etc. Let the missionaries give talks, teach classes, and involve them in every way possible with the members. The special spirit carried by the missionaries will be infectious.

This bishop knew what all bishops should learn: missionary work drives everything else. The spirit that is brought into a ward with a successful missionary program is powerful and all encompassing. It affects everything else a ward does. We had one of the most successful missionary programs the area had ever seen and what was the result for the ward? At the end of the year, the ward was first in every category of which the stake kept track: new members (of course), reactivation, tithing, meeting attendance, temple attendance, etc. It was both astounding and revealing. By putting missionary work first, this bishop achieved all other goals.

## Getting the Members to Help

Sometimes the most difficult part of missionary work is getting the help of local members. This may be due to past trials with bad missionaries, inexperience, lack of leadership, or simply fear. A proactive missionary who understands how to motivate members in a positive way can overcome all these things. Here are some things you can do as a missionary to get the members to help you in your work:

*1.  Be an example.*

This has been previously presented but must be re-emphasized. Members watch missionaries carefully. They want to know they can trust the missionaries before they are willing to work with them. If they see you wasting time, not obeying the mission rules, or actually causing problems in the ward, members will not trust or help you. However, if the members see you working hard, obeying all the mission rules, and actually helping them fulfill their own callings, they will begin to trust and help you.

## Becoming a Great Missionary

*2.   Be an example to the children.*

There is nothing more endearing for parents than to see a relationship develop between the full-time missionaries and their children. Everyone can see it in children's eyes–they look up to and adore the missionaries. I know this was true with my own children, and I know this has been true as my own children served missions. I have received letters from parents thanking us for raising our children to be missionaries who are such wonderful examples to their children.

*3.   Help out in the ward.*

Do not turn down any request to serve in the local ward. Not only will you be able to be an example, but also you will be able to teach them how to serve. By this I mean that many members have not been in the Church long enough to know how things should be done. By serving whenever you can within the ward, you will be able to teach by example. In return, members will be more willing to help when you ask.

One of the best ways to help in the ward is to take the Sacrament to the sick and/or disabled. While serving in Altoona, one of our favorite assignments every week was to take the Sacrament to a bedridden woman in the ward. It was not a burden at all; in fact, we looked forward to it every week. Whether in homes or in the hospital, this is service at its best.

*4.   Give talks and lessons in church.*

One of the most useful ways to encourage and inspire members to help in missionary work is by presenting inspired talks and lessons in church. Since this can be such a powerful tool, it should be approached with great soberness. Many missionaries try to do this on the fly and end up giving unprepared or boring talks or lessons.

Frankly, there is no excuse for this! If you know in advance you have this kind of assignment, take it seriously and take the time you need to do a good job. Even if you are asked at the last minute, you have no excuse for being unprepared! Every missionary should have a well-prepared talk and lesson he can give at a minute's notice. You are a full-time missionary, you are a professional at what you do (or should be!), and you should always be prepared to do a first-rate job in any calling you are given.

5. *Visit the members.*

Visit the members of the ward to get to know them better. Leave a blessing on their home and, when inspired to do so, ask for their specific help in the work. Many times this will be in conjunction with meals they have invited you to share. Now, let me give you the most important advice I can give you in relation to the members: *Do not waste their time*!

There is a problem among some missionaries, called "camping out," in which missionaries take advantage of the good intentions of the members by staying at the members' homes for long periods of time. These missionaries waste their own time and the time of the members, as well. Even if the members encourage this behavior, they will not respect you for it. Camping out at members' homes is inappropriate at any time and for any reason. Even on the holidays, when it is permitted to spend a longer period of time at members' homes, you should not spend all day. This abuse of the members is very destructive to the kind of respectful relationship you should be creating with them. As tempting as it might be to stay longer, don't. If you are invited to dinner, you should not stay more than an hour. Even if they invite you to stay longer, you should say, "No, we are directed to stay only a short time. Also, we have appointments."

## Becoming a Great Missionary

This does three things: It tells the members you respect their privacy and time; it lets them know that you believe in and follow the mission rules; and it shows that you are dedicated and work hard—all of which will build trust.

One of the most important things to remember when working with the members is to show gratitude for anything and everything they do for you. This not only includes a simple thank-you for meals but for splits, service opportunities, or any other thing the members might do to serve or help you.

6. *Always show up and always be on time.*

One of the banes of being a Mormon is living with "Mormon Standard Time." This is the habit by some members of coming ten minutes (or more) late for every activity. While it might sound cute, and might be accepted by most leaders (usually because they come late themselves), it is inappropriate behavior. In the real world, five minutes early is considered being on time. As missionaries, you need to get in the habit of arriving on time for splits, for Church, for teaching appointments, or for any other activity where you have told people you would be at a certain place at a certain time. You will lose respect if you are always late. You will anger people and waste their time (see above).

"Always show up" may seem to be a silly thing to talk about, but it isn't. Often missionaries will find reasons not to show up for an appointment. Perhaps they double-booked appointments or were invited to a member's home or a Church activity. Some of these reasons may be legitimate, but there is still no excuse for missing an appointment. People's eternal souls may be at risk as a result of your mismanagement or shifting priorities. Let me give you an example:

While in my first area, we struggled quite a bit for every single teaching appointment we made. One night we had a conflict. We had a call-back appointment with a family we had tracted out the week before. These kinds of appointments almost never worked out. On the other hand, we had been invited to a party with a member. He had just reenlisted in the military and was having a celebration with his family and all of the missionaries in the district. We had a choice: Go to the party or go to our "maybe" appointment. We chose to go to the party. All night the thought of the appointment nagged me. The next night, we went to the home where we had had the appointment scheduled. The husband came to the door and when he saw us became quite angry. "We waited all evening for you to come. You never came, you never called, you simply stood us up. Anyone that inconsiderate of others is not worth listening to. Good night." He shut the door in our faces. We were absolutely crushed. We knew we would be held responsible for missing the opportunity to teach this family. I never again missed an appointment!

As a ward mission leader, I always monitored the missionaries under my care. If they were late, or missed appointments or splits, I let them know in no uncertain terms that their behavior was unacceptable! I helped them understand that showing up and being on time was part of the integrity a missionary should display. Always be professional!

## Getting Splits with the Members

Of all the varied activities that missionaries participate in with members, getting splits is one of the most difficult. This is real missionary work, the front lines of the war between good and evil, the

## Becoming a Great Missionary

big Mano e Mano. And for that reason, many members fear going on splits. They are afraid they don't know enough, or they will look foolish when they cannot answer questions, or they may suffer from that "personal space" thing where people fear strangers and the unknown. Whatever the reason, you must find a way to help them overcome their fears and say yes when asked to go on splits.

*1.   Start with the priesthood.*

Your best chance for success will come by starting with the priesthood quorums of the Church. They will feel (and rightly so) that it is their duty to help you. You can prepare them by asking for time in priesthood meeting to address the brethren. Tell them your plans for the area (see the chapter on creating a plan and following it) and how they can help fulfill your goals. Let them know you will be calling on them to go with you to appointments, and even tracting, in order to expand the missionary work in the area. Make sure they know you are looking forward to working with them, that you promise to be on time and not waste their time, and that you will be grateful for any help they give.

It is okay to make members feel a little guilty for *not* doing missionary work. After all, that is what our consciences are for—to tell us when we are doing something wrong. However, this should only be done with the priesthood, and only when the Spirit tells you to do so. It can and will work, if done correctly. Just be careful not to offend.

*2.   Start with a solid discussion.*

One of the easiest ways to start members working with the missionaries is to give even one member a good, spiritual experience. You can guarantee this experience by choosing to take them to a scheduled discussion with a family that is progressing and you know will be there. Sometimes missionaries get possessive of their good investigators, but they should be just the opposite. If you have a good family that is progressing, you need to share that experience with as many members as possible. This may mean only one missionary will go to the discussion, but the end result will be much better. The investigator will benefit from getting to know the members of the Church with whom they will soon be associating, and the members will benefit from the spiritual experience of teaching. The good feelings the members will have from this experience will prompt them to come again. It will also help to diminish their fears about doing other kinds of missionary work. And, as the member returns to the ward with positive stories about splitting with the missionaries, it will lead others to do so.

3. *Don't be afraid to ask anyone.*

As usual, one of the problems missionaries have is that they limit their vision of who will do missionary work. Often the sisters of the ward are just as anxious to get involved as the brethren but are never asked. It is more difficult to set up splits with the sisters (you must have a threesome when working with sisters: two elders for each sister, or two sisters for each elder), but it is always rewarding. The mission rules change occasionally but when I served we were able to go on splits with any priesthood holder—that means we sometimes went out with deacons! We even prepared them ahead of time to give part of the lesson. It was a wonderful experience for us and for them. One sister who was bedridden helped us set up splits and dinner appointments. While serving as ward mission leader in Connecticut, we often set up splits with less-active members acting as our companions. They were able to re-hear the missionary discussions and were slowly activated back into the Church because they regained their testimony along with the new member.

## Becoming a Great Missionary

*4. Don't be afraid to tract.*

The last thing you want to do with a member on a split is tract. It is the thing they fear the most and, unless you have worked with the member before, be careful about making their first experience a hard one (most members feel comfortable if they know they were invited into an investigator's home, but uncomfortable about cold calls). However, do not be afraid to tract with members with whom you have worked for a while. In my experience, the Lord finds ways to open doors when members are with you. It is almost uncanny! That is part of the reason we began to seek after splits of any kind with members–it seemed that the Lord opened more doors when we were with members than at any other time.

### Don't interfere

As much as we encourage missionaries to get to know the members, get involved in the ward, and help in any way possible, it is just as important not to interfere with the normal operations of a ward or branch. Often your presence will intimidate and embarrass new members or struggling members who do not know as much. For example, under normal conditions a teacher, no matter how new a member, is required to struggle through a class. This is part of the learning and growing process that we all have to go through. However, if you are in the class, and you always answer the questions, or if you tend to sigh or grumble or make faces when the teacher says something wrong or doesn't "do it the way it should be done," your presence and actions will be detrimental to the teacher and the class. For this reason, President Pinnock gave us the following instruction:

> *Missionaries are not to attend auxiliary meetings or the investigators' class unless there are members in attendance needing the missionaries. It has come to my attention that some*

*missionaries are taking an active role in investigator class activities. May we again remind you that if you are attending an investigator class with your investigator, you are not to disrupt by asking questions or answering questions unless called upon.*

This is such wise advice. As missionaries, you are looked upon as role models. You become natural leaders and people seek you out and constantly request your help and counsel. While acting in your role as a servant of God, this is entirely appropriate. However, once you step inside the ward or branch, your authority ends and is taken up by the local priesthood and those who have been called to run the Church in that area. If you take upon yourself duties that are not yours to take, or if you let others place them upon you, it will end up hurting more than helping the work of the Lord. Sometimes people are called to positions so they can grow, or because they need to learn something from that calling. If they are constantly relying upon you to answer questions, the investigators and new members will not be forced to learn and answer for themselves. If you ask the questions you think the teacher ought to ask, the teacher will never learn. You get the picture. If there is a problem in a class you are attending, or if you see a great need that isn't being filled, you might take the teacher aside privately and kindly talk to them or make suggestions. This can also be done to let them know ahead of time not to call on you but to use the members and investigators instead.

## How to deal with crazy members

Every ward has crazy members; members who are so different from the rest of the ward that they not only stand out, they often offend. Although this is just a normal part of life (we are all human), they can sometimes wreak havoc on investigators and new members.

## Becoming a Great Missionary

It is something every missionary will have to learn to deal with. The more prepared you are, the more likely you will be able to counter problems that arise. Let me share with you a few stories:

1.  *The Holiday Man.*
    In one ward in which I was serving around the holidays, there was a member who was a former Jehovah's Witness and who still held many of their beliefs concerning holiday celebrations. Specifically, he felt compelled to tell everyone at each and every holiday that it was based upon nothing more than pagan rites and rituals. He then set about persuading everyone not to celebrate the holiday. For most of us it was just amusing. However, for some of our investigators it was rather disturbing.

2.  *We don't want your kind in church.*
    All congregations will have a least one bigot. One branch in which I worked had many. We had begun to teach a wonderful black woman the gospel. This was before the Lord permitted blacks to hold the priesthood so it was unusual for us to have progressed so far with this woman, but the Spirit of God had definitely worked upon her. She knew the gospel was true. She had a firm testimony of the Book of Mormon (which she read in one week) and of the Doctrine and Covenants (which she read the next week). She was thrilled with the Pearl of Great Price because, for the first time, she felt she had answers to why God had created different races of men. She wanted to come to Church. She came only once. This all-white branch so offended her she would not return (some members came right out and told her she was not wanted and asked her to leave). Afterward, I was called in by the branch president and scolded for teaching a black woman, let alone inviting her to Church.

We met with her once more after this terrible event. She took it all very well. It had not shaken her testimony at all. She still knew the gospel was true, and she knew the time would come when she would receive all the blessings God had promised her. The reason she could remain so strong in the face of such bigotry was because her faith was based upon the doctrine of the Church, not the people, or even the missionaries. She had gained a testimony that the doctrines we taught were true. Nothing else really mattered. She understood people are weak, and that if we base our testimony on people it will fail. She was wise beyond her age, and I learned a great lesson from her. I learned to make sure the people I teach are converted to the doctrine of the Church.

We left her with a blessing and a promise that if she were patient, times would change and God would provide a way for her. I don't know what ever happened to that woman. I can only hope that some other missionary found and baptized her. In any case, the members of that branch will be held accountable for what they did to this wonderful woman.

3. *The ward bigot.*

A large portion of our ward in Connecticut consisted of faithful black members. One of the priesthood brethren assigned to home teach one of these black families was a true bigot. After just a few visits by this man, this faithful black family was so offended by his prejudice they approached me to get him reassigned. They just did not know what to do. After a great deal of thought, I told this good family that I would not change the assignment. Then I gave them a reason to change their attitude about the situation. I told them this man had been assigned to them *not* for their benefit, but for *his*. We knew this man was a bigot, and we also knew that the only way he would ever be able to rid himself of this terrible character flaw was to get to know a good, loving black family. This was their assignment and challenge: To permit this callous and prejudiced man into their lives so he could learn for himself that his beliefs were false.

After this challenge was presented to the family, they changed their attitude. They accepted this man into their home and their life and, in spite of the abuse they received from him, they tried to treat him as one of their own. In time, this man did change and this good family received blessings beyond their understanding for helping him change.

I'm sure almost everyone has a story they can tell about an unfortunate incident that happened in Church. It is part-and-parcel of being a member of this Church. As missionaries, we just have to learn to deal with the results of these incidents. The best way to deal with any kind of situation like this is by using the truth. Do not try to excuse the behavior or even explain the behavior of other members of the Church. Simply help your investigators by explaining that people are the same everywhere. We are all human and wherever large groups of people gather, there will be some very good ones, some bad ones, and even some crazy ones. So then, what makes this Church different from any of the others? It is the *doctrine* we teach. It is important to explain to your investigators that at some point in time, a member of the Church might offend them. Many who come into the Church because of friends, or the relationship they develop with the missionaries, or for any reason other than obtaining a testimony of the doctrine of the Church, will find that they have a weak testimony that can, and sometimes does, fail them. So if they have a problem with a member of the Church, use it as a teaching moment to insure they gain a testimony of the truthfulness of the doctrine of the Church. If they do that, no abusive member, no incident (no matter how strange or offensive), no earthly cause whatsoever will be able to weaken their testimony.

## Help the Members

Sometimes missionaries think their responsibility is to teach only nonmembers, but that does not catch the true vision of their calling. Missionaries are called to teach the gospel and to prepare people to enter the Celestial Kingdom. If you do a good deed, do you think it makes a difference whether the person is a member of the Church or not? Any good deed, any righteous action that brings someone closer to God, will also help bring about the Kingdom of God.

Just as you seek to help investigators overcome problems, and are willing to help a fellow missionary, be ready to help members of the Church. Yours is a 24-hour job and, like it or not, you need to be a man, suck it up, and do it! After all, the benefits are eternal.

## Lukewarm Members and Missionaries

One of the most difficult thing for great missionaries to deal with is to live and/or work with people who are not as passionate as they, i.e., the "lukewarm." Most of them are very good people (they keep the commandments), but they lack the fire inside that will propel them to good works.

Often, it is those who are converts to the Church and those who have had "colorful" pasts who are the most zealous in teaching the gospel. Christ understood this phenomenon as he talked about how those "to whom little is forgiven, the same loveth little."[1]

---

[1] Luke 7:48.

# Becoming a Great Missionary

It will be those who have had to go through the *full* repentance process that will also understand in full what Christ has done for them, and, as a result, their love for the Savior will be stronger. It's just human nature.

The *only* way that has been found to inspire lukewarm members is to bear powerful, fervent testimony to them of the truth, just as Alma did to the lukewarm members of his day.

> And now it came to pass that Alma, having seen the afflictions of the humble followers of God, and the persecutions which were heaped upon them by the remainder of his people, and seeing all their inequality, began to be very sorrowful; nevertheless the Spirit of the Lord did not fail him.
>
> And he selected a wise man who was among the elders of the church, and gave him power according to the voice of the people, that he might have power to enact laws according to the laws which had been given, and to put them in force according to the wickedness and the crimes of the people.
>
> Now this man's name was Nephihah, and he was appointed chief judge; and he sat in the judgment-seat to judge and to govern the people.
>
> Now Alma did not grant unto him the office of being high priest over the church, but he retained the office of high priest unto himself; but he delivered the judgment-seat unto Nephihah.
>
> And this he did that he himself might go forth among his people, or among the people of Nephi, that he might preach the word of God unto them, to stir them up in remembrance of their duty, and that he might pull down, by the word of God, all the pride and craftiness and all the contentions which were among

*his people, seeing no way that he might reclaim them save it were in bearing down in pure testimony against them.*

*And thus in the commencement of the ninth year of the reign of the judges over the people of Nephi, Alma delivered up the judgment-seat to Nephihah, and confined himself wholly to the high priesthood of the holy order of God, to the testimony of the word, according to the spirit of revelation and prophecy.* (Alma 4:9-20)

I testify that this principle is true. There is only one way to inspire and lead those who are already members of Christ's Church: teach them the truth and then help them live it. We can inspire them to live better lives through our words and actions. As I learned many times from President Pinnock, and as the scriptures make clear,[2] any kind of force or brow beating will not be effective. We must find *positive* ways to uplift and inspire the members to change their lives–to become converted to the gospel they have been taught. As missionaries, we can be influential in helping members become "spiritually born of God"[3] and receive the image of Christ in their countenances. Your testimony, like Alma's, can help them receive a "mighty change of heart."

---

[2] D&C 121:41–44.
[3] Alma 5:14.

# Becoming a Great Missionary

# Nine
## Member Missionary Work

*E*very member should be a missionary. Every member, young and old, should be involved in doing some kind of missionary work. Over the years, I have seen the youngest children to the oldest of members participate in some kind of missionary work. Children can help with Book of Mormon drives, teens can begin to share the gospel with friends and go on splits, and adults can do everything from simply feeding the missionaries to something as elaborate as a ward open house. The following is a list of ways members can actively participate in missionary work.

### The Member-Missionary Class

One of the most useful tools to get members proficient in missionary work is to use the member-missionary class. This is one of the standard, quarterly classes that should be offered in every ward. There is a church manual provided. This is the way this class usually works:

1. The bishop calls a few couples or individuals to attend the class.
2. The class lasts about six weeks and involves learning such missionary techniques as giving away a Book of Mormon or a pamphlet

to a friend, preparing friends and neighbors to accept the gospel, going with the full-time missionaries to teaching appointments, learning to become a friendshipping family, attending an open house, etc.

3.  After the class is over, the members should be familiar enough with missionary work, and motivated enough, that they will begin to participate freely with the full-time missionaries.

Many times the class is simply used to motivate members to do missionary work with no other requirement or calling afterward. However, sometimes at the end of the class, the students are called to a mini-mission for a month or are called as stake missionaries for a year. Over time, all members of the ward should take this class.

## Missionary prep class

These classes are usually held on a stake level for all members who are thinking about, or preparing for, full-time missions, although they can also be held at the ward level if needed. These are intensive classes designed to prepare members to leave for 18 to 24 months to serve the Lord somewhere in the world. The class itself is very similar to the member-missionary class.

## Fellowshipping

One of the most important things the members can do to help the full-time missionaries in their calling is to fellowship a family being taught. Fellowshipping investigators is nothing more than getting to know someone who will soon be a new member of the Church and helping them get to know the members with whom they will soon be rubbing shoulders on a weekly basis. It does not necessarily entail teaching the investigators the gospel, as that is the missionaries' responsibility. It has more to do with simply making friends with new people. Let me give you an example:

One day, the missionaries came to my wife and told her of a new family they were teaching. They were excited about the progress the family was making and wanted to make sure there was member involvement during the teaching process. The missionaries set up a time for my wife to go over and meet the wife of this investigator family. Of course my wife said yes! As she went to drive to the home of this new investigator, Satan tried to interfere; when my wife went to start the car, the battery was dead! What was she to do? She calmed her mind and said a prayer to God for help. Then a miracle happened! Just one of those small "coincidences" that make the lives of the Saints special. I happened to be driving back to the office from an appointment when the thought came to me that I needed to stop at home. I never went home during working hours and had no real reason to go home now. But I listened to that quiet voice and drove out of my way to go home. My wife just couldn't believe it when she saw me coming down the driveway! She threw me out of my truck and shouted, "Goodbye. I'll explain later!" She made the appointment just in time while I stood in the driveway wondering what in the world had happened.

She invited the investigator family to our home for dinner later that week. They had two children who were very close in age to two of our children. When the husband got home that night, he could not believe that his wife had accepted an invitation to go to a stranger's home for dinner! But they did come and it turned out to be a wonderful experience.

## Becoming a Great Missionary

My wife and I discussed at length what we should do while they were in our home for dinner. Should we talk about the gospel? Should we avoid it? We did not want them to feel like we were pressuring them in any way, so we decided not to talk about any gospel subject unless they brought it up first. We would simply treat them as friends and talk about work, school, kids, etc. When they arrived, a second miracle happened. We all got along well, especially the children. They had recently moved to Connecticut and their children had found it difficult to make friends. After they arrived in our home, my children invited their children upstairs to play. To the surprise of the parents, their two children did not hesitate to go with my children to play. The evening went along very well and not once did a gospel subject come up! We simply spent time getting to know one another and becoming friends.

After this family was baptized, we learned that our decision not to talk about the gospel had had a profound effect upon them. They had assumed we were going to do nothing but talk about the Church and try to get them to join. When they discovered that we just wanted to get to know them, they were impressed. The other thing that seemed to help was how well our children got along. We are now very good friends. They eventually moved to Pittsburgh where he was soon called to be the bishop and then to be in the stake presidency.

Although my wife and I never participated in a single discussion with the missionaries, we did have many gospel-oriented discussions with this family and eventually went to the temple with them when they had their family sealed for time and eternity. Fellowshipping this family was nothing more than getting to know them and becoming friends, so that when they did join the Church they were "no more strangers and foreigners, but fellow citizens with the Saints, and of the household of God."[1]

## Member splits

Another thing members can do to help the full-time missionaries is to go on splits with them during the week. Often missionaries will have more than one teaching appointment on the same night. In order to cover both appointments, they need two members to go with them. One member and one missionary go to one appointment while the other member and missionary go to the other appointment. The members usually meet at the missionaries' apartment or at an agreed-upon meeting place. There are several things that both the member and missionary need to do to prepare for the split.

*1. Be on time.*

Since splits are usually required due to multiple teaching appointments, it is important to be on time at the meeting place, so you can be on time to the appointment. This is true for both the member and the missionary.

*2. Set a specific time to return.*

Since no missionary can be left alone, it is important that a specific time be set to meet after the appointments. This means that if one appointment ends early, that pair will need to wait for the other pair to arrive. It also means that if the appointment goes over time the other pair will be stuck waiting until they come. When on splits a missionary should never let the appointment go over time. Even if it is going very well you shouldn't be afraid to end the discussion. In fact, you should always leave your investigator wanting more! Timing is everything on a split! If everyone arrives on time, ends their

---

[1] Ephesians 2:19.

appointments on time, and arrives back on time, no one will have to wait or be inconvenienced.

### 3. *The member should be prepared to teach.*

At the very least, the member should be prepared to bear their testimony several times during the discussion, testifying of the truths being taught by the missionary. By knowing in advance what will be taught, the member should be able to teach part of the discussion (as directed by the missionary). While working with the Aaronic Priesthood, we even had deacons teaching part of the discussion! These discussions are not hard; most members should be able to teach one or two concepts without any study or preparation at all!

### 4. *Always have alternate plans.*

It is not uncommon for scheduled teaching appointments to fall through at the last minute. Therefore, the missionary should always have a back-up plan if the appointment does fall through. This can be visiting another investigator, going on a call-back, or even tracting (if the member is willing). Make sure you have a back-up plan for every split!

Ideally, the ward mission leader should set up splits well ahead of time. However, if there is no ward mission leader, or if the split is needed at the last minute, then it is appropriate for the missionaries to call members directly to see if they can go.

## *Member referrals*

The most important work members can do for the missionaries is to refer them to interested friends, neighbors, and other acquaintances. When a member is acting as a missionary, they are constantly looking for opportunities to introduce the gospel to the people with whom they associate or meet. This does not have to be an intrusive situation, it should come naturally as you talk about your life and what your family does on a day-to-day basis. After you have introduced a person to gospel concepts, and they have shown an interest, you will need to cultivate that interest until you feel they are ready to accept the missionaries into their home. At that point, you ask if they would like to learn more and offer to send the missionaries to their home. If they accept your invitation, you can refer them to the full-time missionaries to be taught. The following is a step-by-step process you can use to develop referrals for the missionaries.

A. *Going fishing.*

Missionary work is like fishing; the first thing you do is throw out the bait—you have to somehow expose nonmembers to gospel principles that will interest them. Once they nibble on the small morsels you give them, they will be ready to eat a full meal. Like fishing, it takes patience and the understanding that not all fish will bite.

The way you "fish" for people who are interested in the gospel is to introduce them to gospel principles you use in your daily life. If you are a faithful member of the Church, much of your time is taken up by Church activities. Often these activities intermix with your business and social life, so when these activities come up simply elaborate on them more than you normally would. For example:

1.  If you cannot make a meeting due to a Church activity or Sabbath worship, instead of just saying, "I'm sorry I cannot make it," you say "I'm sorry, I have to go to Young Men's that night. Young Men's is the name of an activity night that my Church holds for the youth. One night each week, all of the youth meet to participate in some kind of activity. It's really fun and I don't like to

miss it." See the difference? You can give people lots of information without having to ask their permission or get involved in a serious discussion. However, by elaborating upon what you do in association with the Church, you will often find that people become curious and want to know more; the whole situation changes. Suddenly they are asking you about the Church! They are the ones who want to know more! And it is so easy to do.

2. If you are at a party with nonmembers and are offered alcohol or coffee, instead of saying, "No thank you," you should say, "No thank you, my religion does not permit drinking, smoking, or the use of other harmful substances." Most people will then be surprised and say "Really?!" at which point you can elaborate even further. "Yes, we have what is called the Word of Wisdom, a revelation given to the Prophet Joseph Smith that teaches us the proper use of these kinds of things. It is one of the reasons I am so healthy." Once again instead of giving a short answer, simply expand what you would normally say. If you see they are interested in hearing more, then continue. If not, no harm, no foul.

You will become a fisher of men by throwing out your line every day, looking for that one person who will hear about your Church activities or the principles you live by and ask more about them. Once they ask for more information, you go to the next step.

B. *Preparing them to hear.*

The next step in missionary work is to prepare people to hear the fullness of the gospel—in other words, to prepare them to accept the full-time missionaries into their home. Once you sense a person is interested in the Church, or the principles of the gospel you live, it is time to be a little bolder. Until now the work has been easy. You've just cast out your words and waited for someone to show interest. But once you find someone who has shown an interest, you need to be forward enough to begin to talk about religion. This does not need to be pushy or offensive in any way. Just start to talk about your religion and ask about theirs. As you share with one another the beliefs that each holds, they will naturally discover that your religion has much, much more.

> "I have noticed that you showed an interest in some of the church activities in which I participate. Are you a religious person, too?"
>
> "You have asked questions about some of the things my church teaches. Do you go to church? What does your church teach?"
>
> "I do believe in what my church teaches about drinking and smoking! What does your church teach about these things?"

By getting people to talk about themselves, what they believe, and what their religion (if any) teaches, you will automatically have *many* opportunities to discuss what your Church believes! It will be a natural part of the give and take in the conversation.

After one or several conversations about religion, you will be able to discern whether they are satisfied with their own church, their own beliefs, and their own religion. You will be able to tell whether you have deepened their interest in your church and the principles it teaches. If you see that their interest in the Church continues, or that their feelings about the Church have deepened, it is time to ask them to accept the missionaries into their home.

C. *Inviting them to hear.*

After you have properly prepared people to accept the missionaries by (1) introducing gospel subjects to them, and (2) developing their understanding of the gospel through conversations, it is time to take the brave step of asking if they would be interested in having the missionaries teach them about the Church.

**181**

## Becoming a Great Missionary

> "We have talked quite often about religion and the things my Church teaches. You have seemed interested in the things we have discussed. Would you be interested in learning more about my church and the things we believe in?"

If they say yes then explain to them how it works. "We have full-time missionaries who teach people about our church. They have a series of six lessons they teach in the privacy of your home. There is no obligation or pressure of any kind." Offer to hold the lessons in your home if that would be more comfortable. Remember, all they can do is say no. And even if they say no, it does not mean that their life circumstance might not change and they might come to you later and say yes. Always leave the door open.

> "I'm sorry, I'm really not interested in joining another church right now."

> "That's OK! But if you ever do have an interest, or just need to talk to someone, I'm always willing to listen!"

See, no harm, no foul. Even if they turn you down, their respect for you will grow because they will know you have their best interest in mind.

If they say they would like the missionaries to come to their home, it becomes an "official" referral, and you can give their name to the missionaries. It is very important to understand that there are three things that make a true referral:

1.  You have already talked to them about the Church.

2.  You have asked them if they want the missionary discussions.

3.  They are *expecting* the missionaries to contact them.

Just giving the missionaries names of people you know, or with whom you work, does not count as a referral. If the missionaries simply cold-call at a person's home, it is no different than tracting. A true referral is one where the people are prepared to hear the missionaries. The reason so many referrals end in baptisms is that the people are *prepared* to hear the missionaries.

Like Christ, you, too, can be fishers of men. It isn't hard. It simply takes time and patience. Like fishing, you must cast your line into the water again and again before you have a strike. But if you are patient, and diligent, I promise you will catch your share of fish!

*Set-a-date program*

The set-a-date program is just another way of working directly with the angels of God by letting them know ahead of time what you are trying to accomplish. Just as missionaries "map out" an area to work, thereby letting the angels of God know in advance where they will be working so the way can be prepared, the set-a-date program lets the angels know with whom you are trying to work and gives them a timetable in which you expect to accomplish this work.

The program works like this. In an effort to find people for the missionaries to teach (in order to obtain some "official" referrals), you look over your friends, neighbors, and co-workers and choose one or two who seem to be the most likely to be interested in the Church. Or, if you prayerfully and sincerely see that no one you know is a candidate (some of us who have remained in the same area and have been using this technique for years have run out of acquaintances) then prayerfully explain to the Lord that you will be actively seeking someone outside your circle of friends and acquaintances, who is ready to hear the gospel. Then, working with the missionaries, you set a specific date when you would like this person to be ready to accept the missionaries into their home;

perhaps a month or six weeks. Then you kneel before God, explain your plan to Him, and ask His help in reaching your goal.

At this point, you must begin to do everything in your power to see that this goal is reached. You talk to those people you have chosen and, most importantly, *look for signs that God is helping you in your work*. Since you have laid this burden on the Lord, you should assume He will indeed help you to reach this righteous goal. God and his angels will help by placing situations and opportunities in your path whereby you can reach this goal. However, in order for you to take advantage of the opportunities that God and his angels place before you, *you must watch for them*!

As you progress in your effort to prepare the people you have chosen to receive the missionaries, you will find the path has been made much easier than it had been in the past because of the help of God. This program has been very successful for those members who have actually tried it.

Knowing how this principle works, and knowing that it works for any righteous cause, my family decided to use it when selling our home. I had gotten a new job in Cleveland, so we had to sell our beautiful home in Connecticut. We were having trouble doing so due to the economy of the area at that time, so we decided to enlist God's help. We knelt as a family and set a date for two weeks hence in which someone would make an offer on our home. This seemed somewhat risky because we involved our children in this request in an effort to teach them this important principle. Would God meet our request? Two weeks passed without a single offer on our home. We fasted on the last day (Sunday) and went to Church with both hope and fear in our hearts. When we got home there was a message from our realtor. Someone had made an offer on our home!

*Stake mini-missions*

I do not know how this program got started or who started it, but this has to be one of the most inspired programs ever to have been developed to promote missionary work. The program is designed to help young men and women experience real missionary work prior to becoming old enough to go on a full-time mission. This is not just going on splits; it is a program that allows young people to actually live and work with the full-time missionaries for a week or so. This is how it works:

1. During spring break or summer vacation, while school is out, young men (and women in areas lucky enough to have a pair of sister missionaries) are interviewed by the bishop to be called as full-time missionaries for a short period of time.

2. These young people are then each assigned to a pair of missionaries. They live together, eat together, work together, and teach together. For those one or two weeks, these young people are missionaries in every sense of the word.

3. After the time is complete, they are given a formal and honorable release and a certificate of merit showing the time they served.

4. The next Sunday, they are asked to speak about their experience to their ward so they can share their experiences and their revitalized testimonies.

Almost without exception, when the time comes for these young men to go on missions, they go! Between their mini-mission and their two-year mission, they become a great asset to the ward and the missionaries, as they carry that special spirit with them.

### Ward mini-missions

Like all wards, we had a missionary prep class for young men and a member-missionary class for members, to teach and encourage members to be missionaries. But after seeing the success of the stake mini-mission program for the youth, we decided to modify it for the use of all members, so everyone could have the experience of doing full-time missionary work, even for a short time. This is how it worked:

1. Starting with the leadership of the ward, a few members were called to serve a one-month mini-mission. They were released from whatever callings they had at the time and called and set apart as stake missionaries.

2. Under the ward mission leader's direction, the member-missionaries were used as much as possible in missionary work going on at the time: splits, teaching, fellowshipping, teaching new members, providing support for Book of Mormon programs, open houses, etc.

3. After one month, these members were released as stake missionaries and returned to their previous callings.

4. Once a month, the members who had completed their mini-missions were asked to speak in Sacrament meeting to talk about what they had learned, and experienced, and in what ways they had grown.

5. The next month, another group of member-missionaries was called. Eventually, every member was given the opportunity to serve a mini-mission.

The success of this program was astounding! In fact, some of the couples serving mini-missions took the opportunity to set up missionary projects of their own. One such couple had a very musical family and served some time in the fall of the year. They decided to approach churches in our area (not LDS churches) to participate in an evening of Christmas music. The choir from each congregation prepared one or two pieces of Christmas music. Then we all congregated in one of the participating churches (this rotated on a yearly basis) and had a wonderful evening of Christmas music sung by each choir with congregational carols in between each choir. Refreshments were provided by the host church. This evening became so important to the area that the local cable company broadcast it on television!

Almost without exception after this experience was over, these members continued to work with the missionaries. Slowly, the entire ward became focused on missionary work. The powerful Spirit they felt while being missionaries carried over into their callings. Everyone seemed to become more energized, more focused, and more willing to sacrifice. How could they teach others about the law of tithing if they were not paying tithing themselves? How could they teach others about service and sacrifice—how could they watch new members sacrifice so much—and not be willing to do the same? How could they teach the importance of temple covenants if they were not fulfilling the covenants they themselves had taken? And, as the work progressed, they began to seek out the less-active—because they needed them for the work. So now, even the less-actives became involved and active in the work of the Lord. You can clearly see how missionary work benefits the entire ward.

# Becoming a Great Missionary

## *Book of Mormon drives*

Book of Mormon drives are a wonderful way for members to be involved in missionary work. There are several ways to do this, depending upon resources and member willingness.

1. *Book of Mormon testimonies.* In this activity, members put their testimonies inside copies of the Book of Mormon that are given by the missionaries to those they teach. This is very simple to organize. All you need is a testimony from the member typed on a piece of paper small enough to be glued or taped inside the front cover of a Book of Mormon. Then you add a picture of the member and/or family to put on the inside back cover of the book.

2. *Book of Mormon placements.* In this activity, members are encouraged to place copies of the Book of Mormon with friends and neighbors. This can be done as a purely missionary effort or they can be given away as gifts.

3. *Book of Mormon gifts and tapes.* In this activity, members give Book of Mormons or Church tapes to friends and neighbors as gifts during holiday seasons or other special times of the year.

One year the Church provided cassette tapes with Christmas stories on them. These tapes were given out with copies of the Book of Mormon. They were wrapped and used as gifts for people, usually delivered by the missionaries. I obtained a list of all of the employees in the company where I worked and had the missionaries deliver a tape and Book of Mormon to each one. This seemed like a great risk at the time, since I had only been with the company for six months, and the owner and most of the office employees were Jewish. It turned out to be a wonderful experience. All but one person graciously accepted the gift. But this one person, a devout Jew, was very upset with me. The day after the missionaries visited this man, I came to my office to find the unwrapped gift on my desk. I went into his office and apologized for offending him in any way. He told me he was angry that I would try to interfere with his family life and that for me, a Christian, to send missionaries to him, a devout Jew, was unacceptable. Well, the best defense is a good offense I always say, so I told him that his premise was just not true. I told him that if he had given me a copy of the Talmud as a gift, I would have been honored. I told him that I was not trying to interfere with his family in any way—it was simply a gift, nothing more. Amazingly, this good man soon became a very good friend.

This experience was similar to one I had with another man in the company. The superintendent of the men was a hard drinking, womanizing, ill-tempered man. Most of his sentences were laced with profanity.[2] Once he received my gift and discovered I was very religious, his attitude toward me changed. Over a period of time, while he watched my every move and decided that I actually lived my religion, he gained and showed respect to me. Within a few months, his vulgar language was toned down whenever he was around me. This was true for almost everyone in the company. After they saw that I walked the walk, they all began to show me greater respect. Several times at company dinner parties I was requested to say a prayer.

---

[2] "I love that man better who swears a stream as long as my arm yet deals justice to his neighbors and mercifully deals his substance to the poor, than the long, smooth-faced hypocrite. . . . God judges men according to the use they make of the light which He gives them." (Joseph Smith, *Teachings of the Prophet Joseph Smith*, p. 303).

**189**

## Becoming a Great Missionary

Another extension of this experience was the yearly Clawson Christmas presentation. My children had all practiced songs, musical instruments, and games in school and Primary. One year, I decided to ask my boss (remember, he was a Jew!) if my family could come to the office and put on a "Christmas program." I explained that my children would sing a couple of songs, play some instruments, and wish everyone a happy holiday season. Once again, to our surprise, this was warmly accepted! So, there we were, my wife, our five children, and me standing in front of twenty or so nonmembers, presenting our version of a typical Primary program! It was a smash hit! We did the following:

♦ One son played a Christmas carol on the clarinet.

♦ The children sang an "unauthorized" version of Deck the Halls:

> "Deck the halls with poison ivy...fa la la la la la la la la."
> "Tis the season to be naughty...fa la la la la la la la la."

The last line went:

> "Throw the baby in the drier..fa la la la la la la la la."
> (Well, you get the picture!)

♦ My daughter, who was 3 or 4 years old, sang, "Once there was a snow man, snow man, snow man, . . ." Of course, she was too shy to do this alone, so Dad helped her! Even our hardened superintendent had his heart softened by the sight of a grown man pretending to be a melting snowman with his tiny daughter!

♦ Finally, we all sang, "We wish you a merry Christmas."

Each year we were invited back and each year the "Primary program" got more and more elaborate. Over time, others got involved and other families and children participated.

What started as a scary and daring challenge turned out to have wonderful consequences. The same will be true for members who are willing to share the gift of the Book of Mormon with their friends and neighbors. Few, if any, will be offended by such a gift. I know by personal experience that the opposite is true—their respect for you will grow.[3] Even if they never become interested in the Church, your relationship with them will deepen.

## Open Houses

An open house is a ward or stake building set up to recreate a Visitors Center. Information booths and activities are set up for nonmembers to come and learn about the Church in a nonthreatening atmosphere. This is very effective in areas of the world where there are not a lot of members, a new chapel has been built, or a ward has been split. Almost everyone is curious about the Church, but many feel threatened and uncomfortable inviting missionaries into their homes. Open houses provide people an opportunity to learn about the Church in a comfortable atmosphere.

Not very many members try open houses because they are a *lot* of work and they need to be coordinated with *all* priesthood quorums and auxiliaries of the Church. But when done correctly, they can be a powerful tool in attracting people to come and learn about the Church. The process is really very simple. Each Church organization creates an information booth or activity. When people come into the building, they go from room to room, or from booth to booth, learning about different aspects of the Church's organization.

---

[3] "Devotion to the Gospel—There is not a wicked man on the face of the earth but what reveres a pure servant of God. They may not acknowledge it with their organs of speech, but in their hearts, sentiments and feelings they revere such a character." (Brigham Young, *Discourses of Brigham Young*, p. 229).

# Becoming a Great Missionary

For example, the person who teaches the genealogy class is in charge of setting up a booth about genealogy; the Sunday School President a booth about the Sunday School classes that are taught each week; the seminary teacher a booth about the early morning seminary program, etc. You might even have people assigned to perform a variety of musical numbers (piano, organ, instrument, voice) in the chapel during the entire open house so people will feel free to come in and out of the chapel, feeling the special Spirit there. The larger the number of people involved, and the greater the variety of things for people to see, the more successful the open house will be.

The open house can be set up in a number of ways. One is to use the gym for the entire thing, having all of the booths and activities held there. Another is to use the classrooms, which will give each organization more room in which to work. Or, use a combination of both. The evening should begin and end in the chapel. For example, the open house may run from 7:00 p.m. to 9:00 p.m. You start in the chapel with a song, prayer, and short explanation about what will go on, what activities are available, and when things will end. This opening should last 10 minutes. Then everyone is released to man their booths or classrooms. About 10 minutes before 9:00 p.m., everyone is called into the chapel again to have a closing song and prayer.

During the evening, people will come at various times and stay various lengths of time. This is to be expected. This is what you *want* to happen! People should be free to come and go as they please, or go to one or all of the booths, as they desire. No pressure should be placed on people to stay any set length of time or see all of the exhibits. It must remain very low-key for those who come.

The real key to a successful open house is advertising. You *must* call one person to do nothing but advertise the upcoming open house. This should begin at least *two months* before the open house is actually held (because it will take two months to properly set up the open house and get everything organized properly). The advertising can include flyers delivered around the local neighborhood by the missionaries and the youth of the church. It can also be in the local newspaper, which is a great excuse to create an article about the Church to give to the local paper and have them run it—which they will gladly do. Then there is word of mouth by the members to their friends and neighbors, current investigators, etc.

Obviously, since many people are involved in this activity, it must be planned well in advance and coordinated directly through the PEC and the bishop. The ward mission leader or activities committee should be the one in charge of organizing the open house and following up with each organization to make sure everything will be ready on time. As long as *everyone* is involved and does a good job, the open house will come off without a hitch and be very successful.

## The key to successful missionary programs

The key to every successful missionary program or activity is the principle we have talked about before: planning and prayer. Remember what we learned about how angels work. If you plan an activity carefully, present it to the Lord for His blessing, and then follow through exactly as planned, the angels of the Lord will make sure it is successful. I testify to you that this is a true principle. It really does not matter what program or activity you do in an effort to help missionary work in the area; it will succeed if done correctly and according to plan.

## Becoming a Great Missionary

The reason these programs work is not because of the programs themselves. *Any* program you try will work if done the right way. The real reason these kinds of programs work is because of the principle of laying out a plan and asking for the help of God in achieving the plan. Whether it is tracting, a Book of Mormon project, an open house, or setting-a-date, these are nothing more than different attempts to reach the same goal: introducing nonmembers to the doctrines of the gospel. The reason they work is because it is not what we do or say that converts or touches people, *it is the Spirit of God!* All we have to do is find a way to introduce people to the gospel, and God will do the rest. *Anything we do or say will work—if we make sure God is working with us.* All we need do is commit to a reasonable course of action, turn the key to unlock the path for the angels of God by asking for God's help and blessing, and then follow through with what we have planned. God will do the rest. Our actions and words simply provide an opportunity for the Spirit to work. The more opportunities we make, the more contact members and missionaries have with nonmembers, the more success we will have. It is that simple.

When the Brother of Jared asked God to provide light within his boats, he was required by God to determine how this was to be done. He then asked God to touch the stones he had chosen to make them shine. In the same way, we must choose our method of obtaining God's help in doing missionary work; we must find our own stones for God to touch. I testify that he will touch them, and your life will be filled with light.

# Ten
## Teaching the Gospel

Now we get down to the real business of being on a mission: teaching the gospel. Everyone teaches the gospel differently. That is the way it is supposed to be. The *doctrine* that is taught must be the same, but the *way* it is taught can be completely different. The reason the Church has provided discussions for every missionary to learn is to ensure the *doctrine* taught by 60,000 missionaries is always the same. But once the information has been learned, *how* it is taught is up to the missionary. Hopefully, through the inspiration of the Holy Ghost, the missionary will be able to understand the perfect way to touch the individual they are teaching. For example, it does not matter which discussion you teach first. You can teach number one first, or number six, or you can teach number three and go back and forth and upside down or in a circle. It doesn't matter. There are only two things that matter. Do not change the *doctrine* you have been taught, and make certain the individual you are teaching understands. If they do not understand what you have taught, you have not done your job properly.

## Create the Right Atmosphere

When teaching someone, the first thing you must do is create the right atmosphere. This is not always easy and means that sometimes you must be bold with total strangers. As you enter the home, before you even ask anyone to pray, you need to take stock of your surroundings. What is the atmosphere in the room? What are the people you are going to teach doing? Is there anything in the room that will detract from what you will be teaching? Are the people you will be teaching prepared to listen? Here is what you must do:

1.   *If there is music playing, or if the TV is on, you must ask them to turn it off.*

The room should be as quiet as possible in order for those you are teaching to fully concentrate on what you are saying, so they will be able to feel the Spirit when it comes. If they don't comply, refuse to teach. This is a deal breaker. If they are not willing to give their complete attention, it will be a waste of your time anyway.

2.   *If those you are teaching are smoking and/or drinking liquor, you must ask them to stop.*

Ask them to put their cigarettes out and put their liquor away. If they ask why, tell them that your religion prohibits these products and that you would appreciate it if they would cease using them, at least while you are in their home. If they refuse, this is also a deal breaker. If they are blowing smoke in your face, or continuing to drink in front of you, it is a sign of disrespect. If they do not honor the calling you have as a servant of God, they will not listen anyway.

3.   *Talk to those you will be teaching for a little while before starting the lesson.*

Get to know them. By learning something about them, you will have a better understanding concerning what lesson to teach them.

Do not simply assume you will teach lesson number one! Remember the lesson of the well. The more you learn about them, the easier it will be for the Spirit of God to inspire you as to what lesson to teach and what words to say in order to touch their hearts and minds. Let me give you some specific examples:

Lesson One:
They have shown interest in the Church.
    (God has a plan for everyone)
They are dissatisfied with their current church.
    (The Church contains the *truth*)
They have little understanding about God or doubt that God exists.
    (We know who and what God is)
They are obviously dealing with problems of sin.
    (Jesus Christ has provided a way to escape the problems of sin)
They ask or wonder about modern prophets.
    (The story of the Prophet Joseph Smith)

Lesson Two:
They have had a recent death in the family.
    (Christ has overcome physical death)
They are sick, or old, and may die soon, or have a relative who may die soon.
    (Christ has overcome physical death)
They are handicapped or maimed in some way.
    (In the resurrection we are made perfect)
They have shown a willingness to repent.
    (Show them how to *change* their lives for the better)
They want to know how they can be forgiven.
    (The principles of repentance)
They want to know how the Spirit of God works.
    (The Holy Ghost)
They show a willingness to commit.
    (Get them to commit to taking *all* of the discussions)

Lesson Three:
They are confused about religion in general.
    (We have the *truth*)
They show a belief in prophecy, miracles, angels, or other supernatural phenomenon.
    (Restoration of the Church)
They struggle with some of the tenets of their own church, like the baptism of children.
    (The apostasy)

# Becoming a Great Missionary

They wonder why there is a need for church—why not a mountain top.
   (The organization of th Church)
They are interested in the specifics of our church, such as what our meetings are like.
   (Tell them about our meetings; invite them to church)


Lesson Four:
They believe in reincarnation.
   (Premortal life)
They have always wondered about a life before this.
   (Premortal life)
They have experienced déja vu.
   (Premortal life)
They believe religion is oppressive and controlling.
   (Agency; the war in heaven)
They wonder why there is so much pain and suffering in the world.
   (Why we receive mortal bodies; this life is a test)
They wonder why we are here or the purpose of life.
   (The plan of salvation)
They are interested in genealogy.
   (Temples, genealogy)
They wonder what we do in our temples.
   (Temple work, eternal ordinances)
They are afraid of death.
   (Life after death, the Spirit world)
They wonder what happens after we die.
   (Life after death, the Spirit world)
They want to know what they have to do to get to heaven.
   (The commandments, three degrees of glory)
They have been recently married or seem to be in love.
   (Temple ordinances, eternal marriage)
They have a close-knit core and extended family.
   (Temple ordinances, eternal marriage)
They want to know what is required to join our church.
   (The commandments, ordinances)
They specifically ask about the Word of Wisdom, or our "strange ways."
   (The commandments)
They are "living in sin," or have Word of Wisdom problems.
   (The commandments)


Lesson Five:
They are struggling to become a happy family.
   (The gospel brings love and harmony)
They have problems with some of their children.
   (The gospel brings harmony and love)

They have financial problems.
> (Tithing and sacrifice brings blessings)

They are poor.
> (Sacrifice brings blessings)

Lesson Six:
This lesson is simply an overview for those ready to be baptized.

Once you get to know the family, *choose an appropriate lesson* as inspired by the Spirit of God within you. Do not be afraid to be bold, even with strangers.

*4. Always start with a prayer and ask them for permission to kneel.*

If they say no, accept their hesitation and pray while seated. However, getting them to humble themselves by kneeling is a good sign of what their attitude towards God will be.

## Preparing men's hearts to listen

This instruction comes from Elder Gene R. Cook:

> *"You, as the teacher, must do all in your power to prepare the hearts of men so the Spirit can teach. May I suggest seven scriptural performances (see* Alma 31:10) *that, if humbly employed, will immediately invite the Spirit into your heart and the hearts of others.*

1. *Pray.* Pray for the Spirit. Ask those you teach to pray for you and for themselves while you are teaching. Ask for discernment to understand the needs of those you visit (see 3 Nephi 17:2–3; 20:1; D&C 136:29, 32).

2. *Use the Scriptures.* They are the words of the Lord to us, and the Spirit of the Lord will speak through them to all, both young and old (see 2 Nephi 32:3; Alma 31:5; D&C 32:4).

3. *Testify.* If you follow His promptings, the Lord will direct you to testify frequently throughout these visits. Testify that the Lord

has sent you. As you do, "the Holy Ghost carrieth it unto the hearts of the children of men" (2 Nephi 33:1; see also Alma 5:44–47).

4. *Use music.* Using recorded hymns or singing the songs of Zion with or to the Saints in their homes, as prompted, will always bring the Spirit of the Lord (see D&C 25:12, Matthew 26:30, Colossians 3:16, I Samuel 16:23).

5. *Express love and gratitude to God and man.* Express love openly for God and for His children, and the Spirit will be felt profoundly (see John 13:34–35, I Nephi 11:21-23, Moroni 7:47–48).

6. *Share spiritual experiences.* Spiritual experiences have great impact upon men's souls. Share them as prompted by the Spirit (see D&C 50:21–22, Luke 10:25-37, Acts 26:1–32).

7. *Perform priesthood ordinances.* "In the ordinances . . . the power of godliness is manifest" (D&C 84:20). Bless the Saints. Bless the sick. Bless the homes of the Saints. Encourage others to seek priesthood blessings (see 3 Nephi 20:2–9).

> *Brethren, these seven suggestions—one or more as needed—will always bring the Spirit of the Lord into your visits. Are these not some of the spiritual gifts that Christ gave that prepared the way for the Holy Ghost to testify and change men's hearts? Spiritually give of yourself, and your visits will not then be routine, but you will discern the needs of the Saints. You will commit them in the Spirit to act. They will repent and come unto Christ. (Elder Gene R. Cook,* Conference Report, *October 1988)*

### Don't be afraid to be bold

One of the things that separates a good missionary from a great one is his ability to be bold. The Spirit of God makes men bold. It also prepares those whom you teach to accept what you will ask of them, even though at the time it might be totally against everything they currently believe. Being bold means using your faith and the Spirit of God to convince people to do what is right, even if they are not yet prepared to do so. This is especially important in helping people get over physical addictions. Let me give you an example:

This is an idea that came from President Pinnock. He challenged us to challenge those whom we taught to change their lives immediately. There was no need to wait until they received several discussions before confronting them about changing their lives for the better. It all had to do with being bold enough to get people to commit to actions from the first moment of contact. It had to do with something every salesman knows (President Pinnock was an insurance salesman). The more you get people to say yes, the more you get them to make some kind of commitment—any kind of commitment—the more often you will be able to bring them all the way to baptism. One of those commitments was to convince them to get rid of their cigarettes, alcohol, drugs, etc., at the first meeting. This was done directly and without fanfare.

"We have taught you concerning the Word of Wisdom and the importance of keeping our bodies clean and pure in order to be able to feel the Spirit of God in our lives. We know you also believe these substances are harmful. We want you to commit to get rid of (whatever it might be). You know this is the right thing to do. We know you will feel good about your decision and yourself if you follow through with this commitment. Will you get rid of (whatever it might be)? We will help you."

"Show us where your alcohol is and we will help you pour it down the drain." Then get up and help them actually do it.

# Becoming a Great Missionary

> "Tell us where you keep your cigarettes and we will take them with us." Then get up and get the cigarettes. Promise you will throw them away (don't throw them away there, or they may just get them again).

There were many times we were able to do this in the first discussion! We would teach the Word of Wisdom and the commandments as a first discussion, especially on Sundays. Over time, and as we saw people respond to our requests, we became increasingly bold and soon had absolutely no hesitation in asking people to give up their habits and their addictive substances.

## *Don't be afraid to start with the hard stuff*

Many missionaries are afraid to start with the "hard stuff" under the assumption that people will not accept doctrine that is new. But, from long experience, I have found this is just not true. People crave the truth; they long to know that there is something bigger than themselves out there. When confronted with large ideas or concepts, they are actually comforted.

Missionaries sometimes try to "sneak" doctrine, ideas, and commitments by investigators, as though they will say yes without really understanding what they are doing. But this is deceptive and is not consistent with the open and honest spirit you should be developing with your investigator. Besides, it rarely works. Sooner or later you will have to actually ask them the hard questions: "Will you give up your coffee?" "Will you come to church?" "Will you be baptized?" Why beat around the bush? What makes you think their answer will be any different if couched in subtle language? And if you do somehow get them to agree without completely understanding, what good have you really done? Are you also going to deceive the Lord and sneak this person into the Kingdom of God? I don't think so.

It is always better to be up front and honest with people and do it right at the beginning, then you don't have to do it again and again. For example, why ask if you can come back again? Why not come right out and say, "We have six discussions that will teach you about our church. Would you be willing to listen to these discussions?" If they say yes (and most people who would invite you back anyway, would also agree to *all* of the discussions), then you do not have to go through this process for every discussion. When you see they agree to take all the discussions, broach the subject of baptism right off the bat. Don't wait! This does not mean you have to *commit* them to be baptized. It just means you broach the subject so when the time comes to ask them to make the commitment, it is no longer a surprise—they are actually expecting the question to come.

> "Many people who listen to these discussions ask to join our Church and be baptized. While you listen to the things we teach will you think about your own baptism?" Of course they will feel a little uncomfortable and say they were not thinking of joining the Church! "We don't expect you to feel that way now. After you have heard all of the discussions, if you have no desire to join the Church and be baptized, then, of course, that is your decision."

There, it is done. It wasn't hard, and from then on, in the back of their mind, they will have the question: Should I join the Church? And when the time comes that you feel good about actually asking them to be baptized, there will be no surprise; no need to try and sneak it past them or hide the commitment in subtle terms. They will already know that baptism is the end result of these discussions. The most important thing you have done, however, is plant the idea of baptism in their minds so the Holy Ghost can prepare them for when you do ask them to be baptized. Remember the lesson of the well! You have now planted knowledge in the well of their minds so

## Becoming a Great Missionary

God can work upon, and draw upon, that knowledge for their eternal salvation.

### *Stop and listen*

An extension of spending time learning about the family is stopping and listening to them during the discussions. After every concept, ask questions to make sure they understand. *Never* continue to the next concept or discussion until you are sure they understand and are ready, and the only way to know they are ready is to ask questions. Then listen. Just as you listened to them at first, to discover with which discussion to begin, listen to them during the discussion to discover their problems, objections, concerns, and hesitations. Many times, even most of the time, the thing you think is holding them back from committing to baptism is not their only, or even their real, concern. It takes a lot of questions and spiritual perception to discover their *real* concerns. Take the time to find these concerns, and your challenge will be easier.

Listening also provides you with the inspiration you need to discover what to teach them next. Most of the time the concepts within the discussion will proceed exactly as outlined. However, always let the Spirit guide you as to the direction you should take. As noted in a previous chapter, a good missionary knows the discussions backward and forward. If necessary, you should be able to jump from one discussion to another and back again without a hitch. That is the reason the last discussion is an overview. If you have had to jump around during the discussions, the overview will pick up anything you may have missed.

Don't be afraid to create your own discussions, if required. Every once in a while, those you are teaching will have problems that are not addressed in the standard discussions. Since it is imperative that you resolve all of their problems prior to committing them to baptism, there will be times you must teach a discussion that addresses their specific problems. This is completely appropriate. Just make certain the doctrine you teach is correct. If you are unsure, talk to your leaders or make sure an adult member goes with you to the discussion (this works well when dealing with any sticky situation—an adult member can help bring wisdom and experience to a situation with which you have never personally dealt).

As you proceed with the discussions, remember you are preparing people for eternity, not just a quick jump in the font. You will do yourself and those you are teaching a disservice if you go too quickly through the discussions. If those you are teaching come into the Church unprepared, they will quickly leave. Why rush through a baptism that will mean nothing in a few months' time? I have seen missionaries and leaders push for baptisms, looking only for the numbers without focusing upon those whom they are teaching. Oh, they get the numbers, but the numbers mean nothing if people fall away a short time later. Let me state again, with emphasis: *Never* continue with the discussions until they understand what you have taught and are ready for the next concept. *Never* bring someone into the waters of baptism who you know is not ready to make that commitment.

When I was ward mission leader in Connecticut, we had a young man seeking baptism who clearly was not ready. The elders became upset with me when I told them he should not be baptized. However, as I had predicted, he did not pass the interview. A year later, some sister missionaries tried to get him baptized. I told them he still wasn't ready to be baptized and to be patient, but all they wanted was to see him become a member of the Church. Again, as I had predicted, he did not pass the interview. Another year went by and another set of elders with the same result. Finally, the young man came to me humbled and repentant. He had taken the time to clear up the problems in his life and was now ready. It was worth the wait. He passed his interview, was baptized, and became a faithful member of the Church.

There are many stories of people "rushed" into baptism. You have all heard the stories of "basketball" baptisms, where young men are baptized so they can play on Church basketball teams. I know of one boy who had just been ordained a priest in the Aaronic Priesthood and wanted to "practice" on someone. His best friend, a nonmember, agreed to be baptized to please his friend. Of course he went inactive immediately. The stories are numerous and the results are usually the same—those rushed into baptism for any reason before they are truly converted quickly fall away.

### *Resolve all of their problems*

Every discussion will bring up problems your investigators have which prevent them from accepting the gospel and being baptized. It is *very* important each and every problem is resolved as it comes up. Many missionaries ignore or gloss over these problems in an attempt to get their investigators baptized. This path is filled with pitfalls and will ultimately end in failure. First of all, if you do not resolve their problems, most of the time you will *never* get them baptized. They will simply follow along until it is time to commit to be baptized and then begin to give you one excuse after another until you either give up in frustration or finally solve their problems. Secondly, if you do get them into the waters of baptism before their problems are resolved, they will just fall away. Their problems will slowly pull them back into their previous life. Either way, this path leads to failure. So take the time up front to resolve the problems presented to you.

*All problems can be resolved!* Some problems may seem so confusing or difficult that you fear there cannot possibly be a solution. But I promise you, through the inspiration of the Holy Ghost you can find a solution to every problem. Here are some of the most common problems you will find:

*1.   What to do if investigators are not married but living together.*

This is very common today. In foreign countries it is even more acceptable; it is called "common law" marriage. However, even if it is acceptable in the country in which you are serving, it is *not* acceptable for entrance into the Church. The solution is simple. First, teach the law of chastity (discussion 4) and commit them to living it. This does not mean you require them to not be intimate anymore (a requirement they would not fulfill), but you convince them to get married. Once they are married, and if they are living the other commandments, you will be able to baptize them.

One couple I taught on my mission had been living together for some time. Once it came out they were not married, we immediately told them there was a problem. We taught them the law of chastity and convinced them to get married. The funny thing is, even though we were able to persuade them to get married they never joined the Church! In spite of this, we felt very good about making their lives better.

*2.   What to do about the Word of Wisdom.*

This is the most difficult of all problems you will face. You will be dealing with physical addictions, not moral ones. The reason this is not a moral problem is because few other religions believe any part of the Word of Wisdom. Many of these addictions can be classified as sicknesses, which may take a doctor's care or even hospitalization. Should the addiction be too serious to overcome by the individual, he should be encouraged to first seek professional help to correct his addiction, and then, after his addiction is resolved, he can try again to meet the requirements to join the Church. If you see honest progress, you may go ahead and baptize him. However, we come back to the same principle we have covered before: *never* knowingly baptize anyone who still has a problem. They will simply fall away from the Church when the addiction returns.

### 3. *Traditions.*

Most people and families have traditions: religious traditions, family traditions, ethnic traditions, etc. It is important to realize that the gospel of Jesus Christ is not just another religion but a *lifestyle*. This lifestyle will profoundly affect their lives and the lives of everyone with whom they associate: family, friends, coworkers, etc. You should be honest and up front about the changes that will occur in their lives. Most, if not all, of these changes are positive ones, but that doesn't mean there won't be profound changes in their lives for which they must prepare. It is always better to help people understand these changes and face up to them. People often leave the Church when they find it is harder than they thought it would be. It always works out better if they are prepared for the trials that lie ahead.

The best and only way to deal with the problem of *religious and ethnic traditions* is to convince your investigators of the *truth*. Sometimes this means you have to do some research. For example, most of the people in Pennsylvania were Catholic. In order to overcome their problems with religious tradition, I bought a Catholic Bible, which had the Catechism, the Apostles Creed, and a section on doctrine of the Catholic church. Once I was able to show people what their church *really* taught (such as a child who is not baptized goes to hell), it became much easier to overcome their doubts about the truthfulness of the doctrine we were teaching.

The best way to deal with *family traditions* is to get investigators to read the Book of Mormon. As they read about the Lamanites and the damage that false tradition had on their lives, you can show them that if they continue to live their own false traditions they will simply perpetuate damaging lies into their own posterity. However, if, like Abraham, they decide to obey the Lord and change their family traditions, they will take the strait and narrow path that will create generations of righteous posterity. Help them understand that their posterity will look back upon *them* like Abraham, as the father of the faithful.

All problems with tradition can be overcome. You simply use wisdom and your knowledge of the truth to dispel false traditions. Some prior family traditions will have to change after baptism, and those extended family interactions may become strained. These will be overcome by the faith and testimony of your investigators. It is simply a trial they must face. If they face it head on, their faith will grow stronger. It is not easy for people to face their family with these changes. When married in the temple, their family cannot come. If they usually have wine with their meals, or toasts at celebrations, they may feel uncomfortable sitting these out. Many people have daily habits that are a big part of their lives that will change and destroy relationships. There is *nothing* you can do about this. It is part of life, part of becoming a Mormon. All you can do is to strengthen their faith, be honest and up front about the trials they will face, and assure them that the eternal blessings they and their family will receive will be worth it.

### 4. *Fear of rejection.*

This problem is similar to family and ethnic traditions. The only way to resolve your investigators' fear is with a strong dose of faith. Do not lie and tell them their friends and family will not reject them, because it is very possible they will. You can tell them *most* of their friends and family will eventually come around, because they will learn to respect the new life they will lead. This is true, since your investigators will become better people as a result of living the gospel. Others will see that change, eventually accept it, and develop a new and better relationship with the investigators. Having gone through this myself, I know this is how the process works. Almost all my friends, who at first rejected me after joining the Church, became my friends again. The relationship was different, we could not do many of the same things together, but they learned to respect the choice I had made. The end result was a positive one, but it was *very* difficult to go through. Do not hide the trials they may face; prepare them for it!

## *Teach how to recognize the Spirit*

Most people do not know what the Spirit of God feels like. They have felt guilt. They may have even felt the Holy Ghost at times, but only briefly, and they probably did not know what it was they were feeling. So it is up to you to teach them. This principle is so important you should actually stop the lesson to teach it. Do it at least once per discussion for perhaps the first three discussions, or at least until you are certain they understand. Let me give you an example:

◆◆◆

When I was ward mission leader in Connecticut, I went out on splits with the missionaries to a wonderful family they were teaching. It was clear they were interested, but they were struggling to know if it was true. They had obviously felt the Spirit already, but it was also obvious they did not know they had. So, during this discussion and after bearing my testimony to them about the concept I was teaching, I recognized the presence of the Spirit in the room. As soon as I felt the strong presence of the Spirit and saw they were being affected by it, I stopped the discussion and told them what they were feeling at that moment was the Spirit of God testifying to them what I was teaching them was true. I told them this was what the Spirit of God felt like and asked them to remember it. I waited a few moments in silence, as we all concentrated our minds on what we were feeling instead of what we were teaching. I then continued with the discussion.

Over time, your investigators will *learn* to recognize the Spirit of God. Once they begin to recognize it, they will also begin to accept what you are teaching is true. They will know you are a true servant of God because you have brought this feeling of peace and light into their home, perhaps for the first time. This experience of feeling the Spirit of God is the most powerful tool you have. Use it.

## Investigator Followup

Another important thing you will learn is to help those you are teaching progress towards baptism through proper *followup*. Especially in the beginning, the only reason people let you in the door and listen to you is because of the Spirit you carry. When you are gone, the Spirit fades and resistance sets in. To prevent this, you need to follow up with each and every person you contact and teach, sometimes several times a week. By going the extra mile in this area you will find your labors will not have been in vain. Why tract day after day, finally finding someone to teach, only to lose them again because you are too lazy or forgetful to give them a call or send them a note? Once you have made that first positive contact, you *must* continue to monitor them carefully or you will lose them.

For clarity on the subject I again turn to President Pinnock:

> *EFFECTIVE INVESTIGATOR FOLLOWUP AND CALL-BACKS: Contact all investigators every two or three days. The best contact is to teach them a discussion. With the pressures of living in today's world, the special Spirit you bring into homes as you teach the gospel is lost when there is too much time between meetings. Take time to do the little things for your investigators. It's the little things that show people we really care. Call or send a card when there is sickness. Send thank-you cards after dinner appointments. Take special interest in children if they have problems, remember birthdays and anniversaries, etc.*

> *There is a need to spend more time doing call backs. Our work is often wasted when we fail to get back to those who have expressed an interest in our message but can't see us when we initially contact them.*

### *If you don't ask, they can't say "yes"*

The most difficult question for most missionaries is asking people to be baptized. Some are so intimidated by the moment, they never ask the question. Let me tell you a story:

Soon after I arrived on my mission, I met an elder who was fearful and disappointed that he was about to go home and had never baptized anyone. He had been homesick from the first day he came on his mission. He had spent his time and effort complaining about mission life and all the rules he had to keep. He had never learned how to teach or how to commit people to baptism. When I met him, he and his companion were teaching a family that was ready for baptism but the missionaries were just too afraid to ask the question. I went on a split with the elder to this wonderful family. After leaving, I asked him why they were not yet baptized, as they were obviously ready. He gave me some lame excuse about the time not being "exactly" right. Two weeks later, we heard a most astounding thing. This family had been baptized into another church! They were so anxious to be baptized and cleansed of their sins they could no longer wait for the elders to ask them. They simply went to the nearest church and had it done. Now the elders were anxious to talk with this family about baptism, but it was too late. When they brought up the subject, the family simply said they had no need as they had already been baptized. Now instead of participating in the baptism of this family, these elders had a whole new hurdle to jump over. This elder never did experience the joy of bringing a family into the waters of baptism, but I learned a powerful lesson I never forgot: Don't be afraid to ask!

## Professional Investigators

One of the problems many missionaries face is collecting professional investigators. A professional investigator is a person who *loves* the missionaries but will not commit to be baptized. These are people who are always willing to meet with, feed, and listen to the missionaries. They open their home and let the missionaries watch TV and play video games because they *love* the missionaries. But when it comes down to their true interest in the Church and its doctrine, they have none. They may agree to listen to the missionary discussions several times in order to please the missionaries and keep them coming back, but when it comes to making any commitments or becoming members of the Church, they will not do it.

As hard as it might be, missionaries must walk away from these people! Since they are not willing to commit to becoming members of the Church, they are simply wasting the missionaries' time. Wasting a lot of time. The missionaries would actually find more success tracting than continue working with professional investigators. For most missionaries, this is a tough decision. Let's see, having dinner with good friends in a warm home or going out tracting on a cold night. What would you choose? I remember when I had to choose.

I had just been transferred to Pittsburgh from Altoona. Altoona was a place of miracles and unbelievable success. Pittsburgh was immediately a trial of long days with little or no success. However, we had a whole box of call-back numbers—people who had been taught before who were still willing to listen to the missionaries. So, rather than tract every day, we began to go through the call-back list to see what we could find. I was amazed at how many people asked us to come over, have dinner, watch TV, and talk about home. When I asked them about giving a lesson they would say, "Oh, we've already heard them all before! Would you like some dessert?" I had never experienced professional investigators before. President Pinnock had talked about them, and told us to avoid them, but, until now, I had not had to make that particular choice. And it was a *choice* that we had to make. On the one hand, we had nothing to look forward to but endless days of tracting. On the other hand, we had a number of families that *wanted* us to come over and spend time with them. It was easy to try to believe these people would someday join the Church, that it was our duty to visit these people as long as they were willing to let us into their homes. It would have been so easy....

But, of course, it was all a lie. They would never be baptized because they had no real interest in hearing the discussions. They would never be baptized because they had never once picked up the Book of Mormon to read it. They would never be baptized because they did not believe what we taught. But they *loved* the missionaries! As a person of conscience, I had no choice but to drop the professional investigators from our lists. I had no choice but to leave the comfort of their homes, go into the cold, dark streets, and begin again to knock on doors.

So, how is it done? How did we go into the homes of these nice-but-misguided people and tell them we would not be back? We did it with candor and the slight hope that something would touch them and they would finally commit. After all, what did we have to lose?

We decided to challenge them, nicely. We told them that because of our commitment to the Lord we would no longer be able to come to their home unless they were serious about taking the discussions and becoming a member of the Church. We said there were many people who wanted to be taught, and join the Church, and make a commitment to the Lord through baptism. Then we asked whether they were willing to be baptized (remember, most of them had already taken the discussions; sometimes several times). If they said no, we told them we understood, thanked them for all they had done for us, and said goodbye. We hoped that at least a few would tell us they really were interested in joining the Church, but they just weren't ready yet or something like that. I was truly surprised at how many of them, who had been willing to meet regularly with the missionaries, were unwilling to make any kind of commitment to join the Church.

We had started with a whole box of referrals and call-backs. After weeding out those who had no interest, we were left with only two families, one that was eventually baptized and the Brown family. We were back on the street, all day long, knocking on doors, but it was worth it. The time came when our *real* missionary work paid off. We began to teach every day and soon had many families working toward baptism. What would have happened if we had decided to continue working with the professional investigators? Nothing at all.

I will talk about the Brown family at length, so first let me tell you about the other "professional" family that was actually baptized during this period of time. The first time I met this family was at Church. In fact, I had been to Church several times before I realized the members of this *active* family were not members of the Church at all. And by *active* I mean just that. Both parents had callings in the Church, paid a full tithe, and both their young children attended and loved Primary. For all intents and purposes, they were one of the most faithful and active families in this branch, yet they had never been baptized! The father refused to be baptized because he said he didn't "know" the Church was true. In other words, he was looking for some kind of sign—or at least that is what he said. Personally, I believe that he just didn't want the responsibility that came with obtaining the priesthood. Week after week, this wonderful family would come to Church, participate, and refuse to be baptized. Finally, I decided to do something about it.

I asked the father of this family if we could talk with him the next Wednesday about being baptized. He grumbled and hemmed and hawed but finally said that I could come over—letting me know it would do no good. Then, I went to the bishop, the elders quorum president, and the Relief Society president and asked them to attend. They all told me they had reservations about confronting this family because they didn't want to lose them! I told them to simply show up—I would do all the talking and needed them there for support. If they did not come, I was going to do it anyway. They all agreed to come.

When Wednesday came, we all showed up at this family's door. The father was very surprised that the bishop and others had come (I did not tell him I was bringing back-up!). He invited us in and we all sat down. We exchanged a few pleasantries and then I asked if we could start the evening with prayer. He said yes and I asked the elders quorum president to say it. After the prayer, I dove right in. "We are all here to commit you and your family to be baptized next Saturday." You could hear everyone in the room gasp a little as the gauntlet was thrown before this stubborn man. As the father began his usual excuses, his wife became so nervous she left the room to fuss in the kitchen; however, we all knew she was listening very carefully. The priesthood leaders were rather silent, too, nervous and afraid to offend this man and his family. However, I continued to press ahead, letting this father know that we were not leaving until he agreed to be baptized! At one point he said, "I will not be baptized until I know that it is true. That is what I have been taught . . . that I should know for myself if it is true or not!" I was not about to fall for his ruse and simply confronted him again. We want you to be baptized and officially join this Church! Besides, if you did not believe the gospel was true, you would not be attending Church every week, paying tithing, and filling callings! As James would have said, I can prove your faith by your works!" I could tell that he was beginning to break a little, and so could the others. Finally, they also jumped in and bore their testimonies of how much they thought of he and his family, and how much they wanted them to join the Church. He continued to battle with us, a little less confident and a little less confrontational. Finally, I threw down the ace I was holding. "Besides, I *know* your wife and children want to be baptized. You know they want to be baptized. Would you deny them this blessing just to be stubborn?" I could see by the look on his face as he looked towards the kitchen (where his wife had suddenly become very quiet) that I had finally found the key to this stubborn man's heart. I explained to him that answers come *after* the trial of faith. I promised that if he and his family were baptized on Saturday the Lord would reward his faith, and he would know within himself that he had done the right thing. Then, once again, I threw down the challenge. "Will you and your family be baptized Saturday?" His shoulders sagged a little as he quietly said, "Yes."

The entire room seemed to explode with excitement. His wife came running out of the kitchen, tears running down her face as she hugged and thanked her husband. The bishop and elders quorum president were shaking his hand and pounding his back with congratulations. The Relief Society president and this good sister embraced as neither could hold back the tears any longer. As for me? I sat back filled with that quiet, peaceful feeling that comes when you know you have been used as an instrument in God's hands to bring about something marvelous.

This family was baptized the next Saturday. I believe every member of the ward turned out to see it. About a year later, this wonderful family was sealed in the temple. I had not taught this family one lesson—not one. But I know I had a profound effect upon them and the whole ward as a result of this one evening. I had listened to my mission president and the Spirit of God concerning how to deal with professional investigators. It was not an easy decision, but the rewards that came from being up-front and honest with those we taught, and being firm in committing them to actually listening to the discussions and to being baptized, were beyond my expectations.

## Brother Brown: Part I

The most powerful teaching experience I ever had was teaching Brother Brown and his wife (they had two children under the age of 8). We found his name while going through a file of old contacts. He had been taught the discussions before and was obviously a professional investigator. We called and he invited us to come over. When we confronted them about taking the discussions again, they agreed. They also agreed to be baptized, if they found what we taught to be true.

By this time, I had begun to develop a very confident teaching style (as presented in this book). We started right and did all the right things: set the atmosphere, talked to them and chose an appropriate discussion, and convinced them to kneel with us to pray. The Spirit was immediate and powerful. It became clear right away that this was going to be different. The depth of the questions that

## Becoming a Great Missionary

Brother Brown asked, and the power of the Spirit I felt while answering, was just incredible! Instead of taking an hour or two per discussion we were taking an hour or two per *concept*. We literally went through every doctrine of the Church with a fine-tooth comb. I did not have to worry about making sure that all of their problems were resolved before we moved on to the next discussion, as *they* would not permit me to go on until they fully understood and accepted the doctrine we taught.

I spent several *months* teaching Brother Brown. I had three companions and numerous members of the ward who came with us on splits who became a part of bringing this family into the Church. Brother Brown was a General-Authority-in-waiting; everyone who met him came away with the same impression. This was a powerful, spiritual giant of the Lord. He had been in the Marines. He had gone to West Point and graduated with honors. He had become the youngest Captain ever commissioned in the Marines. After serving two tours in Vietnam, he became disillusioned with the military and decided to leave. He graduated from MIT and was working as an atomic scientist in a secret lab in Pittsburgh. He was about 6 feet 6 inches tall and still had an intimidating military bearing and physique. He was an overwhelming presence to be around. He was far more intelligent than anyone I had ever met: accomplished, spiritual, and physically intimidating. Teaching Brother Brown and his family was an experience I will never forget.

I remember when the second companion I had in this area went to his first discussion (Elder T and I arrived in the mission on the same day). He was physically shaken by the experience. He had never in his life experienced the Spirit so strongly. Members were the same way; they almost fought over the opportunity to go on splits with us to teach Brother Brown and his family. It was the perfect teaching experience, and it came by committing them right up front to take *all* of the discussions and to prepare to be baptized. This gave us the time and confidence we needed to teach them correctly. I will tell you more about Brother Brown later.

## Permit People to Sacrifice

Missionaries often are hesitant to allow people to sacrifice. They assume that the difficulty the sacrifice brings will be too hard, or will drive people away from the Church. As with many things in life, just the opposite is true! Sacrifice creates faith, strengthens testimonies, and prepares people to accept the gospel. What does this mean in day-to-day terms?

1. Whenever possible, accept invitations to eat or be with your investigators. Just the fact that you are present with them, your spirit touching theirs, will strengthen them and build their testimonies.

2. Accept gifts of money or help when offered. People *need* to be given the chance to help you in your service because they *need* the blessings and knowledge that will come as a result. If you deny them the opportunity to give, you will also deny them the blessings they need to progress.

3. Always make people pay for the Book of Mormons you give them, unless you were given them for free. First of all, you need whatever money you have. Second, they need to know the book is worth paying for. While I served in Altoona, we were teaching so many people we would sometimes give out a case of Book of Mormons a week. There was no way we could afford to pay for all of those books, so we made sure that they paid at least the *cost* of the book, which at the time was $1. By making sure people paid for their books, we were able to continue our work. Many

times they would offer us more money. We always accepted donations that were offered, knowing they would, in turn, receive
*needed* blessings as a result. We would then either buy more
books or turn the money into the bishop.

## Leave Your Area Better Than You Found It

As the Boy Scouts do on a camping trip, you should always
leave an area better than you found it. This means several things, on
several levels.

♦ First, you should have improved the members' relationship with the
   missionaries. The next missionaries should not have to work as hard
   to get splits and help from the members. You should have kept good
   records (names and phone numbers) of the members who were willing to go on splits.

♦ Second, your teaching pool should be larger, better prepared, and well
   documented as to what has been taught and what your investigators'
   problems are.

♦ Third, your records should be in order and up-to-date. There is nothing worse than coming into an area where there are no records showing who has been taught, who is currently being taught, and possible
   call-backs and first-time contacts. Keeping some type of logical record
   of your work immeasurably helps the next missionaries.

♦ Fourth, you should leave an up-to-date map of where you have
   tracted. It is frustrating to be transferred into an area and have no idea
   where the previous missionaries had worked. More than once, I have
   tracted an area worked a few weeks earlier by the previous missionaries. This can be avoided by simply keeping a map on the wall to keep
   track of where you have worked by marking streets with a highlighter.

# Eleven
## The POWER of Prayer

*O*ne of the most useful tools that a missionary is given is prayer. Prayer can be used to obtain forgiveness and gain strength. It can be used to obtain knowledge and inspiration concerning doctrine you don't understand. It can be used to send blessings to others. It can be used to receive instruction from the Lord as to where to find those who are ready to hear and accept the gospel. Let me share a few stories about the power of prayer.

◆◆◆

### Pray for Strength

When I first came out on my mission, I set a few goals. One of those goals had to do with obtaining the physical strength and endurance needed to fulfill the other goals I had set: I wanted to be able to get up at 5:00 a.m. so I had more time to study and prepare for the day's work. I had an alarm to get me up, and the willpower to get up when it went off, but actually staying awake and being able to concentrate was another thing. I prayed every day for the ability to stay awake and study without falling asleep or forgetting what I had studied. In a short time, the Lord answered my prayers. Not only was I able to get up early and stay awake, but the clarity of my thoughts and my ability to remember what I had read was magnified many times beyond what I could have imagined. Almost daily, I was surprised to find the things I had studied that morning were needed during a discussion later that day. I began to feel as though I had daily personal study with the Savior himself. Not only was it no longer hard to get up in the morning, I actually looked forward to this study time with great anticipation.

## Pray for the Spirit

One of the important reasons to pray every day is to obtain the Spirit of God. We have discussed how important it is to have the Spirit of God at all times. It is the Spirit that touches people's hearts. It is the Spirit that converts. It is the Spirit—the countenance of God—that shines forth from you like a candle on a candlestick and touches everyone with whom it comes in contact. But before you can let your light shine, before you can obtain His countenance, before you can literally expand your spiritual aura to touch others, you, yourself, must have that mighty change of heart. You must be-come *converted.*

> *And now I ask of you* on what conditions are they saved? *Yea, what grounds had they to hope for salvation? What is the cause of their being loosed from the bands of death, yea, and also the chains of hell?*
>
> *Behold, I can tell you*—*did not my father Alma* believe in the words *which were delivered by the mouth of Abinadi? And was he not a holy prophet? Did he not speak the words of God, and my father Alma believe them?*
>
> *And* according to his faith there was a mighty change wrought in his heart. *Behold I say unto you that this is all true.*

> *And behold, he preached the word unto your fathers, and a mighty change was also wrought in their hearts, and they humbled themselves and put their trust in the true and living God. And behold, they were faithful until the end;* therefore they were saved.
>
> *And now behold,* I ask of you, my brethren of the church, have ye Spiritually been born of God? Have ye received his image in your countenances? Have ye experienced this mighty change in your hearts? (Alma 5: 10–14; *emphasis added*)

Alma understood the importance of obtaining the Spirit of God. Notice he was speaking to "my brethren of the church!" He was not trying to bring new members into the gospel; he was trying to *convert* members of the Church. He laid out the process, step-by-step, so we could understand it:

1. We must *believe.* We must gain a *testimony* of the gospel of Jesus Christ.

2. As we grow in *faith* our hearts are changed and we become *converted.*

3. Our conversion produces physical changes in our appearance; we take upon ourselves the countenance of God himself. This countenance, or presence, is the Spirit of God that dwells within us, that people can *see* and *feel* whenever they are around us.

And how do we as individuals know whether or not we have had this "mighty change" in our hearts? How do we really know if we have been spiritually "born of God?"[1] King Benjamin gives us the answer:

---

[1] "The nearer we get to our heavenly Father the more are we disposed to look with compassion on perishing souls to take them upon our shoulders and cast their sins behind our back." (Joseph Smith, *The Words of Joseph Smith,* p. 123).

# Becoming a Great Missionary

*And they all cried with one voice, saying: Yea, we believe all
the words which thou hast spoken unto us; and also, we know of
their surety and truth, because of the Spirit of the Lord
Omnipotent, which has wrought a mighty change in us, or in
our hearts, that we have no more disposition to do evil, but to
do good continually.* (Mosiah 5:2)

We know we have finally been "born of God" when all desires
to do evil have been banished from our hearts, when we begin to
live the commandments of God willingly, and when we begin to live
the mission rules without complaint or regret. All God requires of
us is to keep His commandments[2] and willingly obey our leaders
and the Spirit of God within us that testifies each day of the truth. If
we do this, we, like Alma, will have the testimony of God in our
hearts and the countenance of God in our faces.

*And this is not all. Do ye not suppose that I know of these
things myself? Behold, I testify unto you that I do know that
these things whereof I have spoken are true. And how do ye
suppose that I know of their surety?*

*Behold, I say unto you they are made known unto me by the
Holy Spirit of God. Behold, I have fasted and prayed many
days that I might know these things of myself. And now I do
know of myself that they are true; for the Lord God hath made
them manifest unto me by his Holy Spirit; and this is the Spirit
of revelation which is in me.*

*And moreover, I say unto you that it has thus been revealed
unto me, that the words which have been spoken by our fathers
are true, even so according to the Spirit of prophecy which is in
me, which is also by the manifestation of the Spirit of God.*
(Alma 5:45–47)

---

[2] Mosiah 2:22.

226

Each morning after you get up, every evening before you go to sleep, and in your mind during the day, pray for the Spirit of God to be upon you and your companion. By the sheer force of your will, expand the aura of that Spirit around you so others will see and feel the Spirit of God for themselves. Let your light, the very countenance of God, shine for the entire world to see!

## Pray for Blessings Upon Those You Teach

As you progress in becoming a true servant of God, your thoughts will turn from focusing on yourself to focusing on those you teach. This is a natural progression that should not be forced. In the beginning, you need to focus on yourself. You have to learn the discussions, you may have to learn a language, and you have to become acclimated to mission life and fully living the mission rules. In addition, you have to become converted yourself in order to convert others. But once you are prepared, and once you begin to see that mighty change take place in your heart, you will also find the *need* to share that light and love with others. Like Enos, your heart will turn to your brothers and sisters, and your desire to bring them to God will grow and expand.

> *And he said unto me: "Because of thy faith in Christ, whom thou hast never before heard nor seen . . . thy faith hath made thee whole. Now it came to pass that when I had heard these words I began to feel a desire for the welfare of my brethren, the Nephites; wherefore, I did pour out my whole soul unto God for them.* (Enos 1:8–9)

## Brother Brown: Part II

Teaching Brother Brown and his family was a spiritual feast.

## Becoming a Great Missionary

Each discussion was filled with insight and revelation. Truly the scripture was fulfilled which says:

> Therefore, why is it ye cannot understand and know, that he that receiveth the word by the Spirit of truth receiveth it as it is preached by the Spirit of truth? Wherefore, he that preacheth and he that receiveth, understand one another, and both are edified and rejoice together. (D&C 50:21–22)

All who were present at those discussions were filled with the Spirit, understood the revelations of God as never before, and were edified by the entire process. But, as missionaries, we had to close the deal. We had to bring this wonderful family into the waters of baptism, but Brother Brown was a stubborn man. He would not commit until he *knew* the gospel was true. We were determined to give him that testimony! Finally, when all other options seemed to have run out, we decided to fast and pray that Brother Brown would obtain a witness for himself that the things we had been teaching were true.

Our regular appointment with the Browns was on Thursday. We decided to fast all day Tuesday. As we got up that morning, we knelt in mighty prayer, each of us taking a turn praying for God to accept our fast and sacrifice and give Brother Brown a testimony and witness of the truth. That night, as we closed our fast, we again prayed with great fervor that God would answer our prayers. Little did we know the power our faith had generated. Little did we know how powerful prayer *really* was!

On Thursday, we arrived at the Browns' home, as usual, but as soon as Brother Brown came to the door we knew something had changed. Instead of taking us into the living room as usual, he ushered us into the basement to speak to us in private. He then told us a wondrous tale: He had seen a vision. God had granted him a vision, a revelation of knowledge and power few people ever have an opportunity to experience! He told us that one night he had been reading the Book of Mormon in bed and pondering the things he was reading. Suddenly the Spirit of God fell upon him, and he was given a wonderful vision concerning who he was and what he could become. He saw himself standing among great leaders in the premortal life, arranging the great plans of God to move forward. Then his mind was moved quickly ahead and he saw his future state: living as a God in the Kingdom of Heaven!

As he spoke to us, he was visibly shaken. We had *never* talked to him about becoming Gods. Though our discussions covered almost every conceivable subject, we were never foolish enough to delve into the "mysteries." Nonetheless, this powerful doctrine had been revealed to him, and he wondered if he was crazy or being deceived somehow. It was clear to us by the way he talked and the knowledge that he had received, that this vision was from God. Brother Brown saw my expression and asked why I was smiling. I told him I knew what day this wonderful experience had happened. It had happened to him on Tuesday. The shock of my knowledge made him actually step backward. Without his asking, I answered the question he had on his face: How did I know? I related that my companion and I had fasted and prayed for him to receive a witness from God on Tuesday. It simply made sense that this great manifestation would have occurred as a result of our prayers. He confirmed what I had said—it was Tuesday night he had experienced this vision.

After this experience things changed rapidly. The Browns began to come to Church for the first time and openly began to prepare for baptism. Brother Brown was still stubborn—he would not be baptized until he had a few more questions answered—but their progress increased and the Spirit of God continued to pour out upon this wonderful family.

## Pray to Know Where to Teach

The culmination of your spiritual progress should be the ability to know where you should teach. If you remember, this was one of the goals for my own mission—one I never thought I would achieve. But an event occurred that changed my life and forced me to reconsider the relationship I had with God.

I had just been transferred from Altoona to Pittsburgh to become a district leader. In Altoona, we had smashed every mission record for teaching and had worked like madmen just to keep up with the work. In Pittsburgh that all changed. Suddenly we were teaching one or two discussions a week, instead of five or six a day. We struggled for months, our only source of spiritual food being our weekly discussion with Brother Brown. Eventually, even that ended and we were left with nothing but tracting, day after day, through the cold of winter. We were looking forward with great anticipation to the next zone conference, if for no other reason than as a break from the daily grind. I would be able to talk to President Pinnock again (this shows you the powerful effect a good mission president has on his missionaries—they actually look forward to meeting with him, knowing they will be uplifted). To our surprise and eventual delight, we had a guest speaker at this conference, a Regional Representative who shortly was to become a General Authority. He talked to us about the power of prayer and shared with us a personal story of how he had used the power of prayer, like Alma the Elder, to help his own son.

He had read how Alma the Elder had prayed for his son and how God had responded by sending an angel to intervene.[3] He did not expect anything so dramatic, but he did expect God would answer his prayers. In fact, he demanded it! Yes, we were all shocked to hear the words, but as he related the story it began to make sense. As this great leader knelt in prayer, he reviewed with God all the time he had spent in His service; how he had always fulfilled his callings; and how he had been absent from home so much doing the work of the Lord. He called to mind the scripture, "I the Lord am bound when ye do what I say; but when ye do not what I say, ye have no promise" (D&C 82:10). He realized he had done what the Lord had commanded him and therefore God was *bound* by law to help him. So he cried unto the Lord to live up to His part of the covenant by hearing his servant's cries and helping his son. God heard his prayers and shortly afterward answered his request.

I was shaken to my very soul by this great man's talk. For the first time in my life, I recognized how powerful and binding the covenants were I had taken upon myself in the temple of God. I realized that if I lived up to my part of the covenants I had made with God, He was *bound* by eternal law to live up to His part of the covenants. I could see that as we grow in spiritual strength, as we take upon us the countenance of God, we do become like Him. We move from being servants to becoming friends, and as friends[4] we can speak to God man to man, face to face, friend to friend.

---

[3] Mosiah 27:14.
[4] John 15:14–15; D&C 84:63.

## Becoming a Great Missionary

I then took a long look at my own life. Had I lived up to my part of the covenants I had taken? Was I worthy to approach God and develop the kind of relationship that this great leader had developed with his God? I realized I *was* ready for this step, at least I was ready to try. I knew I was not perfect, but I also realized that no one was—so it wasn't necessary to be *perfect* to develop this kind of relationship with the Savior. Then what was it? It had to be one's attitude. It had to do with becoming confident in the presence of God. It had to do with that mighty change of heart that comes with conversion! A time when we no longer have the *desire* to do evil but only the desire to do good continually. It did not mean we were perfect but meant that our hearts had pure *intent*. With this change of heart, we could approach God in a new way. We could not only learn *from* God, but we could learn *about* God—about who and what He really is. We could become His friend!

And so I decided I must also experience this great friendship with God. I must place myself in a position to develop a personal relationship with the Savior of the World. But how? And for what reason? Both Alma and this Regional Representative had a specific reason to approach the Lord. What was my reason? And then it came to me, as though God himself had planned it all along. What was it I needed most at this time? It was to find people to teach. And what was the one goal I had not yet fulfilled while on my mission? The ability to receive direct revelation from God concerning where to find people to teach! And so it was that I started on a journey of discovery. How would I communicate with God? Not just in some vague feeling but in a way that would specifically direct me to people who were ready to be taught the gospel. How did others do it? The answer came to me through the story of the Brother of Jared:

*And the Lord said unto the brother of Jared: What will ye that I
should do that ye may have light in your vessel?* (Ether 2:23)

God did not, would not, simply solve the problem the brother
of Jared was having. God wanted to make sure that the brother of
Jared *knew* He had solved his problem. If God had fixed the problem without the brother of Jared asking Him for help, he might
have thought it was just a coincidence, or good fortune, that the
problem had been solved. No, God wanted to make sure the
brother of Jared knew it was Him to whom he should look for
blessings! By making the brother of Jared choose what God would
do, the brother of Jared would not be able to deny it was God who
performed the act when it actually happened. After the brother of
Jared decided *how* he wanted the Lord to fix his problem, the Lord
answered his prayer and request:

> . . . *touch these stones, O Lord, with thy finger, and prepare
> them that they may shine forth in the darkness* . . .

> *And it came to pass that when the brother of Jared had said
> these words, behold, the Lord stretched forth his hand and
> touched the stones one by one with his finger* . . . (Ether 3:4, 6)

Now, not only did the brother of Jared have his problem solved,
but he *knew* it was God who had solved it! And his testimony and
faith grew as a result of this process. I realized that I would have to
do the same thing. In order for me to *know* that what I was receiving
actually came from God (and not by imagination or coincidence), I
would have to choose how I wanted God to communicate with me
that which I wanted: finding people to teach. Now I knew *what* I
had to do, but I still had to decide *how* I wanted God to do it. The
brother of Jared had asked God to touch stones with His finger to
make them shine. I had to choose some specific way that God

would communicate with me the knowledge I needed—where to find people to teach. My next answer came from a revelation given to Oliver Cowdery:

> *Yea, behold, I will tell you in your mind and in your heart, by the Holy Ghost, which shall come upon you and which shall dwell in your heart. Now, behold, this is the Spirit of revelation . . .* (D&C 8:2–3)

This is how I would have the Lord communicate with me the information I needed. I would have him tell me in my mind the area in which I was to work to find the people He wanted me to teach. Before I knelt down in prayer to communicate with God, I would review the different areas to which we had been assigned and bring them before the Lord; then, I would ask God to somehow let me know into which specific area we should go.

The first morning I attempted this great experiment was a real struggle. I had never attempted such a thing before and had no clue whether it would really work. However, I felt good about the process I had worked out and had faith that somehow God would work with me, even in my weakness. So I knelt down and began to pray. I prayed fervently to the Lord, explained my plan to communicate with Him, and begged him to agree. I tried to approach the Lord with confidence. I reviewed with the Lord how I had lived my life since I had come back into the Church, how I had faithfully followed the mission rules—even going the extra mile by getting up early and working hard. And, finally, I expressed my true conviction that I was not asking this for myself, but was asking so I could magnify my calling and bring souls to Him.

As I prayed, I could feel the presence of the Spirit and thus grew more and more confident before the Lord. Then I made my first request: I asked God to somehow help me picture in my mind the area He wanted me to work that morning. Then I simply began to run through my mind the different townships, boroughs, and even streets we had in our area. Time went on and nothing seemed to happen, so I concentrated harder. I focused all of my energy in trying to discern some difference in the names and places that ran through my mind; something, *anything* that would make one name stand out over another, but there was nothing. Finally, it became almost embarrassing. I had been on my knees for quite some time, and I knew I had to go out and work. So, almost as a guess, I picked the name of an area that seemed to be "brighter" in my mind than others. As I got up from my knees, I was greatly disappointed. I had expected so much more. As we prepared to leave the apartment to go to the area I had chosen during my prayer, and almost as an afterthought, I looked through my appointment book to see if we might have forgotten something. This was just a habit from my last area, since we had been getting in so few doors and none of them had been more than a one-discussion visit. To my surprise, we actually had a call-back visit written down for that day, a woman we had tracted who told us to come back in two or three weeks, so I had written it down and forgotten about it. And then it hit me. The call-back appointment was in the very same area I had chosen that morning during prayer! Hallelujah! God had indeed answered my prayers, in spite of my struggles and my doubts. I would not doubt again! When we went to that call-back, the woman let us in and we taught her the first discussion. It was the beginning of a miraculous transformation.

I had been in this area for about three months. In that time, we had taught hardly anyone and had not one family we could put down in our teaching pool, but that all changed. I began to pray

# Becoming a Great Missionary

three times a day seeking the Lord's guidance as to where we should teach, in the morning before we left the apartment, at our lunchtime break, and at our dinnertime break. Each night, I would get on my knees to thank the Lord for the answers He had given me during the day. Within 30 days—one month—we had over 15 families in our teaching pool, all progressing towards baptism! We began to teach every day, almost all day long. Each day, my communication with the Lord became more and more clear, and the amount of time I had to spend on my knees to get the answers I sought was less and less. It never failed. From the first day I tried it until the end of my mission, it never failed me. Even after my mission, as I sought for and found my eternal companion and married her in the temple, it never failed me. Even now, the legacy of that moment, of that time of discovery, still lives on in my life.

You must do the same. As a missionary and servant of God, you *can* do the same. However, do not try to duplicate specifically what I did. I have learned over time that different people receive revelation from God in different ways. If you were to try exactly what I did, it might fail. You must find your own stone for God to touch with His finger. The *process* will be the same: choose a method with which you feel comfortable communicating with God, making it as simple, yet as specific, as possible. Do not make it complicated! What I mean is that if you get too complex, your mind will get lost in all the detail. For example, if you were to try and pick the specific house to go to, you would have so many houses to run through your mind it would be impossible to pick one. But if you make your request more general, like an area or a subdivision—something you will be able to do in a day's time—then there will not be as much confusion in your mind and you will have better success. But make sure you do it your way. As with the brother of Jared, God wants *you* to choose how you will receive the answers to your prayers and requests, so you will know it comes from Him.

There is one more key to prayer you should understand. It is the importance of learning to use the great spiritual power that resides within us. First of all, we must ask God in the name of Christ. We have been told specifically to "seek ye earnestly the best gifts."[5] We have been told specifically to ask so we can receive. God wants us to develop our faith. He wants us to be successful and experience the great powers we have at our disposal. It is part of His eternal plan for His children, so He will do whatever He can to insure our success.

> *To ask is one thing; to seek is a greater thing; and to knock at the very doors of heaven assures that those holy portals will be opened and that the desired blessings will be forthcoming. Those who take no thought save it be to ask are denied the blessing. "Let him ask of God . . . But let him ask in faith" is the divine decree* (James 1:5–6; D&C 9:7–9). *Nothing is withheld from those who seek the Lord with all their heart. Those whose search falls short of the utmost bounds to which it should extend shall not find the desired treasure.* (Bruce R. McConkie, The Mortal Messiah, *Vol. 3, p. 188).*

What does this mean? It means that when we pray for an answer or a blessing we must do so with great desire and *intensity!* It is not enough to say our prayers like we did as children: "Now I lay me down to sleep. . . ." We must consciously increase the power and mental exertion of our thoughts so we can break through the veil of heaven and insure our prayers are both heard *and* answered! This is not easy. It takes great desire and effort for someone to pray "with

---

[5] D&C 46:8.

**237**

all their heart." But if we truly desire to *know*, if we really need that blessing from God, then our faith will be effective and we will receive the desired result.

## How to Pray as a Group

One of the most misunderstood principles about prayer is *why* we pray as a group and *how* to properly pray as a group. The most exalted form of prayer is to pray as a group within a prayer circle. Why? What is it about praying as a group that is better than praying as an individual? The answer is all about *power*.

Proper and intense prayer is nothing more than a person focusing his spiritual and mental *powers* on a subject or person. If his prayers are righteous and appropriate, they will be accepted by God, who will then enhance and magnify his personal power so that his prayers will be answered. When a *group* of people is praying, their combined spiritual and mental powers have more effect than one individual has. However, group prayer must be done correctly in order to be effective.

Just as any organization needs a leader, just as God has organized His Church with *one* Savior and *one* prophet, and each family has *one* head, when group prayers are said there must be *one* speaker. For example, if both missionary companions pray to find where to teach, there would inevitably be conflict and confusion. Therefore, only *one* companion should be designated to pray for guidance and thus only *one* companion should be expected to receive an answer. But what then does the other companion do? What does the rest of the congregation do when there is *one* person praying? The answer leads us to understand the proper way to conduct group prayers. It all has to do with *power* and *focus*.

The Prophet Joseph Smith first taught this principle to Hyrum Smith. Joseph explained that the other members of the group should focus their prayers and mental energy upon the person praying. Their spiritual power should be directed to the person praying with the intent that his prayer will be heard and answered. The person acting as voice becomes the conduit for the spiritual power of the group. The person praying also acts as the receptor for any knowledge or revelation coming to the group from God. As a group, we focus on the individual praying in order to insure he will receive an answer to his prayer on our behalf.

For example, we as a Church focus our prayers and spiritual power upon the prophet of the Church. Why? Because we want to insure the prophet will receive revelations from God for all of us. Each individual does not pray that God will reveal to each of us doctrine and direction for the Church. This would lead to chaos! Instead, we focus our prayers and powers as a group upon *one person*, the prophet. In return, God answers this group prayer by giving that one person, the prophet, the answers we are seeking. This is the proper way to proceed; this is how group prayer is supposed to be performed.[6]

Let me give you a personal example of how this works. One day while looking at some land on which to build our home, we lost our 2-year-old daughter. We were in the middle of a heavily wooded area and when we turned around, she was gone. After some time of

---

[6] "There are times and places when all should vocally repeat the words spoken, but in our prayer meetings and in our family circles let every heart be united with the one who takes the lead by being mouth before the Lord, and let every person mentally repeat the prayers, and all unite in whatever is asked for, and the Lord will not withhold, but will give to such person the things which they ask for and rightly need." (Brigham Young, *Discourses of Brigham Young*, pp. 44–45).

fruitless searching, we decided to kneel and pray as a family. Each of us knelt and tried to get an answer as to what to do and where to look for this child. After we each ended our prayers, each of us had a different answer as to what to do! This left us more confused and anxious! Just then, my wife remembered reading the story of Hyrum Smith and after she explained the principle of group prayer we decided to try it. It was decided that I would pray and all the other members of the family would focus their prayers on *me*. As I prayed to God for an answer, my family prayed for *me*, that I would receive the answer I was seeking. This time our group prayer worked. I was told very clearly to go to a phone and call the police immediately. We went to the nearest home and called the local police. They told me they already had our daughter and that she was sitting in a police car at the end of the street! One minute later, we were reunited with our daughter who was calmly devouring an ice cream cone (the family that found our daughter had immediately called the police to come get her). We learned a great principle that day, which will never be forgotten.

## The Book of Prayers

One way to *learn* how the Spirit of God works and to *learn* whether your prayers are being effective is to keep a prayer book. This is a principle I learned from a little old lady in Cleveland. She was a faithful member of the Church who had the wonderful desire to help others. She was too old and poor to do anything else, so she turned to prayer. She had faith in God and knew He would do what she could not. Her faith was so great, she began keeping track of all of the things she prayed for, just to make sure everything was covered. She prayed for members of the ward who were sick or who were facing problems at home or at work. She prayed for her family members, neighbors, and friends—even perfect strangers, if she knew they needed help. She wrote down all of her prayer requests in a book, and each day she began her prayers by reciting each name and request that appeared on her list. As people were made well, as problems were solved, as friends and neighbors had their wishes and prayers answered, she put a check by their name: one more item off her list.

Of course her list was *never* completed, because she always added someone to the bottom of the list as she was made aware of new problems. Most people didn't even know about this dear woman and her "prayer book." She did it quietly, just a humble servant of God working behind the scenes to make people's lives better. My wife and I had the privilege of being the recipients of the power of her prayers. We were moving back to Utah and, unknown to us, she put us on her list to have our home sell. We had been struggling for months to sell our home, but a short time after our names had been placed in her "prayer book" our home sold and my family was able to move. One more prayer answered, one more check in her book, one more item on her list completed.

A short time after our house sold, this good woman called my wife to chastise her. She complained we had not called to let her know our house had sold. When my wife told her yes, it had sold, and how grateful we were, this dear lady explained to my wife how she had put our names and the desire to sell our home into her prayer book. She explained it was very important she learn when her prayers had been answered so that she could check us off her list and thank God for answering her prayers. We learned a great deal from this sister.

## Becoming a Great Missionary

This humble woman knew how to get things done. She knew how to pray and get answers to her prayers! By keeping track of her prayers and God's answers, she *learned* how the Spirit of the Lord worked, she *learned* what didn't work, and she *learned* the difference between them. She had also learned that gratitude to God was an important component in completing the prayer circle. A true prayer is not complete until we acknowledge that the answer to the prayer came from God—that it was not just a coincidence. We make that acknowledgement when we express our thanks to God for answering our prayers. She learned there are steps to prayer: asking, persistence, patience, receiving answers, acknowledgement, and gratitude. She had perfected a God-given talent and used it fully and graciously for others.

If the idea of a prayer book seems new, it isn't. The Prophet Joseph Smith talked about this principle in learning how to receive and understand revelation:

> *A person may profit by noticing the first intimation of the Spirit of Revelation; for instance, when you feel pure Intelligence flowing unto you, it may give you sudden strokes of ideas—so that by noticing it, you may find it fulfilled the same day or soon; (i.e.) those things that were presented unto your minds by the Spirit of God, will come to pass; and thus by learning the Spirit of God and understanding it, you may grow unto the principle of Revelation, until you become perfect in Christ Jesus.* (Teachings of the Prophet Joseph Smith, p. 151).

As you attempt to communicate with God by keeping record of your prayers and the insights you receive, and then *watching for the signs* that God is answering you, you will be able to learn how the process works. This is not easy; it takes time and great effort. But it *will* work if you persist.

## True Humility

After reading this section, some may have mixed feelings. Was I arrogant to think I could do the same thing as the brother of Jared and Alma? Some may consider themselves unworthy even to attempt this great blessing, as they look back on their lives and recognize the many sins they have committed. Perhaps you have not been living the mission rules as you should, or working as hard as you should. All of these thoughts are just excuses. It comes down to understanding the real meaning of humility.

Most people do not understand the real meaning of humility. They see humility only in one way, as Christ described it for two men praying:

> *Two men went up into the temple to pray; the one a Pharisee, and the other a publican. The Pharisee stood and prayed thus with himself, God, I thank thee, that I am not as other men are, extortioners, unjust, adulterers, or even as this publican. I fast twice in the week, I give tithes of all that I possess. And the publican, standing afar off, would not lift up so much as his eyes unto heaven, but smote upon his breast, saying, God be merciful to me a sinner. I tell you, this man went down to his house justified rather than the other: for every one that exalteth himself shall be abased; and he that humbleth himself shall be exalted. (Luke 18:10–14)*

Based on this scripture, many people believe the only way to be humble is to beat up themselves, emotionally and spiritually.[7] They berate themselves about even the smallest transgression, thinking

---

[7] "Some of the company thought that I was not a very meek Prophet; so I told them: 'I am meek and lowly in heart,' and will personify Jesus for a moment, to illustrate the principle, and cried with a loud voice: 'Woe unto you, ye doctors; woe unto you, ye lawyers; woe unto you, ye scribes, Pharisees, and hypocrites!' But you cannot find the place where I ever went that I found fault with their food, their drink, their house, their lodgings; no never; and this is what is meant by the meekness and lowliness of Jesus." (Joseph Smith, *Teachings of the Prophet Joseph Smith*, p. 270).

this abusive behavior will make them humble. In fact, it does just the opposite. It lowers a person's self-esteem, destroys their self-confidence, and places them in a position of depression and sadness, ultimately leaving them vulnerable to the power of Satan. Not exactly the attitude a good missionary should have!

> *It (humility) is not self-abasement—the hiding in the corner, the devaluation of everything one does or thinks or says; but it is the doing of one's best in every case and leaving of one's acts, expressions, and accomplishments to largely speak for themselves.* (The Teachings of Spencer W. Kimball, *p. 233)*

God is kind and judges men with knowledge and love, not with a desire to punish and/or destroy. He can see within our soul, knows the intent of our heart, and understands that even though we are imperfect we are capable of doing great good. He permits us to serve Him, knowing that even though we may make mistakes, the good we do edifies both us and those we try to serve. There are times, after we have committed *serious* sins, like the publican in the scripture above, that we must smite our breasts with despair and let the pain we feel motivate us to repent. But most of the time, we simply need to beware of pride. We *need* self-esteem. We *need* self-confidence.[8] We need to understand that as children of God we have inherited abilities far beyond our mortal understanding. We have the ability in this life to follow in the footsteps of Jesus Christ. We have the ability to use our faith for good and to experience spiritual gifts and blessings. We have the innate ability to become like God; therefore, humility cannot be something that destroys our

---

[8] "Instead of pleading with the Lord to bestow more upon you, plead with yourselves to have confidence in yourselves, to have integrity in yourselves, and know when to speak and what to speak, what to reveal, and how to carry yourselves and walk before the Lord." (Brigham Young, *Discourses of Brigham Young,* p. 93).

self-confidence and self-esteem. It cannot be something that will injure us. It must be something that has a positive effect on our lives.

> *Among the cardinal virtues of the gospel is the praiseworthy virtue of humility. . . . I interpret humility as being strength. Humility expresses itself in lowly service, in volunteering for any service which will ameliorate the conditions, particularly the spiritual conditions of mankind. Humility does not mean to grovel, to be a sycophant. Humility is inward strength outwardly expressed in good works. Great souls attain to humility. (Charles A. Callis,* Conference Report, *April 1942)*

True humility is nothing more than seeing yourself as God sees you. If you see yourself as more than you really are, you have pride. If you see yourself less than you really are or, if you think that you are not worthy to receive the love and blessings of God, you are being self-destructive.

Like most things in life, the extremes at either end of the spectrum are never good. There is a strait and narrow path through the center of life that provides balance. This is the path we must find. This is the path the Savior walked. Christ did not think himself more than he was—he did not have pride. But neither did he think of himself as a terrible sinner, incapable of receiving the love of God. He knew who he was and what he was capable of. He knew when he needed help and when he could handle things himself. This is the same balance we must have in our lives.

> *In our time and in such settings, our need for virtues like humility and obedience will be very great. Humility is not the disavowal of our worth; rather, it is the sober realization of how much we are valued by God. Nor does true humility call*

## Becoming a Great Missionary

*for the denigration of what truth we already know; rather, it is
the catching of one's breath, as he realizes how very little that
which we mortals presently know really is! (Neal A. Maxwell,*
All These Things Shall Give Thee Experience, *p. 127)*

Humility has the ability to see through both the flattery and derision of others. A servant of God seeks to please the Master, not others, and as a result becomes comfortable in the presence of God. A person with self-confidence before God is humble because he knows his place in life and does not worry about what others think or say.

*When a person sees things as they are, flattery and reproach are
all the same to him, he sees no difference. If he finds that he is
pleasing God and his brethren, he is exceedingly rejoiced, and
feels an increase of humility and resignation. When a man is
proud and arrogant, flattery fills him with vanity and injures
him; but it is not so when he is increasing in the faith of God.*
(Discourses of Brigham Young, *p. 228)*

*Humility is not weakness but strength. One can be bold and
meek at the same time. One can be courageous and humble. If
the Lord was meek and lowly and humble, then to become
humble one must do what he did in boldly denouncing evil,
bravely advancing righteous works, courageously meeting every
problem, becoming the master of himself and the situations
about him and being near oblivious to personal credit. (*The
Teachings of Spencer W. Kimball, *p. 232)*

*How does one get humble? To me, one must constantly be
reminded of his dependence. On whom dependent? On the Lord.
How remind one's self? By real, constant, worshipful, grateful*

*prayer. . . . Humility is teachableness—an ability to realize
that all virtues and abilities are not concentrated in one's
self. . . . (*The Teachings of Spencer W. Kimball, *p. 233)*

As usual, it is only through inspiration that we can see ourselves
as God sees us, and therefore have true humility. Only God can
show to us our weaknesses and turn them into strengths.[9] Only
God can draw us out of our self-pity, shower blessings upon us, and
give us the inward strength to go forward with faith.

---

[9] Ether 12:27.

# Becoming a Great Missionary

# *Twelve*
# *The Point of Baptism*

The most important and sometimes most difficult process to learn is how to commit people to baptism. Most people perceive the truth when they hear it, but understanding the truth and being willing to live it are two different things. Developing the ability to convince people to commit to living the truth—to commit to baptism—is the final step in learning how to be a great missionary. This chapter will deal with how to approach this subject, how to deal with investigator concerns, and how to deal with your own fears.

## How to Commit People to Baptism

For most missionaries, the most difficult discussion to teach is the one where they commit the investigator to live the commandments and be baptized. It is stressful because missionaries want so *badly* for them to say yes, but fear they will say no. You don't want to scare them away by being too pushy, on the other hand, you know you need to broach the subject and prepare them for "the question:" Will you be baptized?

# Becoming a Great Missionary

*1. Be up front and honest.*

As stated in a previous chapter, the best way to prepare people to say yes to the question of baptism is to let them know up front that baptism is a requirement for joining our church. This is such an important principle that it deserves repeating! Almost everyone will say no the first time you bring up the subject of baptism. They will say they are interested in hearing what you have to say, but do not want to join the Church. You should always come back with an assertive and positive response, stating that you *knew* all along how they felt and that you did not expect an affirmative response, at least not now.

> "Of course we don't expect you to join our Church right now. In fact, we would not permit you to join right now! You see, God has a plan for all of us. He expects each and every one of us to make covenants with Him to prove our worthiness. In these covenants, we promise to do certain things for God, such as keeping his commandments; and God promises to do certain things for us, such as bless our families and us on earth and inherit the Kingdom of God after this life. Because these covenants are so sacred, we do not permit anyone to enter into them without first making sure they are prepared to live them. The discussions we teach will give you an understanding of what God expects. After you hear all of the discussions, the decision will be totally up to you: you can either decide to go on with your life as it is, or you can decide to accept the promises God has given and enter into the covenant of baptism."

At this point, two things have happened. You have calmed their fears about making a commitment *right now*, and you have given them something very deep and sacred to ponder. They will want to know what these sacred covenants are! After you have broached this subject once, you never have to worry about it again. Whenever it comes up, if they are still nervous or say they don't want to join, you can remind them that you told them up front it was *their decision* and if they are not ready, it is okay. Then continue to teach them until they are ready.

*2. Don't wait.*

The longer you wait to bring up the idea of baptism, the harder it will be to get them to commit. People must have time to ponder before making a life-changing commitment. If you "spring" it upon them at the last discussion, of course they will say no! "You never told us you expected us to join your Church!" "You never mentioned we had to get baptized!" People need time to decide. More importantly, people need time for the Spirit of God to work upon them. This is a recurring theme in this book. God cannot draw from an empty well. If your investigators have *never* been taught about baptism, if the thought isn't even in their mind, how can God then work on that thought? Paul understood this when he said, "And how shall they believe in him of whom they have not heard?"[1] The Spirit must have something to work upon. If you place the idea of baptism in their minds, even if they reject it at first, it will give the Spirit of God a chance to work upon them over a period of time. Then when you do ask the question, they will be prepared to say yes.

*3. Make sure they are ready.*

For most missionaries, this is not a problem. By the time they find the courage to ask their investigators to be baptized, they are more than ready! But occasionally there will be some missionaries, even some entire missions, so zealous to get baptisms they do not wait until the family is truly ready. This creates a frightening scenario, because it almost ensures the family will eventually leave the

---

[1] Romans 10:14.

## Becoming a Great Missionary

Church. They will be the seed in the Savior's parable of the sower[2] planted in soil without dirt; therefore, they did not grow roots. As a result, it was just a matter of time before they withered and died.

You *must* make certain your family is ready to take upon themselves the sacred covenants of God. This does not mean you take upon yourself the responsibility to decide for them (God forbid) as only they can say yes or no; only they can decide, only they will be held responsible for whatever decision they make. What does it mean, then, to make sure they are ready?

A. It means you make sure you have not taken any shortcuts.

B. You teach them *all* the discussions.

C. You make sure they *understand* what you have taught.

D. You make sure you have resolved all their problems and concerns.

E. They are going forward with full knowledge of all of the commitments and responsibilities they will be taking upon themselves. If you help them hide their sins (oh, it really isn't *that* bad) or pretend to overlook the problems they have with the doctrine (I know they don't believe in prophets, but they *want* to be baptized!), you will be doing both them and the Church a great disservice.

You cannot make the *decision* for them, but you can make certain you have taught them correctly and well!

*4. Get the members involved.*

When investigators are hesitant to be baptized, it is rarely due to

---

[2] Matthew 13:3–9.

the doctrine (after all, it *is* the truth). It may be a result of their fear of the change in their lifestyle or of meeting and associating with so many new people. The way to overcome this fear is to make certain they meet as many members as possible while you are teaching them the discussions. I promise you, the members can do a much better job of overcoming their fears about baptism than you! Put away your pride, realize you cannot do it alone, and get some help from the members.

Even if you find it hard to get members to split, as your investigators near baptism the *leaders* of the ward should come and help you. For example, the elders quorum president should come to meet the father and talk about the priesthood, the Relief Society president should come meet the wife, and the Young Men's and Women's presidents and Primary president, etc. (or their counselors) should come meet the various members of the family. The more members that visit the family prior to baptism the better, as your investigators will then feel more comfortable coming to church because they already know people.

5. *Make sure they go to church.*

One of the natural fears people have is the fear of the unknown. Getting your investigators to come to church as soon as possible is the best way to get them over this fear. They need to meet other members of the church, know where the church is, where to park, where the door is, and which class to go to. These things may seem small but can loom quite large in the minds of your investigators. This also means that *before they go to church,* you are to tell them all about it. Not just what time it starts, but *everything* about it. You tell them, "We start in this class for an hour, then go here for an hour, then go into sacrament meeting for an hour. The sacrament is bread and water, and you should not partake of the sacrament yet, until after you are baptized." The more you tell them about church and the more specific you get, the more at ease they will be when they get there.

*6. Don't turn them into professional investigators!*

If you have taught your investigators all the discussions and they still refuse to be baptized, it is time to move on. Occasionally, people take a long time to make up their mind (I have seen some people take a year or more). As missionaries, you do not have that kind of time. When it comes to extended teaching assignments, it is appropriate to turn these investigators over to stake missionaries to continue the work. As full-time missionaries, you should *not* continue teaching a family very long after they have progressed through the discussions. If you continue to visit and eat dinner with them without having them make any kind of commitment to the Church, you will create *professional investigators!* It is better to leave them for a time—months, even years—so another missionary might have a better chance of committing them to baptism when they are ready.

I had an example while serving as a Seventy in Utah. We were teaching the discussions to a young couple who, after all the discussions were given, declined to be baptized. We were not sure what to do. We could not simply give them the discussions *again*, and we did not feel it was in our best interest to meet with them every week, as though we were their home teachers, since they were not members of the Church. After some discussion, we turned them over to an older stake missionary couple. They were wiser and more patient than we could have been with this young couple. A year later, the diligence of these stake missionaries paid off—the couple was baptized.

Another example happened in Connecticut while I was serving as ward mission leader. One of the part-member families I was home teaching finally committed to taking the missionary discussions. It was another example of simply being bold and asking the nonmember husband, directly and forcefully, to hear *all* the missionary discussions. Once he said yes, the path seemed clear: have the full-time missionaries teach this family and get the husband baptized. Everything seemed to be going exactly as planned, until all the discussions had been taught and the husband still refused to be baptized. He was not yet ready. What should we do? Once again, we decided to turn the family over to someone older and wiser. We assigned this family to one of the senior missionary couples serving in our ward. About eight months later, this good husband and father was baptized.

This is how it should work. Full-time missionaries teach only those who are prepared to be baptized into the Church. If all the discussions have been taught and your investigators still refuse to come to church and be baptized, they should be turned over to the local priesthood—the stake or senior missionaries—to continue contact. This will prevent them from becoming "hooked" on the missionaries. It will prevent them from becoming professional investigators.

## What Happens if Only Part of the Family Wants to Join?

One of the most difficult decisions to be made occurs when only part of the family is ready to be baptized. Generally speaking, it

## Becoming a Great Missionary

is good to wait as long as possible before creating a part-member family. If one family member is not ready, wait a while longer, especially if it is one of the parents. If the father is not ready but the rest of the family is, wait. It is better to be patient and baptize the family as a group rather than create tension within the family unit by baptizing only part of the family.

Remember that the family is the most important unit in God's kingdom. It is inappropriate to be about the work of splitting up families. Whenever possible, the family should be taught together, progress together, and be baptized together. No missionary should be so zealous as to tear a family apart by baptizing only part of the family when, with patience, they could have been baptized into the Church together.[3]

Sometimes you just have to let them go and let time resolve the issues and problems. Let me give you an example.

We were teaching an older couple who seemed very interested in joining the Church. After a while, the husband became disinterested and even antagonistic toward us while the wife continued to progress toward baptism. It became clear they were going in separate directions. They had been perfectly happy as a couple until we had introduced the gospel into their family, but now it seemed as though the gospel would break up their family. Finally, it came to a crisis. If the wife continued with the discussions, their marriage would probably end. The husband demanded she stop meeting with us. What should we do? What should they do? All I can tell you is

---

[3] "And if children embrace the Gospel, and their parents or guardians are unbelievers, teach them to stay at home and be obedient to their parents or guardians. . . . But if a man forbid his wife, or his children, before they are of age, to receive the Gospel, then it should be the duty of the Elder to go his way." (Joseph Smith, *Teachings of the Prophet Joseph Smith,* p. 87).

what finally happened and I believe the Lord accepted it. The wife, with our blessing and encouragement, decided to stop taking the discussions. Her relationship with her husband had to come first. We knew that God would bless this good woman either way. It was a tough decision and we believed that, in time, her husband might come around. I knew that God could see the desires of her heart, and she would be blessed and, in time, be rewarded for her faith.

There is another principle involved, however. Every man, woman, and child will have to stand before the bar of God to be judged by their works. What they did in this life and the decisions they have made, including the decision to accept the gospel and be baptized will all be a part of this judgment. Since this is a personal decision, not a group one, each individual must be accepted on their own merits and desires. What this means is that in spite of our desire to bring families into the Church *together*, sometimes this is impossible. If it becomes clear some members of the family will not join the Church and others are definitely ready, we should not, *can not*, deny them the blessing and opportunity to be baptized. There is another profound principle behind the decision to proceed with baptism. The spiritual growth within the faithful spouse will eventually save the husband or wife.

> For the unbelieving husband is sanctified by the wife, and the unbelieving wife is sanctified by the husband: else were your children unclean; but now are they holy. (1 Corinthians 7:14)

I believe this principle is much broader than stated here. I believe a parent or parents can sanctify their children and faithful children can sanctify their parents. I believe we underestimate the

power of the Spirit to influence those around us. The presence of
the Spirit of God touches and influences everything around it.
When thinking about this principle, I always think of a little history.
Just a few years before the Iron Curtain fell and eastern Europe and
the Soviet Union opened their doors to the preaching of the gospel,
a significant event happened. A temple of God was built in East
Germany, *behind* the Iron Curtain. I believe the building of this temple was directly responsible for the eventual change in the hearts of
the people of Germany, which, in turn, led to the fall of the Iron
Curtain. This being true, what influence can a faithful member have
on their spouse who lives with them day after day?

Even in part-member families, the family must come first. This
is a principle that must be affirmed over and over if the entire family
is to one day become united in Christ. Let me give you an example.

We were teaching a wonderful family in Connecticut. The wife
had been a Jehovah's Witness, which almost cost her her marriage.
The Jehovah's Witnesses demanded she always put their church
first, so, time after time, she was choosing strangers over her husband and children in matters that directly affected their family like
tithing, finances, and the time she spent away from her family.
Eventually the family was in crisis, and the wife had to choose between
the Jehovah's Witnesses and her husband. She chose her husband.

Not long afterward, she met the Mormon missionaries and was
converted. But once again, perhaps because of her recent history
with the other church, there arose a conflict within the family. Her
husband did not want her to be baptized. As ward mission leader, I
went with the missionaries to help resolve the conflict. After assess-
ing the situation, I told the husband that, considering the circum-

stances, we would not baptize his wife without his permission as we did not want to break up his family or do anything that would cause problems for them. We decided to follow the principle we had been taught in almost every priesthood meeting we attended: The family comes first.

Within a few days after our meeting with this family, the husband gave permission for this good woman and her son to be baptized. Our concern for the unity of his family had convinced him this Church would be *good* for his family. I was assigned to be their home teacher. Not long afterward another problem arose—tithing. This sister had been faithfully paying tithing on the money she earned at her job. The family was going through some tough financial times and the husband demanded she stop. I was brought in to resolve the problem. Once again, I put the family first. I told this sister she was to obey the wishes of her husband and *not* pay tithing. I told her that God knew her heart and knew that she would pay tithing if she could. I told her it was more important to keep a good relationship with her husband than to fight over money. I told her I knew the time would come when she would be able to participate in this law and receive its blessings. I told her how lucky she was to have an honorable husband who worked hard, financially supported her and her children, and did not abuse them but loved and cared for them. This was not a man for whom she wished to cause problems, but one with whom she wanted to stay! I read her the scripture quoted above and promised she would have a much greater influence on her husband by loving him than by doing things to disrupt her family.

Once again, her husband was surprised and touched by the tone of my words. How different from the other churches he had experienced! Instead of trying to divide his family, we were doing everything we could to keep them together. It wasn't long before she began to pay tithing again with the full blessing of her husband. Soon he was attending Church socials and participating in Church at various times. We eventually moved, so I don't know their status now, but I'm sure we did the right thing. She remained faithful, her son was married in the temple, and her husband fully supported her membership. In time, I know he will join the Church, too.

We will never know, nor can we as mortals adequately judge, the trials people must go through to become members of the Church and remain active. I remember one wonderful young woman for whom I was a home teacher. She had been converted and had been a faithful member for about two years when she came up against a real problem—marriage. There were no available men in the ward and she wanted children and a family. She fell in love with a nonmember. She had to choose between the Church in which she believed and loved, and the man she loved and could have a family with. She chose to experience the love of a good man and have a family, and I could not tell her she was wrong! I could not judge her heart or the path on which the Lord might take her. I wished her all the blessings that could come to her in her life, prayed she would find joy, and said goodbye.

These are *hard* decisions! We are but mortals with limited understanding about how God works in the lives of men on earth. Therefore, we *cannot* presume to judge the decisions of others, especially when it concerns something so sensitive, private, and personal as love and family. We are fortunate to be able to leave that judgment in the loving hands of Jesus Christ.

*If they say yes, baptize!*

I have stressed a lot the need to make certain you teach people properly, so they understand what you have taught, and that you do not baptize them if they are not ready. But the bottom line is, if they desire to be baptized, you *must* baptize them! You cannot judge their hearts, only God can. You cannot *assume* they are lying, or *assume* they are not ready, or assume anything else about them. You must take them at face value and ask the standard questions prior to baptism. If they say yes, baptize them!

> *In the first place, I want to say to the Elders who go forth to preach the Gospel—no matter who may apply to you for baptism, even if you have good reason to believe they are unworthy, if they require it, forbid them not, but perform that duty and administer the ordinance for them; it clears the skirts of your garments, and the responsibility is upon them.*
> (Discourses of Brigham Young, *p. 327*)

## What to Do After They are Baptized

People fall away from the Church for a variety of reasons but primarily as the result of two things: either they were not prepared properly before being baptized, or the members of the Church did not properly follow up after baptism. Let us talk about the followup that *must* take place with every new member of the Church.

### 1. *Joint member/missionary visits*

Preferably these visits should begin *before* investigators are baptized, but it must certainly occur after they are baptized. There must be a formal "passing of the torch" from the missionaries to the home teachers. There should be at least two visits where *both* the missionaries and members go together to visit the new member.

# Becoming a Great Missionary

The new members know the missionaries and trust them. This feeling of comfort and trust must be passed from the missionaries to the home teachers. This is very simply done by teaching a few joint lessons together. This will show the new members that the missionaries trust the home teachers, so the new member will trust them as well. By teaching together, they show a united front that the doctrine taught is the same, and the Spirit of God is present. There is a *transfer* of trust.

2. *New member discussions.*

All new members should be given the new member discussions in the weeks following the baptism. The stake missionaries, senior missionaries, home teachers, or any combination of the three can teach these lessons. These discussions are simply a review of the missionary discussions with a greater emphasis on the temple, so they can begin preparations for the temple. These discussions will reinforce everything taught by the missionaries. The new members will remember the sweet Spirit they felt and why they made the commitments they did. The lessons will solidify their testimonies and give them another chance to bring up, and overcome, any doctrine they did not understand or principle they hesitated to believe.

3. *Give new members a calling.*

Every new member should be given a calling as soon as possible. Some bishops are hesitant to call new members to positions of trust, assuming that because they are new they will not do a good job or will make mistakes. These bishops must overcome their misgivings because it is in error. *Everyone* makes mistakes in their callings; no one is perfect. The growth these new members will gain far outweighs any problem they might create or experience while serving in that calling. What do branches do? Some countries have *branch presidents* who have been members of the Church only four months! If they can survive and grow with the help of the Lord, surely your branch or ward can continue to grow by placing inexperienced new members in positions of trust within the ward.

*4.    Give them a new goal: the temple.*

Make sure new members understand their eternal progression has just begun. As they begin to serve faithfully, they must begin preparations to enter the temple of the Lord. Obtaining their temple endowments and having their family sealed for eternity should be a well-established goal for every new member, even before they are baptized.

*5.    Frequent interviews with the bishop.*

The bishop should set aside time to interview all new members on a regular basis. Not only should he interview them after baptism and for new callings, but he should interview them every few months to gauge their progress, foresee any problems, and make assignments to other leaders in the ward to help them through the first few difficult years as members.

# Becoming a Great Missionary

# Thirteen
# Dealing With Other Churches

One of the most important things a missionary must do while on his mission is deal with other churches. Not just the members of other churches, but their leaders, i.e., ministers, pastors, priests, rabbis, etc. How you communicate and work with these people will have a profound effect on the success of your mission. Most of the people with whom you talk on your mission will already be members of another church. If you are not tolerant of other people and their beliefs, or if you tend to judge them because they believe differently than you, you will fail. However, if you learn to see that *all* churches teach some truth, and then build upon that truth instead of tearing it down, you will have great success.

> The great religious leaders of the world such as Mohammed, Confucius, and the Reformers, as well as philosophers including Socrates, Plato, and others, received a portion of God's light. Moral truths were given to them by God to enlighten whole nations and to bring a high level of understanding to individuals . . . We believe that God has given and will give to all peoples sufficient knowledge to help them on their way to eternal salvation. (Statement of the First Presidency regarding God's Love for All Mankind, 1978)

## Becoming a Great Missionary

### Bible Bashing

Something that happens to every missionary is having a negative confrontation with someone of another church. To put it bluntly, confrontations are unwise. They solve nothing, do nothing positive, and usually end up causing so many bad feelings on both sides that the repercussions can last a long time. As a new missionary, I was naïve enough to be dared into Bible bashing with the minister of a small church near where we lived.

I was one of four missionaries who had been out on splits and, being the "green" elder, I was dared to go into this church and Bible bash with the minister. This was on a weekday night, just after their church service had ended. After most of the people left, all four of us entered the church, and I walked up to the minister who was still surrounded by some of his parishioners. I introduced myself and asked to speak with him. I'm sure he knew what was coming, but rather than be embarrassed in front of his members he complied with my request and we moved toward the front of the chapel, sitting on one of the pews. We spent a few minutes talking about different doctrines, and he made it clear he was not happy with what I had done. After it was over, I felt very badly about it. I knew I had accomplished nothing good and had, in fact, caused a great deal of harm. Those members who saw us talking would look badly upon Mormons, and the minister would look badly upon Mormons and might even talk to his congregation about us. Nothing positive, everything negative. Don't do it.

### Learning from the gentiles

Many Mormons have an air of arrogance. Their testimony that

ours is the only true and living Church on the face of the earth (which is true) has made them prideful and judgmental. They begin to believe that *only Mormons* have the truth (which is not true)[1] and that *only Mormons* will go to heaven (which is also not true). This arrogance and pride prevents them from learning great truths from people of other faiths.

> *One of the grand fundamental principles of Mormonism is to receive the truth let it come from where it may. (*Words of Joseph Smith, *p. 229)*

> *It is our duty and calling, as ministers of the same salvation and gospel, to gather every item of truth and reject every error. Whether a truth be found with professed infidels, or with the Universalists, or the Church of Rome, or the Methodists, the Church of England, the Presbyterians, the Baptists, the Quakers, the Shakers, or any other of the various and numerous different sects and parties, all of whom have more or less truth, it is the business of the Elders of this church (Jesus their Elder Brother, being at their head) to gather up all the truths in the world pertaining to life and salvation, to the Gospel we preach, to mechanism of every kind, to the sciences, and to philosophy, wherever it may be found in every nation, kindred, tongue, and people and bring it to Zion. (Brigham Young,* Journal of Discourses, *Vol. 7, p. 283)*

It is our *duty* to learn truth from other faiths! Let me give you two examples of wonderful things I learned from members of other faiths that have continued to touch my life for years.

---

[1] He [Joseph Smith] closed by referring to the Mormon Bible, which he said, contained nothing inconsistent or conflicting with the Christian Bible, and he again repeated that all who would follow the precepts of the Bible, whether Mormon or not, would assuredly be saved." (excerpted from a letter by M. L. Davis, *History of the Church,* Vol. 4, p. 80).

## Becoming a Great Missionary

*1. The ordinance of the washing of feet.*

One day, while knocking on doors, we came across a woman who was "saved by grace." She would not let us into her home but talked for some time standing at the door. I don't remember what was said, or how we got on the subject of the ordinance of washing of feet which was performed by the Savior upon his apostles,[2] but I will always remember the parable she taught us as to what this marvelous ordinance really means.

In Christ's time, when there was a wedding and wedding feast to attend, everyone who was invited would wash, put on his or her best clothes, and then walk to the wedding feast. Since in those days everyone wore sandals, or no shoes at all, by the time they arrived at the groom's home their feet would be dirty. Prior to entering the home, the guests were required to wash their feet, which was usually done by a servant at the door as an act of kindness provided by the groom to his guests. It was not necessary to completely wash again before entering the home, because they had already been washed, anointed, and clothed in proper clothing *prior* to coming to the wedding feast. However, no matter how clean their feet were prior to the journey, and no matter how careful while traveling to the feast, their feet became dirty and had to be cleaned. So when arriving at the feast, the only preparation left prior to entering the home of the groom was to wash their feet.

After pondering this story, I received the insight that this is like our own path into heaven. Even after we have made our temple covenants and put on the temple garments, we are not quite prepared for the Kingdom of God, because no matter how hard we try not one of us is perfect. We all sin, but most sins committed after

---

[2] John 13:3–10.

going through the temple of God should be very minor in nature—
a little dust needing to be washed from our feet by the Savior prior
to entering the Kingdom of God.

No matter how one reads this parable of washing the feet, you
cannot deny the truth of it, the simple power of it, and it came from
a gentile!

*2. The Atonement.*

One day while tracting, we ran into a Baptist minister who had a
lively conversation—you could even call it a debate—with us about
the differences between our faiths with regard to the atonement of
Christ. I would not call it Bible bashing because I was careful to actually *listen* to his side and try to *understand* his point of view. Since I
was actually listening, he taught me a profound lesson about the
Atonement of Jesus Christ which started me on an odyssey lasting
over 10 years—a personal goal to fully understand the atonement of
Christ and how it really works.

As our gospel conversation turned to the doctrine of "saved by
grace" and the atonement, this wonderful minister began to ask me
questions about my own understanding of this doctrine. It was during this questioning that my life was changed.

"Do you believe that Christ atoned for the sins of the world?"

"Of course. Mormons believe in the atonement of Jesus Christ-
that Christ paid for all of our sins!"

"Do you believe that Christ took upon himself your personal
sins? That he bled and died so you could be forgiven of your sins?"

"Of course. Our religion teaches that the atonement of Christ was
necessary for anyone to return to the presence of God."

"We look upon the atonement of Christ like a scale, or balance,
with men's personal sins on one side, and Christ's atonement on the

other side. For every sin that has been or will be committed, Christ in turn suffered for, or atoned for, each and every one of those sins. Every sin for every person who will ever live."

"Yes, we believe Christ paid the price for all sins. That he suffered the punishment for our sins so we would not have to suffer, so we would not go to hell for our sins but be able to go to heaven. However, we believe there are certain conditions a person must fulfill in order to get to heaven. We believe in works as well as faith."

At this point in the conversation, I began to worry. I knew our religion did not believe or teach the doctrine of "saved by grace;" however, so far I was *agreeing* with everything this minister said! I could feel myself being drawn into a trap but had no knowledge of how to get out of it.

"You believe Jesus Christ paid the price for the sins of all mankind. He paid for your personal sins. He was punished for, or suffered the consequences for, our sins. Just like that scale, justice was paid in full by Christ's suffering on the cross?"

"Yes, we believe everything you have said; we are taught that God requires us to do certain things in order to get into the Kingdom of Heaven. For example, baptism." I specifically used this example because he was a Baptist.

"Well, if you agree that Christ paid for your sins, that He has already met all the demands of justice, why are you required to do anything else? If Christ has paid the debt, then the debt is paid and nothing else should be required!"

He closed the trap. He had me. All of my arguments would fail from this point. He knew it and I knew it. How could I believe that Christ paid the price for all sins and at the same time believe we would be required to work out our own salvation? I knew that something was wrong. I knew our Church did not believe or teach the doctrine of "saved by grace," but, as far as I could tell, *I believed it!* Why would I believe false doctrine? I came into the Church as a convert, knowing almost nothing about God. I had to have been *taught* to believe this doctrine. Now I was really confused. Everything I seemed to believe, and most other Mormons seemed to believe, was the same doctrine being taught by the "saved by grace" churches. But it is clear that Mormons also believe in works. We are taught that works are necessary for salvation. *I was taught that works are necessary for salvation.* I had faith that what our Church taught was correct, but the minister had a valid point! If Christ paid for our sins, if Divine Justice had already been paid in full, what need was there for works? Were these arbitrary requirements made by God to provide a reason for the three degrees of glory? My mind raced for days, for weeks, for years trying to find the solution to this question about the atonement. Finally, after many years, I found the solution I had been seeking. Brigham Young taught that the purpose of the atonement was to reverse the effects of *Adam's* original sin and bring to pass the resurrection of the dead.

> *The Gospel that we preach is the power of God unto salvation; and the first principle of that Gospel is, as I have already said, faith in God, and faith in Jesus Christ His Son our Savior. We must believe that he is the character he is represented to be in the Holy Scriptures. Believe that he told the truth when he said to his disciples, "Go ye forth and preach the Gospel to every creature; he that believeth and is baptized shall be saved, but he that believeth not shall be damned." We must believe that this same Jesus was crucified for the sins of the world, that is for the original sin, not the actual individual transgressions of the people; not but that the blood of Christ will cleanse from all sin, all who are disposed to act their part by repentance, and faith in his name. But the original sin was atoned for by the*

**271**

## Becoming a Great Missionary

> death of Christ, although its effects we still see in the diseases,
> tempers and every species of wickedness with which the human
> family is afflicted. Again, if our Gospel be hid, it is hid to them
> that are lost. (Journal of Discourses, Vol. 13, pp.143–144,
> Brigham Young, July 11, 1869)

However, the point of this story is not to discuss the doctrine of
the atonement. It is to show the importance of respecting the beliefs
of others, even if you don't agree with them. *All people have and live by
some truth.* The problem for many is that lies and false doctrine are
mixed in with that truth. Our job as missionaries is not to condemn
the religion of others. How can we make a blanket condemnation of
a religion—any religion—that has *some* truth in it? We must not. We
must accept the truth they do have and build upon it. We should
*never* condemn any religion! We should respect and honor  every religion because of the truth they *do* contain!


## What is the Purpose For Other Churches?

In God's plan, there is a significant purpose for the existence of
other churches. First of all, other churches' doctrines, though mixed
with error, do prepare people to accept the fullness of the gospel
taught by the missionaries. Second, not all people are destined to
inherit the celestial kingdom. Some will *choose* to inherit the terrestrial or telestial kingdoms. Other churches prepare people for these
other kingdoms! The missionaries teach a gospel designed to attract
and prepare those who will inherit the celestial kingdom. Just as
God inspires the missionaries to find and teach those prepared to
obtain the celestial kingdom, God inspires and works with the good
men of other churches to make bad men good and make good men
better. They prepare people to inherit the other kingdoms of God.

# Dealing With Other Churches

> *We do not teach and preach just to bring people into the Church or to increase the membership of the Church. We do not preach and teach to persuade people to live better lives. Ministers and others are involved in the kind of ministry that makes bad men good and good men better, and we honor and appreciate those who do so. (Elder Dallin H. Oaks, Church News)*

It is important to see and understand the good that other religions do for people willing to accept and live the principles they teach. If we simply condemn other churches out of hand, we are being intolerant and evil. Just as God is willing to bless the good and the evil, we, too, must be willing to bless, accept, and help all people, regardless of what they choose to believe. Jesus Christ did not tolerate sin, but He was tolerant of people who, in their weakness, accepted sin as part of their lives.

> *It may have been Christ's reference to deeds done in His name that prompted John to interject a remark at this point: "Master, we saw one casting out devils in thy name, and he followeth not us: and we forbad him, because he followeth not us. But Jesus said, Forbid him not: for there is no man which shall do a miracle in my name, that can lightly speak evil of me. For he that is not against us is on our part." The young apostle had allowed his zeal for the Master's name to lead to intolerance. That the man who had attempted to do good in the name of Jesus was evidently sincere, and that his efforts were acceptable to the Lord we cannot doubt; his act was essentially different from the unrighteous assumptions for which some others were afterward rebuked; he was certainly a believer in Christ, and may have been one of the class from which the Lord was soon to select and commission special ministers and the Seventy. In the state of divided opinion then existing among the people concerning Jesus, it was fair to say that all who were not*

273

*opposed to Him were at least tentatively on His side. On other
occasions He asserted that those who were not with Him were
against him.*

*Even John, traditionally known as the Apostle of Love, was
intolerant and resentful toward those who followed not his
path; and more than once had to be rebuked by his Master. And
again, while traveling with their Lord through Samaria, the
apostles James and John were incensed at the Samaritans' lack
of respect toward the Master, and craved permission to call fire
from heaven to consume the unbelievers; but their revengeful
desire was promptly rebuked by the Lord, who said: "Ye know
not what manner of Spirit ye are of. For the Son of Man is not
come to destroy men's lives, but to save them."*

*Intolerance is Unscriptural—The teachings of our Lord breathe
the Spirit of forbearance and love even to enemies. He tolerated,
though he could not approve, the practises of the heathen in
their idolatry, the Samaritans with their degenerate customs of
worship, the luxury-loving Sadducees, and the law-bound
Pharisees. Hatred was not countenanced even toward foes. His
instructions were: "Love your enemies, bless them that curse you,
do good to them that hate you, and pray for them which
despitefully use you, and persecute you; that ye may be the
children of your father which is in heaven: for he maketh his
sun to rise on the evil and on the good, and sendeth rain on the
just and on the unjust." The Twelve were commanded to salute
with their blessing every house at which they applied for
hospitality. In the Parable of the Tares, Christ taught the same
lesson of forbearance; the hasty servants wanted to pluck out the
weeds straightway, but were forbidden lest they root up the
wheat also, and were assured that a separation would be
effected in the time of harvest.*

*In spite of the prevailing Spirit of toleration and love pervading
the teachings of the Savior and the apostles, attempts have been*

*made to draw from the scriptures justification for intolerance and persecution. Paul leaves us not in doubt as to the character of the Gospel he so forcefully defended, as his later words show: "But I certify you, brethren, that the gospel which was preached of me is not after man. For I neither received it of man, neither was I taught it, but by the revelation of Jesus Christ." Let it be remembered that vengeance and recompense belong to the Lord.* (James E. Talmage, Articles of Faith, *pp. 390–401*)

## Know Your "Enemy"

The leaders of other churches are not our enemy; however, we do struggle with them for the souls of those who attend their church. We battle for the minds, hearts, and souls of people who have been taught to believe differently than we do. We must recognize this is a battle, the same battle begun in the premortal life. Since so much of what we do is to counter the errors and false doctrine of other churches, it simply makes sense to get to know what other churches believe, what they teach, and how they live. We turn again to Brigham Young:

> *I always feel to urge our youth to attend meetings when strangers preach, that they may be able to understand that which is not of God, and learn the differences between the doctrine taught by us and others.* (Journal of Discourses, *Vol. 13, p. 323*)

Sun Su, in the *Art of War*, taught that we should never go into battle unless we know ahead of time what our opponent is like. If we go to war blindly, we are sure to lose. However, if we get to know our enemy ahead of time, we can properly prepare to defeat him. For this reason, it is incumbent upon us to attend the services of other churches, read their literature, and talk to their ministers and teachers in an effort to prepare ourselves to answer the questions posed to us by members of various churches. We *know* we have the truth but it is sometimes not enough to know the truth—we must understand the lie the truth defeats.

Some of your most memorable experiences while on your mission will be discovering what other people believe. Sometimes it is comforting to know that so much of what we believe is the same. Just because we believe differently does not mean people who follow other religions are evil. There are many, many wonderful people in this world who *choose* to believe and live differently than we do. Sometimes what we learn about others is simply unbelievable (such as religions that believe we can die and come back as an animal). Sometimes what we learn makes us laugh, or cry, or sorrow for those we meet. But they are all our brothers and sisters, and it is because of our eternal relationship with them that we take the time to share the gospel with them. It is also why, when they choose *not* to accept what we teach, we must understand the BIG PICTURE: God has a plan for *all* his children. Though they may not accept and live up to a celestial law, we may encourage them to live a terrestrial or telestial law—either one of which will bring them into the Kingdom of Heaven where they will find great joy and blessings.

So often we forget that God has blessings that extend to every one of His children, and, while they may not earn the highest reward, they still will earn some reward and place in His Kingdom. That is why, as missionaries, we cannot judge those we seek to teach. Only God knows the hearts and minds of His children. We do not know, nor can we tell, what God has planned for others. We can only do our best to bless *all* we meet and teach as many as are willing to listen. Those who choose to reject our message of hope and gladness we send on their way with a blessing on their heads, and a hope that some day their heart will soften and some other member or missionary will be able to reach them. The most important thing to remember is that no matter what happens, whether they choose to listen to the discussions or not, whether they choose to be baptized or not, we must leave them better off than we found them. We must leave them with a positive feeling of love, so they know the door is always open if they change their mind.

I had many wonderful experiences with people of other churches while doing missionary work. Here are just a few:

When I was serving in Altoona, we were invited by one of our investigators to the ordination ceremony of a group of new priests in the Catholic church. This was quite an honor, and, if for no other reason than curiosity, we jumped at the chance. Altoona had a beautiful domed cathedral in the city where a cardinal was coming to oversee this ordination. As with most Catholic churches, this one was very tall and long, the building shaped like a cross, with the altar and large dome right in the center of the "cross." We sat about halfway back. Behind us was a loft that held the choir, an organ, and, on this occasion, several people with brass horns. As the new priests walked into the cathedral from behind us and worked their way down the aisle to the altar, the organ was playing and the choir singing. It was beautiful. As the priests got to the altar under the dome, they prostrated themselves in front of the altar, lying flat on their faces with their arms stretched out from their bodies on either side so their hands nearly touched. The cardinal, with his flowing robes, large hat, and golden miter, began to speak in Latin with lots of pomp and circumstance, walking back and forth, making gestures with his arms (of course we couldn't catch very much of what he said, except that we heard the word Melchizedek several times). As the cardinal was finished, he nodded to the choir loft and suddenly the horns began to play. It was thrilling! The horns that will blow at Christ's coming can't sound much more beautiful than this music! The sound flowed out of the ceiling and moved through the building with great flourishes. As the horns ended, and with the sound still reverberating through the cathedral, the priests rose and their priesthood robes and vestments were placed upon them. Once they were properly clothed, they were introduced to the congregation and, to thunderous applause, they walked down the long aisle and went outside the building. The service was over.

One of the most amusing churches we ever visited was in Philadelphia. It was a Catholic church that, unlike most Catholic churches, was built like a big gymnasium. The building was split in half by a large room divider that could be opened and closed (like we have between the chapel and cultural hall in many of our churches). This unusual set-up was because the church obtained most of its donations from bingo games it ran during the week. On Sunday the whole building was used, but during the week, the divider was shut to make the back half of the church into a bingo parlor. We were invited by one of our investigators to go with them. It was just unbelievable! In this smoke-filled room were hundreds of people (mostly women) totally focused on bingo cards. Most had three or four cards going at one time. Each card cost one dollar and, if they won, they paid various amounts from $5 to $150 or so. The church took the bingo profits to operate the church. I must say, it was different from our tithing! The highlight of the evening, and the last play of the day, was a basket full of liquor! I am not kidding!

The final prize was a large basket full of wine, bourbon, beer, and whiskey and everyone was excited and cheering over this tremendous prize! What a sight to see. The woman who finally won the prize was at least 80 years old and so small she could not carry the prize to her car, so two men helped her load the liquor in her trunk.

Another interesting experience came one Christmas while I was in Pittsburgh. One of the sets of elders in my district was teaching a wonderful family in which the father was the organist at the local Protestant church. I had met this family several times while splitting with these missionaries and had interviewed them as they prepared for baptism, but things were a bit complicated. They had committed to be baptized, but hadn't yet told their minister. For most people this may not have been a big deal, but it was for this family. Almost all positions and callings in other churches are *paid professions*. The minister is paid, the choir members are paid, and the organist is paid. This brother was well paid because it was a large church in a wealthy area, and he was a very good organist. Not only did he have to leave his church, but he had to leave his job in order to convert to our church (this was his second job, done only on Sunday). He had one more concert before he could leave—the Christmas concert. He was going to tell the minister that night, and he invited us to come hear him play his last concert. We went and were introduced to the minister as the missionaries that converted him to his new church (which did not go over very well), and we sat down with the other members of the congregation. They all sang hymns, prayed, and lit candles—all of which we participated in and it was very nice. Our new convert played wonderfully. It was a unique experience.

## Becoming a Great Missionary

We visited all kinds of churches while on my mission, almost always with an investigator we were teaching at the time. In every case, it was worth the experience. It opened my eyes to the kind of religion most other people have—one based upon the principles of men instead of God, or at least so mixed together they cannot tell one from the other. I learned how confused, and confusing, most other religions are and how much they need what we can give them. Every visit to another church increased my faith in the truths that our Church teaches. Brigham Young was right! How can we know how precious our religion is if we haven't seen for ourselves what other people have? What possible harm can come from visiting and learning about other faiths? I turn again to Brigham Young:

> *Now, then, if our brethren of the Presbyterians, Methodists or any others visit here and want to preach to you, certainly let them preach, and have your children hear them . . . Parents, do not be afraid of having your children learn everything that is worth learning. And if any of our Christian brethren want to go into our Sabbath schools to teach our children, let them do so. They will not teach them anything immoral in the presence of those who are in charge of the schools.* (Journal of Discourses, *Vol. 14 p. 196*)

Why would Brigham Young be willing to let ministers of other faiths preach to his own people? Because he knew that the Church of Jesus Christ of Latter-day Saints and the principles it teaches are true. And because they are true, they will withstand *any* challenge. He realized that when his own people saw for themselves what others had, their faith would not be hurt but would, in fact, increase! They would realize for themselves how precious a thing they had and not rely only on the testimonies of others. The same is true for missionaries. As they go into the world and experience other cultures, learn about other religions, and see how other people live their lives, their faith and confidence in their own beliefs and way of life will only grow stronger.

It reminds me of an experience that happened to my family after a move. Our family has always loved to swim, so almost every place we lived we had a swimming pool; it was no different for this move. One of the first things we did was to build a swimming pool in the back yard. One neighbor went a little crazy with fear. We did not have a fence around the yard yet and would not put one up until after the pool was built (otherwise, how could we build the pool?). But even though we had not yet dug the hole for the pool, as soon as our neighbors heard we were planning to put one in they began to complain. They were absolutely convinced their little children were going to drown! You have to understand this was an above-ground pool that rises four feet above ground level and would take a concerted, if not impossible, effort for a small child to get into. Our neighbors were so filled with fear it made them irrational, which made them unfriendly. Once we started building the pool (by digging a hole, building the frame, lining it, filling it with water, etc.), the police, firemen, city inspector, etc., were called almost every day by our neighbors, complaining about what we were doing. Each day at least one of these officials would come talk to us. We would explain what we were doing, and they would leave, rolling their eyes at having to come out once *again* over some complaint by a neighbor. We finally got the pool built and filled it with water. Then, of course, we built a high fence around the whole area so no one could get in.

The point of the story is to understand the *fear* our neighbors had about the pool and how their fear was handled. The solution to

# Becoming a Great Missionary

the fear was (1) don't build it in the first place, or (2) make sure to build a high fence around the pool so no one can get in. This is typical of how people deal with fear. Our family, on the other hand, had those same fears but dealt with them differently. Of course we were aware of the danger of children drowning in pools! In fact, on two occasions we had children who *should* have drowned in pools but through sheer luck (or help from God) were saved. One son, when he was just two or three, fell into an abandoned pool that still had some water in it. One of his brothers came running in to tell us about it, and we ran out to find him floating in the pool—fortunately face up and breathing fine! Our daughter fell into another pool and was saved by one of her brothers. So what was *our* answer? How did we deal with our very real fears about pools and drowning? We taught all our children to swim beginning at a very young age. The answer seems simple doesn't it? We could not watch our children all the time. We could not guarantee that every pool or lake or river would have a fence around it. Instead of trying to protect our children from water, we taught them how to swim so we no longer had to worry about pools or fences or water of any kind. We had protected our children by teaching them how to take care of themselves.

This same lesson can be applied to dealing with false doctrine and the beliefs of other churches. People have terrible fears about their children learning false doctrine or being led astray by others. In an attempt to protect their children, they try to put fences around them. They refuse to let their children play with nonmembers or members who do not live up to their own high standards. They place high fences around their lives, never permitting their children to experience anything that might endanger their faith. This intolerance of others is unfriendly and unscriptural as well as sinful. Let me share with you an example out of the local newspaper:

> As a non-Mormon born and raised in Utah, I have been the recipient of many acts of prejudice by Latter-day Saints . . . I remember something that happened 35 years ago as if it were yesterday. A group of neighborhood kids were going swimming at someone's backyard pool, and I was invited along. When we arrived at the house, we were greeted by this child's mother, who said she didn't recognize me from the ward. I told her I wasn't LDS and she sent me home, because "only children from the ward are allowed in our home."
>
> A few years ago, my middle-school age son was confronted by missionaries on his way home from school. They would wait for him and block the sidewalk, all the while preaching the virtues of the Mormon faith. This had gone on for days, and did not stop until I threatened to go to their Mission President and complain. When I saw my own children being subjected to the same kinds of discrimination and prejudice I had endured by teachers, neighbors and other children I was, stunned. I realized that many things hadn't changed in the past 20 or 30 years, and how small-minded and intolerant many of the Mormon faith are. As soon as an employment opportunity presented itself, I relocated my family to another state where religion is not the sole topic of conversation, and all faiths are treated with equal acceptance. (Letter to the Editor, *The Salt Lake Tribune* 12/18/01)

This letter gives a dramatic account of what intolerance can do to nonmembers. It is obvious these prejudiced Mormons believed they were protecting their children by preventing them from meeting non-Mormons or experiencing "gentile" things; however, they are doing just the opposite—they are not only sinning themselves by their intolerant actions but are raising their children in sin by their example. As a result, their children are weak and in even greater danger. These protected children will not have faced adversity or had their faith challenged. As soon as they are out in the world alone, they will drown—overwhelmed by false doctrines and new ideas they have not heard before, and an inability to figure out how to handle them; just like my neighbor's children who may have been protected from my pool by a high fence, but what happens when they find a pool or lake or river in their path with no fence around it? They will drown.

## Becoming a Great Missionary

Brigham Young understood this principle. He willingly and openly invited the Saints to compare their religion with others'. He knew that what we have is *true*, and that only ignorance can defeat the truth. He wanted the members of the Church to learn how to swim![3]

Finally, simple logic tells us we need to accept our non-Mormon neighbors. How will we be able to function as member missionaries if we do not associate with, or have any friends among, people who belong to other religions? If the *only* people we deem worthy to associate with are other members, how can we possibly fulfill our responsibility to be missionaries? The answer is—we can't! If we are intolerant of others, we commit sin because we judge them without knowing them, and we prevent them from being able to accept the gospel. Reflect on the letter to the editor above. Do you think there is any way the person who wrote that letter would accept missionaries into his home after what he has experienced? I repeat what has been said many times before in this book. *Do not judge people!* You do not, cannot, know their hearts or the plan that God has for them. You have a choice, either be tolerant and accepting of the beliefs of others (whether they want to listen to the gospel or not) or become intolerant and bigoted by rejecting people because of what they believe or how they might live. The first leads to a path of acceptance, the latter leads to sin and rejection. The choice should be easy for anyone who truly believes in the two great commandments. Love God and love your neighbor as yourself.

---

[3] *"Guides for Child Training*—Now understand it—when parents whip their children for reading novels, and never let them go to the theater, or to any place of recreation and amusement, but bind them to the moral law, until duty becomes loathsome to them; when they are freed by age from the rigorous training of their parents, they are more fit for companions to devils than to be the children of such religious parents." (Brigham Young, *Discourses of Brigham Young,* p. 209).

## Defeat Your Enemy

Occasionally, the battle between truth and error escalates until real battle must be waged against those who spread false doctrine and false accusations against the Church. When that happens, we have no choice but to fight back. We have no choice but to use the Priesthood of God to condemn that person or group.

After I was transferred to Altoona, the Lord began to bless us in a marvelous manner. We were breaking mission records almost weekly, and our names were well known among the clergy of other churches. Almost daily, while out tracting, we would come across people who would say, "Our minister talked about you guys just last Sunday! He said you were working for the devil and that we should not let you into our homes or listen to you." Most of the time, we got in anyway. But we were worried that ministers of other churches were actively speaking against us. One of them actually went on his weekly TV program and talked against us by name! However, we were able to put all of this into proper perspective by realizing that the notoriety was helping more than hurting us. But then things changed. They crossed the line and we had no choice but to act.

Two missionaries were tracting in the area next to ours and happened to knock on the door of the minister who was the head of the ecumenical movement in the city (this is the movement where different churches get together to resolve their differences). Meeting in his home that day were two other clergy (one of whom was the TV evangelist who had spoken against the missionaries). They invited the missionaries in and told them it was quite a coincidence they stopped at the door at this moment, because they were meeting specifically to decide what they could do to stop the Mormon Church from growing in this area! The ministers told these missionaries they were going to do everything they could to stop the work being done in the area and subsequently drive the Church out. This was no longer action taken against the missionaries only (which is just part and parcel of the calling we take upon ourselves—to suffer for the name of Christ). This was action against the *Church* itself, which made it a different matter altogether. These men not only rejected the gospel but fought against God. Because of these actions, a priesthood ordinance was needed to protect the Church against such evil men

> *And whosoever shall not receive you, nor hear your words, when ye depart out of that house or city, shake off the dust of your feet. Verily I say unto you, it shall be more tolerable for the land of Sodom and Gomorrah in the day of judgment, than for that city.* (Matthew 10:14–15)

When the missionaries left these ministers, the Holy Ghost bore witness to them that that's what they should do. They stopped a short way up the road, took off their shoes and socks, and in a small stream, washed the dust off their feet in testimony against these men, with a prayer that God would prevent these ministers from hindering the marvelous work being accomplished in this area. Afterward, we were all a bit worried. Did we do what was right? As usual, we turned to our mentor, President Pinnock, to see what he thought. Would he say we had done the wrong thing? Would he say someone else should have done it, or that we should have checked with him first? He did what he always did. He demonstrated the trust he had in us, uplifted our spirits and confidence, and motivated us to work harder and achieve even greater things. And how did he do this? I told him what had happened, what had been done, and asked him what he thought. He replied, "I just feel sorry for those ministers! They have now reaped the whirlwind by their actions."

He supported what was done in every way, thanked us for our hard work, and promised God would continue to bless us.

## Brother Brown Part III

It is not only those who directly attack the Church that need to be rebuked. Sometimes individuals have to be told their actions will bring condemnation upon themselves and their families. This was the case with Brother Brown.

Brother Brown was the perfect convert; a General-Authority-in-waiting. He had taken time to learn every doctrine. He had followed the direction of the Lord and prayed with all his heart to know the truth. As a result, he had been blessed with a great vision. Afterward, and for the first time, he and his family started attending Church in preparation for baptism. We went to our regular Thursday meeting with them and were shocked to hear they were getting cold feet. They told us they would take the next week to decide whether or not to join the Church and would let us know the following week. Of course we prayed and fasted and sweated the entire week. The next Thursday, we again met with Brother Brown and his family to hear their decision. We had a bad feeling all that week, and our feelings were correct. They told us that they had decided to go back to their old church, the Church of England, and that this was their final decision.

It was only then that the Spirit fell upon me and told me what to say. I told him clearly the consequences of this decision for him and his family. I looked Brother Brown in the eyes and told him that if he rejected the light and knowledge he had received, he would be condemned by God both in this life and the next. I testified he and his family would never again be the same; he would continue to seek the truth and never again be able to find it. I flatly testified to him that by rejecting the truth he had received, he and his would surely face destruction! He did not get angry at my words, nor object to them or deny the truth of them. He simply resigned himself and his family to their fate, thanked us for all we had done, and said good-bye.

What a lesson for all of us. We go on our missions fully believing that once people hear and accept the truth, they will automatically choose to live it. But this is just not true. From the War in Heaven through this life and into the next, people will have every opportunity to *know* the truth and yet many will choose to reject it. Remember, *everyone* will be given the opportunity to hear and then accept or reject the gospel. For reasons I have never understood, some will *choose* to reject what they know to be true. Christ taught this truth from the very beginning. The parable of the sower is nothing more or less than recognizing that some people who hear the gospel will find any number of reasons to reject the truth.

# *Fourteen*
## *Becoming a Leader*

A t some time, almost every missionary will be called to a leadership position. This is a great honor and comes with great responsibility. As a regular missionary, your example and actions influenced the many people with whom you came into contact. As a leader, you will influence many times more people. Every missionary you affect for good or ill will, in turn, affect everyone they meet. This means you must be more diligent about living the mission rules and being a good example, as you have the opportunity to inspire or corrupt those who serve under you.

## Bad Leaders

Bad leaders provide excuses for those who break mission rules. They may even abet them in their efforts. I have seen leaders who arranged district and zone meetings where all who were in attendance broke mission rules. This not only promoted disobedience and dishonesty but completely sabotaged the mission president's ability to manage the missionaries and the mission. Bad leaders are just bad missionaries magnified.

# Becoming a Great Missionary

## Good Leaders

Good leaders take their responsibility seriously. They know they are examples and take extra care to obey the mission rules. They are always on time, always prepared, and always positive with their thoughts or criticisms. They always leave a missionary better than they found him.

*1.  The key to motivation is splits.*

You can only motivate other missionaries when you are with them, by going on splits. Every missionary loves splits. Splits take them away from mundane routine and energizes them with something different, even if only for a few hours. The more often you split with those serving under you, the more influence you have. The more often you split, the easier it is to pick up problems and help resolve them; the better you will be able to see their strengths and bolster them; the more you will see their weaknesses and help overcome them.

*2.  Always be positive.*

The way to any missionary's heart is through positive reinforcement. Instead of trying to find things they are doing wrong and correcting them (any *gentile* can do that), spend your time looking for the good things they do and praising them. The praise will reinforce the good things being done and motivate them to do more. Tell them stories of other missionaries who have found success and help them see how they can have the same success in their area. Help them become better than they are.

*3.  Ask lots of questions.*

The only way to help other missionaries with their problems is to understand them, and the only way to understand them is to ask questions. It is the story of the well again. The more you find out about them, the more information the Lord will have to draw upon to inspire you as to what to say and do while you are with them. Sometimes you will acquire information that will need to be passed on to the mission president. Do not hesitate to do this! A mission president lives and dies by the information he receives from his missionaries. If his information is limited, or if he is lied to, it can disrupt the spiritual flow of the entire mission. A good leader knows when he can directly help those under him and when he must seek the help of the leaders above him.

### 4. *Give spiritual talks.*

One of the characteristics of a good leader is the ability to communicate to large groups of people through talks. There is almost nothing more motivating than a powerful spiritual talk. It can bring clarity to confusing doctrine, it can help people see new ways to solve their personal problems, and it can help them *feel* the Spirit of God. I have already mentioned one example of how powerful this tool can be—the Regional Representative's talk about the power of prayer. That one talk changed my life forever. It motivated me to develop my relationship with my Savior and to bring that relationship to a higher level. It helped me become a more effective servant of God. One talk. You should try to do the same.

### 5. *Always be up front and honest.*

Even though it is absolutely essential to create positive experiences with those you serve, do not exaggerate or mislead missionaries about who they are and what their problems are. Exaggeration and sophistry are simply lies and deception. This *never* helps; it only creates the illusion of helping. If you are asked your opinion, give it to them honestly and to the point—always remembering that you are there to help. If you offer honest criticism, you must also be prepared to offer honest *solutions*. There is nothing more debasing and frustrating than having a problem brought into the open only to have no solution. You are there to help missionaries become better people and more effective servants of God. Make sure your desires and focus are in the right direction.

> *If you are ever called upon to chasten a person, never chasten beyond the balm you have within you to bind up.* (Discourses of Brigham Young, p. 278)

There is a reason the scriptures talk about "reproving betimes with sharpness." Leaders are *supposed* to alter the course and build the character of those they serve. When done with love and the Spirit, there is rarely anything more powerful or influential in a person's life. I cannot count the times I was moved, even required, by the Spirit to talk to people about problems they had and what they had to do to get right with the Lord. I cannot remember a single time it turned out to be a negative experience or had anything but a positive response.

In addition to learning how to do this, you will need to teach others how to confront people and solve their problems.

For example, as a priesthood leader, I used to go on splits with the home teachers in my quorum so I could see how and what they did during their visits. I was surprised at the timidity of home teachers when confronting people about their problems. Even though they were teaching less-active members, no one *asked* them why they left the Church or why they had become less-active, so I showed them how to do it. I went with them and asked the tough questions for them. In almost every case, those being home taught would immediately open up and tell us the hows and whys of their lives. Then, knowing what the *real* problems were, we could begin to help them. The concept is simple, but it does take spiritual courage to confront people about their weaknesses and problems.

I learned this principle on my mission, but it solidified after I got married and was home teaching a less-active older couple in Utah. I had been visiting them for about six months, doing the standard home teaching visit, when one month my youth companion could not go so I went alone. I decided to try what I had learned on my mission. I asked permission to ask them some personal questions. I began asking them the hows and the whys of their less-active status. "Why don't you come to Church anymore?" "Was there something that happened that caused you to lose faith?" At times, the air was filled with tension as my questions brought to the surface uncomfortable feelings and events. But as they were explaining to me their problems, and the reasons for them, it became clear to *everyone* that their reasons were really quite silly. Once they actually voiced their problems, *they* were able to see for themselves how silly they were being. Within two months, they were completely active again and taking the temple preparation class. I have never forgotten that experience and have repeated it many times. It is so simple, but it takes courage! You can do the same thing with the elders you serve and the investigators and members with whom you come in contact. It is a very powerful tool, but, unfortunately, it is a tool very few have the courage to use.

## Help Other Missionaries

Always take time to help other missionaries with problems. Remember, we are God's army, and an army must work together to obtain victory. I can't count the times I had long conversations with missionaries with problems. Most of the time, they just wanted someone upon whom to unburden their souls; sometimes I was able to give counsel I think actually helped.

One missionary, nicknamed "trunky" because he was so anxious to go home, broke down and cried one night as I sat in the car with him. He was just one month away from going home, and he was lamenting all the time he had wasted while serving his mission. He had been so homesick that he spent his time and energy thinking about home and regretting all of the things he was missing while never focusing on why he was on a mission in the first place—to serve the Lord. He knew he had just wasted two years of his life, and, worse, he knew he would regret it the rest of his life. He desperately wanted to be a good missionary; to feel what it is like to have real success—but it was too late and so he cried. I will always be thankful that this elder opened up to me. I did not, could not, help him. But he helped me a great deal. After listening to his story of regret, I swore an oath that I would not waste a moment of time while on my mission. I never wanted to feel as I knew he felt. I never wanted to regret serving the Lord.

I believe I was able, in turn, to help a few missionaries in a positive way by helping them to overcome weaknesses, to work harder, and to find success in a very difficult assignment. It is not just leaders who are supposed to lift and motivate those around them— every missionary should look for opportunities to help and motivate those with whom they serve. It is not only our opportunity; it is our duty.

## What to do with False Doctrine

As a leader in the district, zone, or mission, it will be your responsibility to look for, and combat, false doctrine being taught by missionaries. Sometimes it is very subtle. If in doubt, ask your mission president. While serving as a missionary for over 15 years, I have heard my share of false doctrine. The great majority is harmless and should be ignored. However, some can destroy testimonies and lives and therefore must be combated.

1.   *False doctrine by new members.*

The most commonly heard false doctrine is brought into the Church by new members. This is also the kind of false doctrine you do not have to worry about—it is harmless! There is not a single new member in the Church who knows *everything.* Therefore, what they have not yet learned is filled in by their previous belief system, which is usually distorted and filled with doctrinal errors. This is normal. New members must be given time to progress and learn at their own rate. They were baptized into the Church knowing a few basic truths, such as the truth of the Book of Mormon, Jesus Christ is the Savior, and the restoration of the gospel. Their small testimonies of these new doctrines are primarily based upon the spiritual experience they have had with the missionaries. After they are baptized and receive the Holy Ghost, and as they grow in their understanding of how the Church works, they will begin to gain a more powerful witness of the truth. The Holy Ghost will help them discern between truth and error, and the false doctrines they still believe will slowly vanish over time. Meanwhile, when asked a question about doctrine, they will have no choice but to rely on what they believed *before* they joined the Church.

# Becoming a Great Missionary

*Heresies abound in the sectarian world. But what of the true Church? Are there heresies within even that divine institution? Paul says such was the case among the Corinthians, and it is apparent that the same thing prevails in the modern kingdom of God on earth.*

*Speaking of our day, Nephi said that "because of pride, and wickedness, and abominations, and whoredoms," all men have "gone astray save it be a few, who are the humble followers of Christ." Then pointing to these true saints, he added: "Nevertheless, they are led, that in many instances they do err because they are taught by the precepts of men." (2 Nephi 28:14.) That is, heresies are found in the Church today, even as in the meridian of time. For instance, what of the views of some on revelation, on the age of the earth, on the theories of organic evolution, on the resurrection of the sons of perdition, on a second chance for salvation, on whether God is progressing in truth and knowledge, and so forth?*

*The fact is that a major part of the testing process of mortality is to determine how much of the truth the saints will believe while they are walking by faith rather than by sight. And the more truths they accept, the clearer will be their views on Spiritual matters, and the more incentive and determination they will have to work out their salvation and gain eternal glory hereafter. Heresies and false teachings are thus used in the testing processes of this mortal probation. (Bruce R. McConkie,* Doctrinal New Testament Commentary, *Vol. 2, pp. 362–3)*

Let me give you a personal example. For months after I was converted to the Church, I continued to believe in the false doctrine of reincarnation! Nothing I had been taught or heard had told me it was wrong, so I had no reason to discard a belief I already held to be true. However, as time went on and I came to understand more fully what the resurrection of the dead meant, I came to understand that reincarnation was a false doctrine, and I changed my belief system. For months after coming back into the Church, I went through major doctrinal changes as I learned the truth and discarded my false beliefs. The fact is that this process has never ended! I am still learning new things, and modifying what I know and how I apply what I know, as the truth is revealed to me through the teachings of the prophets or through personal revelation. When you think about it this way, *all* members of the Church believe in and teach false doctrine to some degree or another, because none of us knows all things, and all of us are still learning. The key is to remain humble enough to continue to learn new things about the Kingdom of God every day!

> *I never thought it was right to call up a man and try him because he erred in doctrine, it looks too much like Methodism and not like Latter-day Saintism. Methodists have creeds which a man must believe or be kicked out of their church. I want the liberty of believing as I please, it feels so good not to be trammeled. It doesn't prove that a man is not a good man, because he errs in doctrine. (*Words of Joseph Smith, p. 183)

2. *False doctrine by nonmembers.*

False doctrine distributed by other churches and anti-Mormon groups can be devastating to investigators, new members, and occasionally even naïve missionaries. There is only one way to combat this type of false doctrine—with the truth! Most of the pamphlets, books, and movies that are created by anti-Mormon groups are full of false statements, quotes taken out of context, and exaggerations. In almost every case, if you can persuade those having trouble with these to talk to you, you will be able to overcome it. Without exception, I lost an investigator or new member to false doctrine only when they refused to talk to me about it. If they read it, make their

# Becoming a Great Missionary

mind up about it, and then refuse to talk to you about what they have read, there is not much you can do. They have been deceived and will suffer the consequences. However, if you can get them to sit down and listen, you should be able to take them through the doctrine step by step and alleviate their concerns and fears. Remember, *we have the truth!* There is no reason to worry about discussing with people what they have read or heard; the truth will always win in the end.

I had an experience confronting false doctrine while serving as ward mission leader. A missionary who had been out for about a year was teaching a family that had been given anti-Mormon literature by their minister. This family, in turn, gave the literature to the missionary and wanted him to explain it. After the missionary read what he had been given, he, too, was ready to leave the Church! He finally came and asked if I could help him through this trial of his faith. No sweat. We talked for about two hours, and I took him, point by point, through the information he had been given. At the end of the evening, he was converted again and ready to combat this false doctrine on his own. How did I do it? By knowing the truth *and where to find it.* I was well read and knew where the quotes had been taken out of context. When I was able to show him the full context of what was said, the whole meaning changed!

I also was able to help because I knew the anti-Mormon literature of the time. Since I knew the Church and its doctrine are true, I had no fear of reading any and all anti-Mormon literature that I could lay my hands on.[1] If I found *anything* I did not understand or

---

[1] "Shall I sit down and read the Bible, the Book of Mormon, and the Book of Covenants all the time?' says one. Yes, if you please and when you are done, you may be nothing but a sectarian after all. It is your duty to study to know everything upon the face of the earth in addition to reading those books. We should not only study good, and its effects upon our race, but also evil, and its consequences." (Brigham Young, *Discourses of Brigham Young*, pp. 256–257).

could not easily combat, I took the time to look it up. It did not take long to discover how deceitful this literature was and how easily it could be refuted, given the right information. I remember going to the Hill Cumorah pageant with some very new members we had helped bring into the Church. There were many anti-Mormon pamphlets being handed out by other churches. Most people tried to avoid them. Not me! I walked right up to each one and took as many as I could get my hands on. While we waited for the pageant to begin, I even shared some of the pamphlets with these new members of the Church! We had some good laughs over some of the things they were trying to say about Mormons. I had no fear about doing this because I knew the truth. The new members had no fear because they knew I was confident in my knowledge of the gospel and my ability to combat anything the anti-Mormon groups tried to promote.

Now as a rule, I would recommend trying to keep this type of literature out of the hands of most investigators and new members simply because they are weak in the faith. However, it is not something you have to *fear*, because, once again, *we have the truth!* [2]

### 3.  *True doctrine that is misunderstood.*

The kind of "false doctrine" that is as damaging as that produced by anti-Mormons is true doctrine that is given to those not ready to hear it. This is like giving a slab of red meat to a child not yet weaned from his mother's milk. This is perhaps the most difficult type of "false" doctrine to combat because it is true, and if those who hear it or read it do not accept it, or cannot understand it because they have no foundation to do so, how does one make them "instantly" ready to hear and understand? It is very difficult

---

[2] "No man can disprove a truth." (Brigham Young, *Discourses of Brigham Young*, p. 10).

but can be done if they are willing to be patient and listen to the truth.

One incident I will never forget happened while serving in the Nauvoo Visitors' Center. We spent a lot of time studying while serving there. This was partly because there was a lot of down time we needed to fill and partly because we wanted to be prepared to answer any question asked of us. Since I loved to read and had already read everything they had in their small library, I wrote home and had my family send all 26 volumes of the Journal of Discourses! I was working on volume one (which has many powerful doctrines in it from polygamy to the Adam God theory) when I was called to take a tour. For some reason, I left my book at the front desk at the start of the tour and asked the senior missionary couple to watch it until I got back. They kindly said they would. When I was through with my tour (about 20 minutes), this faithful couple was arguing about some doctrine they had noticed in my book (I always underline important passages), behaving like they were ready to leave the Church over some of the things they had read! I took my book back and never let anyone look at it again.

I was totally astonished that faithful members of the Church could turn away from the Church so quickly simply because they had read something they did not fully understand. The doctrines I had underlined in this book were true. This senior missionary couple, though lifelong members, obviously were not spiritually ready to hear, understand, and accept what they read. This is not uncommon in the Church. Many members struggle to understand some of the deeper doctrines of the Church. How often do you hear a Sunday School discussion about the doctrine of polygamy? Seldom, if ever. Yet this doctrine had a profound effect on both the history of the Church and the people and leadership in it! The "Adam God theory" is a doctrine not one Sunday School teacher in a hundred will touch, yet it is a wonderful doctrine taught by both Joseph Smith and Brigham Young and is, in fact, very easy to understand, if taught *correctly*. That, of course, is the key to all of this. Learning the *truth*. If both members and missionaries will take time to study the scriptures, study the words of the prophets, and gain a spiritual testimony of the doctrines of the Church, nothing will be able to shake their faith. If we come across false doctrine, we need not fear or fall away. We need only to use our faith to have the confidence to know that the Church is *true* and that once we fully understand the *truth*, the false doctrine will vanish and our faith will be enhanced. If done in such a manner, we will always find ourselves on safe ground with our faith firmly established. People have trouble with doctrine only when they jump to conclusions before finding out the whole truth.

4.  *Stand up for what is right.*

When false doctrine is taught in Church (and it happens *all the time*), it is usually appropriate to let it go. Most members will recognize false doctrine when they hear it and will understand the context in which it was taught (usually by an inexperienced member). They can just smile, knowing that, in time, everyone settles into the truth. There is usually no need to make a big deal out of it. Just take the time to take the person aside *privately* to explain that what they said was incorrect, and then lead them to where *they* can look it up and learn it for themselves.

Occasionally though, when the doctrine is taught in such a way, as to truly mislead, or is taught by someone in authority so that it may actually be accepted as truth by the congregation, members or priesthood leaders should step in and publicly correct the doctrine so there is no question as to what the Church teaches on the subject. I have seen this done several times by bishops who felt it necessary to step up to the podium to correct false doctrine that had been expressed in a talk. This can happen often in wards *full* of new members who tend to take anything said over the pulpit as truth. In these cases, the bishop has a responsibility to correct any false doctrine being taught to the congregation.

On one occasion, my wife had to step forward in Relief Society to counter some false doctrine being taught. The lesson was on the priesthood and its value to women. In the course of the lesson, one of the long-time members of the Church felt it necessary to quip, "The only reason the brethren have the priesthood is because women are co-creators with God in bearing children. Men had to have *something* to do!" There were *many* new members and investigators there, all taking what was said as the position and doctrine of the Church. No one was objecting or saying anything that would lead these women to think otherwise. In tears that such a sacred power would be so haphazardly tossed about, my wife rose and corrected the false teaching and replaced it with the truth. It was a lesson no one will forget, and no one in that room will ever again confuse the doctrine being taught that day.

Embarrassing someone in public is the last thing we want to do. Under normal circumstances, it is appropriate to take the person aside in *private* to let them know of their error. However, occasionally, when the group is accepting the false doctrine being taught, we have no choice but to publicly correct the doctrine being taught so no one will be led astray or deceived.


## Always Choose People Over Meetings

True success as a leader comes from working with people, not in holding endless meetings, filling out forms, or measuring statistics. I cannot tell you how frustrating it is to waste time sitting in an *unproductive* meeting, knowing you could be spending your time much more effectively talking with, and working directly with, those you are serving. Leaders who think they are being productive by creating work for those under them are unwise stewards. Their actions are doing just the opposite of what they hope. Instead of inspiring those who are working in the trenches with statistics of how well they are doing, or being able to tell them *precisely* where they are failing through all the paperwork they require of those below them, these leaders hinder the work of the Lord. Instead of spending *productive* time meeting with, and serving, those for whom they are responsible, they end up spending too much time in meetings, doing paperwork, and being a "clerk" instead of a leader.

We all understand there is a need for paperwork, and I know full well how important clerks and secretaries are. Much of the Church could not function without them. In fact, while serving as the priesthood leader in a very small ward, when given the choice of getting a second counselor or a secretary I took the secretary and made sure he was more competent than even my counselor. Why? Because I recognized how important a secretary was to make *any* organization work correctly! However, there are things *required* to be done in order to make sure the work of the Lord goes forward in an organized and proper manner, and there are things that are nothing more than make-work projects that serve no other purpose than to make some leader feel important, or like they are accomplishing something. A true leader *never* places a greater burden upon the shoulders of those below him than he has to. In fact, a true leader spends much of his time trying to find ways to lighten the load of those who serve under him.

## Becoming a Great Missionary

As a leader, make certain any assignment you give someone has meaning. Make sure you only ask people to do things that actually help the work of the Lord go forward. Make sure you do not burden those who serve below you through unthinking decisions. Make sure you make their lives better, their burdens lighter, and their assignments meaningful to them and to those they will be serving.

# Fifteen
## Putting It All Together

*I* n this chapter, I will review some of the things we have talked about so you will have a step-by-step guide of how to become a great missionary and how to begin a successful missionary program in your area.

### Starting out right

1. Go on your mission for the right reason.
   a. Have a desire to serve God.
   b. Have a desire to do your duty to God and your family.

2. Prepare *before* you leave on your mission.
   a. Be honest in all of your interviews.
   b. Set a few goals to achieve.
   c. Start doing missionary work immediately.

### Become a good companion.

1. Be a good example by keeping all of the mission rules.
2. Work very hard every day.
3. Learn something from *every* companion.
4. Go the extra mile.
5. Learn to enjoy the work.

# Becoming a Great Missionary

*Create a proper environment.*
1.  Find an appropriate place to live.
2.  Keep your apartment clean.
3.  Take full advantage of your preparation day.

*Become men of honor and integrity.*
1.  Be willing to make tough decisions.
2.  Be up front and honest with your priesthood leaders, your mission president, your companions, and your fellow missionaries.
3.  Take responsibility for your actions.
4.  Always be productive.

*Find success while tracting.*
1.  Learn many different door approaches.
2.  Change your door approach often.
3.  Keep your mind active, be willing to experiment.
4.  Map out a plan for yourself and the angels of God to follow.
5.  Stop at *every* door.
6.  Go the extra mile every day.
7.  Learn how to project your spiritual aura.

*Find people to teach.*
1.  Place articles in local newspaper.
2.  Stop at *every* door: schools, churches, businesses, etc.
3.  Seek out the places people gather.
4.  Use some of your time doing service projects.

*Develop a good relationship with the local members.*
1.  Always work through the ward mission leader.
2.  Find ways to ease the burden of the bishop.
3.  Always be a good example, develop the trust of the members.
4.  Ask the members to go on splits.

5.   Ask the members to fellowship your investigators.
6.   Ask the members to develop referrals.
7.   Be on time.
8.   Always keep appointments.

*Learn how to teach with the spirit.*
1.   Create the right atmosphere.
2.   Be bold, upfront, and honest.
3.   Listen to their concerns.
4.   Resolve their problems.
5.   Teach them how to recognize the Spirit.
6.   Follow-up with each investigator several times a week.

*Learn how to pray with power.*
1.   Pray for the Spirit to be with you.
2.   Pray to find people to teach.
3.   Pray for your investigators.
4.   Understand and develop true humility.
5.   Find your personal "stone" for the Lord to touch.
6.   Learn the power of group prayer.

*Learn how to prepare people for baptism.*
1.   Be up front and honest about your intent—to baptize them.
2.   Get the members involved.
3.   Don't be afraid to ask people to be baptized.

*Learn how to deal with other churches.*
1.   Don't "Bible bash" or get into arguments.
2.   Show the proper respect for every religion.
3.   Do not judge people of other faiths or lifestyles.
4.   Have confidence in the truth you carry with you.

## Becoming a Great Missionary

*Learn how to become a righteous leader.*

1. Do not ask anyone to do something you would not do yourself.
2. Go on lots of splits with those for whom you are responsible.
3. Always be positive in the things you say and do.
4. Be up front and honest with those with whom you serve.
5. Always choose people over meetings.

# What To Do After Being Transferred To a New Area

Here is an example of things you can do whenever you are transferred to a new area. It is a formula for missionary work in which I have found great success.

1. Get a map that shows every street in the entire area. Mark each street you complete as you follow the "plan of action" you developed to work your area. This will help you, and the missionaries that follow you, keep track of the work that is being done.

2. Go to the local newspaper with a picture and an article about yourself. Ask them to publish the information as soon as possible. This will get your name and face into the minds of the people you will be teaching (an empty well, remember), which will prepare them to be willing to receive you when you knock on their door.

3. Get to know the immediate neighborhood. Meet all of your neighbors. Meet the local clergy. Your influence within any area will start with where you live and expand from there. Find the public gathering areas and meeting places where you might have an opportunity to teach.

4. After you get to know the area well, begin your prayers to the Lord concerning where to find those who will be receptive to the gospel. Develop your "plan of action" as moved upon by the Holy Ghost. Then follow it! This will let the Lord know where

you will be working and permit the angels time to prepare the way ahead of you.

5.  Once you have created a plan of action, make sure you stop at *every* door, building, church, school, etc. Never assume they will not listen!

6.  When you start to have success, begin working with the local members, getting them to go with you on splits to the investigators you are teaching. As the members become involved in missionary work it will motivate them to also fellowship those families and even start producing referrals to their friends. Working with the members will greatly increase your ability to reach a multitude of people.

7.  As you acquire more people in your teaching pool, you will be able to get more members to help. As more and more members get involved, you will begin to get referrals and leads and find yourself teaching more and more people—creating an ever-expanding circle that will continue to grow as long as you continue to work hard to keep up with it.

    Another way to look at the process is to imagine catching a wave while body surfing. At first you have to swim with all your might just to match the speed of the wave so it will carry you with it. Then, if you have swum hard enough, you will be carried with the wave. Once you are being carried forward on the crest of this wave of excitement and success, it will take minimal effort to keep it going. The hard part always is getting started. Once you catch the wave, it becomes very easy to keep the momentum going—as long as you are diligent and careful.

8.  As your success builds, be sure to keep good records of those you have taught and are teaching so you can follow up properly. As you begin to gain success, you will find you have less and less time available to do the work correctly. Most of your time will

be involved in teaching and preparing your investigators for baptism. But that is the precise time you need to make sure you continue to follow-up on every contact and investigator so no one is forgotten. Learning to become organized and efficient with your time, to insure every aspect of your responsibility as a missionary is fulfilled, is just a part of your calling.

Part of that follow-up is making sure those you baptize are properly assimilated into their new ward by having an interview with the bishop, receiving a calling, receiving home teachers, and receiving the new member discussions. If no one else is following up on this process, it falls to you. You must help the leadership of the ward understand and fulfill their responsibilities to these new members.

9. Before you leave the area, sit down with the companion that is staying and review all of your records to insure they are up to date. Make sure no referral, call-back, or investigator is forgotten or lost during the transfer. This will insure all of your hard work and success will continue after you are gone.

## Sixteen
## The **Power** of Faith

*I*n this chapter, we will look at the power of faith and the miracles that can come to pass as a result. We have talked about faith and how, through the power of our *will* and the strength of our fervent prayers, we can begin to produce the fruits of faith. Let's talk about how faith works and how you can, in fact, produce miraculous results beyond your wildest dreams.

### The Key to Faith

If I were to ask members of the Church what is the real key to faith, there would be many answers: prayer, keeping the commandments, reading the scriptures, etc. All of them, though good attempts, would be wrong. The real key to faith for members of the Church, and especially for missionaries, is *work*. This may sound like a strange response to a serious question, but it's true. Work is the key to performing miracles. Remember what we have learned about faith: Missionaries already *have* faith. They just have to learn how to use it. Rather than spend time increasing your faith, you should spend your time learning how to *use* your faith. The key to learning how to use your faith is to *work* and then to work even harder: to go the extra mile. In fact many times the opportunity to experience great miracles is nothing more than being in the right place at the right time. Let me give you an example:

I was serving as ward priesthood leader (it was a small ward and I served as *both* the high priest group leader and the elders quorum president) and had been given the assignment to choose two brethren to give a blessing to a woman who was in the hospital. What none of us knew at the time was this woman had great faith, and her prayers were going to be answered. God had *already* ordained this woman to be healed. This great miracle was simply waiting for two priesthood holders to give her a blessing. Who would it be? Any two priesthood holders would do. At the end of priesthood meeting, I asked for two brethren to volunteer to go to the hospital to give this woman a blessing. Two men raised their hands. Later that day, they went to the hospital and gave the woman her blessing. The next Sunday, they told us of their experience. The woman had been healed almost immediately. It was a spiritual experience that neither of these men will ever forget, and all they had to do was volunteer!

Life is a lot like this event. There are many marvelous experiences just waiting to be had by simply showing up. By working hard, by always being in the right place at the right time, you will experience many wonderful miracles and spiritual blessings. If you work harder and longer than other missionaries, you *will* experience more miracles than they. The first and most important key to making your faith bear fruit is *work*.

## The Second Key to Faith

The second key to faith is *go the extra mile*. Work even harder; push yourself. In my first area, I desperately wanted to succeed. I wanted to be able to *teach* people the gospel I loved so much, but it came so agonizingly slow! It would have been so easy to give up, to start working a little less each day, sleep in a little longer, come in a little earlier, etc., but I knew better. I had learned that a golden family was waiting at the end of that last street, and I was determined to find them. And though it came slowly, the cycle of success finally began for us. We found families to teach, we persuaded members to go on splits, and our teaching numbers went up, week-by-week, and I could *feel* the faith growing within me. I *knew* that God would reward my hard work and desires. One week it all came together, and we knew we would break the mission record for the number of discussions taught in one week! The mission record was 24 discussions. It was only Wednesday and we already had 15! We also had two splits with members set up for the end of the week. We knew it was inevitable we would break the record. We felt such great joy because we knew we had earned it. We had worked and planned and worked even harder. And now, through the grace of God, we were reaping our reward and it was wonderful. By working even harder, by going the extra mile, you *will* find that golden family at the end of the street! The second key to making your faith work is to *go the extra mile*.

## The Third Key to Faith

The third key to faith is *watch for signs of what God is doing*. Righteous servants of God know that God and His angels will prepare the way for them. Therefore, they *watch* for the hand of God to be shown, so they will be ready to serve God properly and effectually. For example, if you have prayed for God to send someone to teach, would it not be wise to begin to *watch* for that person to come across your path? If you are a businessman in trouble and have prayed to God for help, wouldn't it be common sense to *watch* for new business opportunities? If you are a missionary desperately praying for help in the service of God, how will you know when God is reaching down His mighty hand to give you that help if you do not *watch for signs* that tell you what God is doing?

As we earnestly seek God's help, we must look for the signs God will show us. These signs prove that God is working to help us. They also give us understanding about what God is doing to help us and how He is going to do it. We must *watch* for signs, so that when they happen we can use them for our righteous purposes. By actively watching for the signs of God, we prove our faith in God's ability to help us. We activate and energize our faith when we confidently look for the hand of God in our lives and this sacred work to which we have been called.

## Give Blessings

One of the most important duties of missionaries is to give people blessings. *Never* turn down the opportunity to give someone a blessing. You are their link to the eternal God. You may be the first, and sometimes the only opportunity some people have to receive a priesthood blessing. Because of this, you must keep yourself prepared.

Although most missionaries know the mechanics of giving a blessing, they often have no clue as to how to give *powerful* blessings; blessings you know connect our earthly bodies with the powers of heaven; blessings that *always* work. Yes, it is possible to give blessings that *always* work, just as some people can always have their prayers answered. All it takes is a combination of *faith* and *mental effort.*

Most missionaries already have enough faith to produce great miracles; they just don't know it. Many misunderstand how easy it is to acquire and use faith. This is partly because they do not understand the true meaning of scriptures.

There is a misunderstanding concerning the power of faith. Christ said that if people had faith as small as a grain of mustard seed, a person would be able to move mountains.[1] After reading this, most people feel that Christ is criticizing the people for their lack of faith. After all, they have never moved mountains or experienced great miracles! But Christ meant something else entirely. Christ was giving people a glimpse of what is possible with the faith they already have inside of them.

*All* missionaries already have faith. They have *proven* their faith by their works—attending Church, being baptized, going to the temple, accepting Jesus as their Savior and Messiah, and, greatest of all, being willing to go on a full-time mission. These actions have *already* produced enough faith within you to produce great miracles!

If missionaries have problems producing results, the problem does not lie in a lack of faith, but in their inability to use their faith properly. Christ's admonition is this: If a person can move mountains with faith as small as a mustard seed, just think of what he can do with the large amount of faith he already has! Many more people have faith than use faith. The only thing these missionaries really

---

[1] Matthew 17:19–20

need to understand is how to use the faith they already have. Joseph Smith taught us how this works.

> *"We ask, then, what are we to understand by a man's working by faith? We answer—we understand that when a man works by faith he works by mental exertion instead of physical force. It is by words, instead of exerting his physical powers, with which every being works when he works by faith. God said, "Let there be light, and there was light." Faith, then, works by words; and with these its mightiest works have been, and will be, performed. (*Lectures on Faith, p. 59)

As mentioned in the section on prayer, we must use our mental powers to pray with *intensity* and *power*. The same is true for giving blessings. It is not enough to focus on saying the right words (this is important but should not be your focus); you should concentrate on connecting with God and on intensifying your desire to bless this person. In the quiet solitude of your relationship with God, the Spirit of the Lord will act as a conduit as the powers of heaven flow through you to others. Concentration, focus, mental effort, and intensity. Put these things in your blessings and prayers and you will get results.

Keep in mind that this power of faith can be developed and used by *anyone* at any time. Faith is an eternal law, available to all God's children, whether members of the Church or not. This is why members of other churches can, and do, experience the fruits of faith: miracles and answers to prayer. The spiritual gifts and blessings experienced by people of other faiths are not a result of the power of Satan (as some may believe in an attempt to bolster their own belief system). They are the direct result of eternal laws that apply to *everyone*, not just the limited number of people who claim membership in Christ's true church.

> Faith is an eternal principle, an eternal law; it is built into the
> universe itself as a governing, controlling force; it is ordained of
> God and shall endure forever. It takes no special divine decree
> to cause the effects of the law of gravity to be manifest
> everywhere on earth at all times. The law has been established
> and the effects that flow from it are everlastingly the same. So
> it is with faith. He who has given a law unto all things has
> established faith as the power and force by which he and his
> shall operate in righteousness forever. No special divine decree
> is needed to utilize the power of faith; it is like gravity:
> anytime any person in any age conforms to the law involved,
> the ordained results will attend. (Bruce R. McConkie, The
> Mortal Messiah, *Vol. 2, p. 287*)

Because the power of faith can be used by anyone, the blessings
of the priesthood can be used to bless anyone, even nonmembers of
the Church. All that is required is a desire to receive a blessing at
your hands and a belief in Jesus Christ.

> How do men exercise faith? What are we to understand by a
> man's working by faith?
>
> Those who work by faith must first have faith; no one can use a
> power that he does not possess, and the faith or power must be
> gained by obedience to those laws upon which its receipt is
> predicated. Those who work by faith must believe in the Lord
> Jesus Christ and in his Father. They must accept at face value
> what the revealed word teaches as to the character, attributes,
> and perfections of the Father and the Son. They must then work
> the works of righteousness until they know within themselves
> that their way of life conforms to the divine will, and they must
> be willing to lay their all on the altar of the Almighty.
>
> And then—when the day is at hand and the hour has arrived
> for the miracle to be wrought—then they must be in tune with

## Becoming a Great Missionary

> *the Holy Spirit of God. He who is the Author of faith, he whose power faith is, he whose works are the embodiment of justice and judgment and wisdom and all good things, even he must approve the use of his power in the case at hand. Faith cannot be exercised contrary to the order of heaven or contrary to the will and purposes of him whose power it is. Men work by faith when they are in tune with the Spirit and when what they seek to do by mental exertion and by the spoken word is the mind and will of the Lord. (Bruce R. McConkie,* A New Witness for the Articles of Faith, *pp. 169–210)*

You are men of faith, servants of the Most High God. You have been given the authority to use the powers of heaven itself to bless the earth and save the children of God. You *have* the power! Now all you have to do is learn how to use it.

## Destroying the Olive Tree

One of the powers we have been given is the power to destroy. It is not a power used frequently, but one of which you should be aware. The Savior's use of this great power is recorded only once, against a small olive tree.[2] Joseph Smith talked about this power but in another way. He learned that if God determines a person should die, we should not fight against his will.

> *June 24—This night the cholera burst forth among us, and about midnight it was manifested in its most virulent form. Our ears were saluted with cries and moanings and lamentations on every hand; even those on guard fell to the earth with their guns in their hands, so sudden and powerful was the attack of this terrible disease. At the commencement, I attempted to lay on hands for their recovery, but I quickly learned by painful*

---

[2] Matthew 21:18–22

*experience, that when the great Jehovah decrees destruction
upon any people, and makes known His determination, man
must not attempt to stay His hand. The moment I attempted to
rebuke the disease I was attacked, and had I not desisted in my
attempt to save the life of a brother, I would have sacrificed my
own."* (History of the Church, *Vol. 2, p. 114*)

On another occasion, Joseph talked about how our prayers may
hold those back from dying who should be released. He taught that
it is appropriate to let them go if they are called home. Let me share
with you a couple of stories.

A wonderful woman in Connecticut was living a very painful
life. She was *very* old and had cancer. The pain with which she lived
every day was almost unbearable, but she did bear it, and she continued in her faithfulness as an example to her family. You see, her
family did not want to let her go. They prayed to the Lord every day
to keep her alive—for them. One day an elder was called upon to
give her a blessing. Everyone expected the usual. He would raise his
voice to God in prayer on her behalf that she might be healed and
made well. But as he prepared himself to give that blessing and
sought out the quiet place in his mind where he communicates with
God, he was told something entirely different! He was told to let her
go. In essence, he was told to use his priesthood powers to help her
*die!* At first it seemed to go against everything that he was taught as a
priesthood holder. He was not sent forth to destroy but to heal and
send blessings, but he could not deny the message God was telling
him to send. With great trepidation in his heart, he started the blessing. He told this good woman how much God loved her and what a
great example she had been for her family but now God was calling
her home. He told her to prepare herself to be taken into the bosom

of Abraham, to be taken home to God who gave her life. Her pain would be gone and she would experience a peace and joy unlike any she had ever experienced. She had earned it! She had been faithful and God was going to reward her faithfulness by calling her home.

The scene was rather a strange one. The family was in tears, shaken because their mother and grandmother was to be taken. But in the midst of this sorrow was the woman herself, beaming with joy! This is exactly what she had wanted! This is what she had been praying for, for weeks! She *knew* it was time for her to be taken; she just didn't know how to tell her family or prepare them for her death. Now, in one simple blessing, her prayers had been answered and her problems solved. Now her family could prepare for her death, knowing it was God's will. Now she knew the end was in sight; she would not have to endure this terrible pain much longer. She was filled with joy and thanked this humble priesthood holder for having the courage to listen to the whisperings of the Spirit. Though the family was shocked, they accepted the words of God that had come through the blessing and prepared to let her go. It wasn't as hard as they thought it would be, because they knew she was going to a better place. Three days later, this good woman died in bed, surrounded by family just as she had prayed to God it would happen. God was able to answer her prayers because, in spite of the reservations this elder may have had, he had listened to the Spirit.

A similar event happened to me in Cleveland. A woman's brother, who was not a member of the Church, was ill and in the hospital. I knew the family well because I was her home teacher. She had asked me to come to the hospital to give her brother a blessing and of course I agreed. As I got to the hospital and began to run through my mind what I might say (knowing this man was not a member and I might have to explain a little about the Church and how we give blessings), the Spirit began to tell me I was to release him from this life. No way! Using this mighty power for members of the Church was one thing but to do the same for a nonmember? What would they think? As you might imagine, I was not looking forward to this event. I guess my demeanor showed it because his sister could tell I was upset. When I got to her brother's room, it was filled with family members, none of whom were members of the Church. They were talking excitedly. The doctor had just given them some great news. The operation had been a success and he would soon be going home! There was a minister from another church there, and I discovered this minister had given him a blessing. It immediately became clear that I would not be giving a blessing this day, and I was relieved! After we left the room, this good sister asked me what was wrong. She could tell that I was not my normal, happy self. After some hesitation, I told her that, had I given her brother a blessing, I would have told him to get his affairs in order because God was going to take him home. I also told her I was glad I did not have to give such a blessing, and I was now having second thoughts about whether what I had been feeling was correct. One week later, her brother died suddenly and without any hint of further problems; not even the doctors saw it coming. I was glad I had told this good sister my feelings that day because she remembered what I had told her and it gave her incredible comfort to know it was God who had called her brother home. She knew he was in a better place and trusted God had done what was right.

321

# Becoming a Great Missionary

## God Does Work Miracles

We were within days of breaking the mission record for the number of discussions taught in one week. We even had a baptism scheduled for the next week. Everything was going perfectly then disaster seemed to strike. I was transferred to what was universally acknowledged to be the "pit" of the mission. This was an area with such bad karma every missionary dreaded being sent there. When the zone leaders told me where I was being transferred, they tried to console me by saying it really wasn't as bad as everyone said. What was President Pinnock thinking?! Perhaps I was naïve, or perhaps I was still filled with the spirit of joy that had been upon us that week as we experienced so much success, but I trusted my mission president and felt confident in the Lord's plan for me. In spite of any disappointment I may have felt over being transferred, I knew God had a plan for me. I knew He would somehow make everything work out right.

As I was transferred to my new area, I became, for the first time, a senior companion. My companion was a brand new missionary, so I would be training for the first time as well. I remember touring the area for a while and going to see the new chapel that was being built. As we sat in the parking lot looking at the new building, I said a silent prayer. "Please God, let me continue the work I was doing in my last area. Bless me to know that You will be with me here also!" As I prayed, thoughts flooded my mind. This is a brand new church. The people in this area will want to know who will be attending this church! What better place to start than to work in this very area! As we began walking to the first home, once again I had a prayer in my heart. "Show me a sign, Lord! Show me that I am on the right path and that You will continue to bless me!"

God did show me a sign. We got into the very first door and taught a discussion! It was a sign from God, and my faith and energy to do the work of God in this new area skyrocketed! I decided to double my effort and increase my spiritual intensity and energy at every door. The very next week, my new companion and I shattered the mission record for number of discussions taught. From then on, we continued to break the record week after week, as we climbed into the 30s, the 40s, and then the 50s.

Little did I know how profound that sign was to be! It was at this time that God revealed to me a principle that would work for me throughout my mission, although I didn't know why it worked until years later. God inspired me to use a map to lay out a work plan for the entire area. I took a map of the city and mapped out the areas where we would work. As we covered streets, I marked them on the map. Over the summer, we tracted almost the entire city. By laying out the areas we would be working ahead of time, it gave the Lord time to work on the people we would be visiting. It amazed us how the people on the streets we tracted always seemed to be at home and/or ready for us to visit.

Week after week, we expanded our teaching and broke mission records. We began to have frequent visits from our district leader, and then the zone leaders started showing up. Even the assistants started coming on a regular basis. I'm sure it was a combination of checking to see whether we were cheating on our reports and a desire to learn what we were doing differently that made us so successful. We really didn't care. In fact, we really enjoyed being able to work with these great leaders so often! In reality, we were just working hard and letting the Lord do the rest. It was all very exciting.

## Becoming a Great Missionary

We never really knew why we suddenly had so much success. We were simply working hard and praying hard. The only problem that arose during this period of success was that we could not ever get past the first few discussions. We were getting into almost any door at will and trying our best to teach good, quality discussions, but when it came to return visits, they always said no. No one could find an answer. Not even our leaders, who worked with us on a regular basis, could answer this perplexing question: Why did people refuse to listen to more than one or two discussions? It was a mystery.

Our biggest success, besides simply getting into homes, was the distribution of Book of Mormons. At first we simply gave them out, but after a while it was costing us too much money so we started to charge people one dollar. Many paid us extra, so we had money to buy cases of books at a time. I would take a briefcase packed with as many books as I could carry, and would have to return to the apartment several times each day.

We taught thousands of people. We gave out hundreds of copies of the Book of Mormon. But after six months, we had only one baptism. It wasn't until years later, while talking to Elder Pinnock, that he finally explained the difference between "sowers" and "reapers"—that each person has a different talent and my talent was as a sower of spiritual seeds.

As miraculous as all of this sounds, God was just getting started! He had another lesson to teach. He taught me to see as He sees, to catch the *vision* of what is possible when God puts His hand to the work. I had no concept of how far God could go, or would go, in making the work go forward in this area, but I was about to find out.

It happened one Saturday, but it began Friday night. Our week started on Sunday and ended on Saturday, so we had one more day to work. One more day to push ourselves to break the mission record again. We called our district leader and asked permission to leave our apartment early, and work a little late, so we could break the record again. He gave us permission, so we were excited and up late praying and planning where to go the next day. We had our large map on the wall, with each street that we had worked highlighted. You could see large patterns in our work—large sections of the city colored in. We prayed for guidance as to where we should go the next day. We felt strongly we should just keep going where we had been working. God seemed to have prepared people for us to see every single day, so why should we change what we had been doing?

The next day, we got up early and got out on the street. We stood at the head of the street we intended to tract at 8:00 a.m. Saturday morning. It was a beautiful summer day, warm and sunny. The part of town we were tracting was older, but the homes were well kept. Before we started down the street to the first home, we stood together and said a prayer. I prayed that the Lord would open doors for us that day, so we could teach people the gospel we loved. I opened my eyes and took a large breath before beginning that day's work. I looked up at the sky, paused a moment to take it all in, and the Lord opened a wonderful vision before my eyes.

I saw before me a large door and frame that covered the entire street we were about to tract. It was gigantic, maybe 70 feet tall and 30 feet wide (wide enough to block the entire street). As I wondered about the meaning of what I saw, the voice of the Spirit spoke to me and said, "God *will* open doors for you this day!" As I continued to look, I saw this large door begin to open before me until it was fully open and the street was no longer blocked. It was not until later that I fully understood the meaning of this great vision.

As we started knocking at the doors of homes on that the first street, we began to experience success beyond our wildest dreams. We began to get in *every* door. Some people were not at home, or perhaps had not gotten up yet, but *every* door that answered our knock let us in to teach. I wish I had the words to describe it! Door after door, street after street, hour after hour, we knocked on doors and were let in to teach. I quickly came to understand what was happening, so instead of giving a full lesson, we gave a short lesson and set up a return appointment. Door after door, street after street, hour after hour, we tracted and found success at every door. As morning moved to afternoon, we began to physically weaken. After working hard and tracting all summer, we were in good shape, so our weakness was not physical but spiritual. We were spiritually drained from teaching!

The homes in this area were built with large front porches and most had two or three chairs out front. As our strength diminished, we would come to a door, knock, and then sit down to rest while we waited for whoever was at home to come to the door. They would open the door, look at us sitting on their porch and not even ask us who we were. They would just say, "Come in." Finally, late in the afternoon, our strength simply gave out, and we had to rest and get something to eat. We stopped for about 30 minutes to eat and rest and then began to knock on doors again. We found that we had lost the "crest of the wave," and were no longer getting into *every* door but continued to have surprising success. By the end of that day, we had taught almost 30 discussions. At the end of that wonderful week, we had taught over 70 discussions. Almost three times the record we had been trying to break in my last area!

God had shown me how limited my understanding really was. We would have been content, even elated, to teach 20 discussions a week. We thought the world was truly coming to an end when we taught over 40! But who could ever imagine teaching 70 discussions? Who but God! That is the whole point. With the help of God, we really can do anything, achieve any goal, move any mountain, and fulfill any assignment. Now I could, for the first time, grasp the full meaning behind Nephi's statement of faith: "I will go and do the things which the Lord hath commanded, for I know that the Lord giveth no commandments unto the children of men, save he shall prepare a way for them that they may accomplish the thing which he commandeth them." (1 Nephi 3:7) Now I understood that faith was indeed centered in God. We have faith to accomplish great things because we *know* that God has the power to bring *anything* to pass, if He so chooses.

## Faith is Having a Vision of What is Possible

President Pinnock often quoted the proverb "Where there is no vision, the people perish." (Proverbs 29:18). After experiencing that marvelous vision, I had greater understanding of how important it was to have a *vision* of the work we were doing. If we believed that all we could do was 10 discussions, or 10 baptisms, then that was all we would do—and we would be happy to achieve it! But what if that was far less than what God wanted us to do? What if God was ready and willing to extend our abilities far beyond what we could possibly do ourselves? Then the only thing that was limiting us from experiencing that kind of success was our own lack of vision. Fortunately, I learned the lesson well and when I had another opportunity to "go and do the things which the Lord hath commanded," I made sure I did not limit my vision!

### 1. *Preparing for the miracle.*

A short time after moving to Connecticut, the ward we were in split, and I was called to be the Seventies Quorum president (which automatically carried with it the calling of ward mission leader). I had two active members of the quorum and one less-active member, so our numbers were very few, but I was excited because I could begin putting together a missionary program I believed would work.

Shortly after, while driving to an appointment at work, I was thinking of what I should do and how I should proceed with the work of the Lord in this area. Suddenly, the Spirit of the Lord fell upon me. God wanted to help me understand the importance of this calling and that I had been specifically called to this place and time to do a great and special work for the Lord. God wanted me to understand that the events that had taken place prior to our moving to Connecticut were orchestrated simply to get me to this specific place and time. My family and I arrived here because we had been faithfully listening to the Lord and following the *signs* He had given us. Now it was up to me to fulfill the destiny the Lord had prepared for me in this place.

The scripture of Peter came to my mind: When asked what he should do, he was told, "Feed my sheep."[3] The Spirit of the Lord was telling me the same thing. I was to disregard everything else and

---

[3] John 21:15–17.

concentrate on feeding his sheep in order to find and nurture those who were ready to come into the fold. Soon, I was in tears and had to pull to the side of the road. I knew without doubt that God was with me because of the spirit I was feeling. I had the faith and confidence to fulfill this great calling because of the wonderful training I had received from President Pinnock both during and after my full-time mission. And I believed I had the knowledge, ability, and patience to see it through to the end. Now all I had to do was use the *key* to successful missionary service. I had to go to work with all my heart, might, mind, and soul.

In the next few months, I began to feel very strongly that since there were just the three of us, and limited support from the ward, we needed to get back to the basic missionary work of tracting, finding, and teaching. I wanted to place the Seventies on the same level as the full-time missionaries (we had four missionaries working in the ward at that time, two working the inner city and two working the more rural part of the ward). We decided that as members of the Seventies Quorum we would take responsibility for an area of the ward that was not being worked. As Seventies, we would work the area in the same manner as the other missionaries working their areas. We would tract, and take any referrals made in the area. After we made first contact, we would set up a return appointment and split with the full-time missionaries to teach the discussions. In this way, we could increase the number of missionaries working in the ward by one third and thereby increase our success. As I meditated and prayed about this unique direction, I felt *very* strongly this was the way the Lord would have us go. I developed a plan of action, took it to the Lord, and received confirmation that it was acceptable. After the work began to progress, we further developed the missionary program and created a more formal organization.

## Becoming a Great Missionary

From that time forward, my companion and I began to go out
two nights a week: Tuesdays and Thursdays. Each week, we would
work our area those two days and on the other days do home teaching or split with the missionaries, as needed. Sometimes we would
go out four or five times a week! It was difficult, especially with a
young family, but I was determined to do my part in bringing about
God's work.

But it didn't come easily. In fact, there were times I almost gave
up. I had great faith. I knew that God and His angels would come
through . . . but did I have the patience to wait for them? The missionaries and the three of us worked all spring, summer, and fall.
Week after week, month after month, with no success. We taught a
few people here and there, but not one investigator was progressing
toward baptism! I began to hear criticism from members of the
ward. "Why doesn't he do this?" or "Why doesn't he do that?" It
was frustrating and I would often second-guess myself. I was *often*
tempted to change the plan, but whenever I would kneel and pray I
would always get the same answer. Be patient and stay the course.
The angels are working as fast as they can!

You see, I remembered what I had learned on my mission. I
knew that God had sent His angels to prepare the way and that if
we changed course, all their work would be for naught. I also knew
the more faith I had, and the more patience I exhibited, the greater
the reward would be. If I did my part, God would know He had the
*time* to set up a great work without fear the course would be
changed by faithless servants. This is how it is with the prophets of
the Lord as they see visions of the future. God shows them the
works He has planned, knowing these great men will not vary the
course they are on, and, in the end, will reap the rewards God has

prepared. In my case, the angels had to have something big they were working on for it to take so long! Finally, my patience and faith were rewarded.

It was the week after Thanksgiving and my companion and I went out to work, as usual. It was Tuesday, our regular day to work. We had been diligently working every Tuesday and Thursday for an entire year. My companion and I had a referral in the city. It was a part-member family we could possibly teach, if only we could find them. So, we went into the city to look up the referral. Unfortunately, we got the usual result—either a wrong address or the family had moved some time ago. When we knocked on the door, the family that lived there had just moved in. They were from Puerto Rico. Just as he was about to close the door, the Spirit of the Lord fell upon me and I knew I had to get in that door. Without even thinking, I stuck my foot out to stop the door from closing. I told him we were servants of the Lord and had a message to share with his family. To my surprise, he let us in. We taught him part of a discussion and set a time to come back with the full-time missionaries. It was *very* unusual!

As we left the apartment, I began to wonder about the event. I had not felt the Spirit that strongly since my full-time mission, and wondered if it had some special meaning. As we walked along the sidewalk, I stopped to ponder the power of the Spirit and the peculiar event and timing of its coming. As I stood there pondering, a vision suddenly appeared before me. It was the same vision I received when I was on my full-time mission. A large door with frame covered the entire street, only this time the door did not open. The Spirit of God spoke to my mind and said that the door would not open until the members of the ward were fully prepared to receive those who would come through. Then, the door would open and a flood of people would come into the Church. The vision closed and I was left alone in the dark street, wondering what it all meant. One thing was clear. Whatever the Lord and His angels had been preparing was about to burst forth.

The rest of that week, I pondered the vision and what it meant. Somehow the members of the ward had to be prepared. How was *I* going to get the members prepared? I wanted the vision to be fulfilled, and wanted to know how to prepare the members so the door would open. I was reading the Book of Mormon at the time and came across a passage that seemed to speak to me. It seemed to answer every question I had been pondering: Alma 4:19. Alma was trying to re-energize the Church, by having them purge themselves of their sins and change their hearts. Then came the statement that seared my heart. Alma stated there was nothing that moved the people more effectively "save it were in bearing down in pure testimony." That was my answer! I would bear testimony to them and motivate them with the truth. The next Sunday (the first of December) was fast and testimony meeting. What a coincidence . . . .

That fast Sunday, with great fear and trembling, I decided to tell the ward about my vision and try to persuade them to help open the door the Lord had presented. I started my testimony by reviewing the vision and experience I had while on my full-time mission, showing that such things *did* happen and were true. I then told them about my recent vision and testified that if they would help me, if they would begin to support the missionary work in the ward, they would see this spiritual door open. Then hundreds of people ready to listen to the gospel would be drawn into the Church.

The reaction to my testimony was mixed at first. There seemed to be three groups that formed in the ward.

1. Some members were touched by the Spirit, believed what I had testified, and immediately offered their help in the work. Among this group were the missionaries (of course), the small group of blacks in the ward, a few of the white members, and, most importantly, the bishop. It was very important for the bishop to recognize the truth of what I had experienced and back up what I said. He did so with both his words and deeds.

2. There was another group of members who simply did not believe. They held back and waited to see what would happen. However, this group quickly came on board once they saw the success that came to pass. I could completely understand the lack of faith in this group. After all, I had worked all year and had not had a single baptism to show for it. I had no proof, no success behind me, and yet suddenly I was talking about having a flood of people coming into the Church! They doubted. They wanted to wait and see.

3. The last group consisted of those who were offended by my words. They thought my vision was not true, or at least would not happen to someone like me. Perhaps they were jealous because this had never happened to *them*. This group actually seemed to fight against what we were trying to do.

So what happened? How did it all start? Two weeks after my vision, we had our first baptism for the year. The next year would change dramatically.

*2. The miracle begins.*

From the very first day of the next year, everything seemed to change. Family after family began taking the discussions. The members were motivated to go on splits and act as friendshipping families so these investigators would be fellowshipped into the Church.

## Becoming a Great Missionary

The cycle of success had started at last! As the snowball effect grew and grew, no one could imagine how large it would get. It is hard to describe what happened to someone who wasn't there to appreciate it. Perhaps one way to illustrate the dramatic growth is to talk about the gospel essentials class.

As part of my calling and because the ward was still very small, in addition to serving as the Seventies president and ward mission leader I was responsible for the gospel essentials class. The purpose of this class is to teach new members and investigators, and it is always the smallest of the Sunday School classes. After a short time attending this class, the new member would move into the gospel doctrine class, which is always the largest Sunday School class. When I was called to teach this class, we were given the smallest classroom in the ward building, a room large enough for about 10 people. This made perfect sense because we had very few investigators and no new members. However, within a month's time, we had a room full of investigators. Within two months, we had to ask for a regular-sized classroom because we had too many investigators to fit into the small classroom. After another two months, we had to open the room divider so we took up *two* regular classrooms. After another two months, we filled both those rooms and began discussing with the bishop whether or not we could move into the room where the gospel doctrine class usually met. After talking with the gospel doctrine teacher, it was agreed we would use that room for the gospel essentials class.

Within six months, we had so many investigators and new members, we went from being the smallest Sunday School class to the largest Sunday School class in the ward! This was unheard of! But it didn't stop there. After another two months, we had *so* many people coming to Church we could not fit them in the gospel doctrine room! Two choices were left to us. We could move the class into the chapel, or we could open the partitions and take up *all* the classrooms on one side of the building. After a lot of discussion, the bishop decided we should use the classrooms because we needed to use chalkboards as teaching tools. So, we opened the partitions to three classrooms and moved the gospel essentials class there. During that period of time, there were Sundays we had 50 investigators coming to class every week! Add to that the missionaries (we had doubled the number of missionaries, from 4 to 8) and members who attended to support and fellowship our investigators, and you had to see it to believe it!

Another consequence of this growth was that we had to develop a process for the members to learn the new people's names. The bishop issued a directive to everyone in the ward. Whenever a person got up to speak, whether it was in Priesthood, Relief Society, Sunday School class, giving a talk, or during Fast and Testimony meeting, they were first to state their name. Over time, this enabled new members to learn old members' names, and vice versa.

Another way to see and understand the miraculous events that transpired that year is to look at the amount of member/missionary work that occurred. Just a few weeks into the year, it became clear I would have to spend a lot of time setting up splits to cover all the appointments the missionaries were getting. Since we now had four sets of missionaries instead of two, this meant there were many nights I would have to find eight members to go on splits. There were many weeks I had to arrange splits *every night of the week*! There were some weeks I had to make arrangements for over 50 members to meet with the missionaries! Now you can understand why the Lord said the door would not be opened until the members of the ward were ready!

As ward mission leader, I developed a system of dealing with the tremendous growth we experienced. Each Sunday, I would have a 7:00 a.m. coordination meeting with the full-time missionaries. I would get updates on the progress of each investigator and find out the schedule for their discussions that week (i.e., how many splits they would need me to set up). At 7:45, I attended the weekly PEC meeting with the bishop and the other leaders of the ward where I would pass on information about the progress of each investigator and let them know the needs we had. The different quorums would organize the members, assign home teachers (based upon upcoming baptisms), and help to organize the scheduled baptisms (usually every week). About 8:45 a.m., we would end our meeting and prepare for Church at 9:00 a.m. I would then teach the gospel essentials class and run the Seventies Quorum class, handing out additional assignments as needed for the week. Between classes, I would coordinate filling the font for any baptisms, which were usually held just after Church. After Church ended at noon, we would finish preparations for any baptism that week which would start at 12:30 p.m. This would last about an hour (sometimes longer if there was a small reception held afterward). Then I would go home, eat, and begin my afternoon schedule.

Each Sunday afternoon, I got out my calendar and the ward list and began calling members for splits. I set up splits well ahead of time; sometimes up to a month in advance, if I could. I did not let *anyone* say no. I just kept asking, "Well, what about next week? No?

What about the week after that? No? What about the week after that?" until they gave me a date. One week I would start at the "A's" and work to the "Z's" and the next week I would start at the "Z's" and work to the "A's." I went through the list until I filled all the slots for needed splits. At the start of the year, these splits were filled by the Seventies Quorum or other priesthood quorums. Within a very short time I began to see this would not be enough, so I began to call *everyone*, including the sisters, for help (of course splits with the sisters meant the discussion had to be held at their home, or *two* sisters would have to go with each missionary). *All* the youth were involved in missionary work. Anyone over twelve years old could go on splits and even the younger children were sometimes invited to participate in the missionary discussions. I became so desperate for help, I began calling the totally inactive members to help. In fact, this worked so well we were able to reactivate quite a few members through this big missionary push! It was fantastic!

At the end of the year, we found that about 75 percent of *all* members in the ward had been active in missionary work that year. That was *all* members, including the less active and children! When you consider that less than 40 percent of the ward was considered active, we had 35 percent more people doing missionary work than were considered active members!

In the end, the results were miraculous! We went from one baptism in 1985 to *38* baptisms in 1986, and about *25* baptisms in each of the years 1987 and 1988. Perhaps the most remarkable thing about the whole experience was the ward's statistics at the end of that second year. Our ward was at the top in every possible category: tithing, reactivation, new priesthood, etc. It was the first time the stake had ever seen such a thing.

## Becoming a Great Missionary

In the end, three great missionary principles were reaffirmed.

1. You have to have a *vision* of where you are going, a plan of action with which God and His angels can work.

2. The key to success in missionary service is hard *work*.

3. You must have enough patience for God and His angels to prepare the way before you. Nephi was right after all. Go forth and do the work of the Lord, *knowing* that He will prepare the way before you!


# Faith and the Priesthood

Faith is at the core of everything we do, everything we are, everything we will become, and even everything that *exists*. It is not only the "moving force" of the universe, as Joseph would say, but it is *power*. It is the power behind everything—even the priesthood.

Most people think the power of the priesthood is somehow separate from faith, as though men who hold the priesthood have obtained some special power that others cannot obtain, but this is not true. *All* power comes from faith. The priesthood is *authority*, not power. The priesthood is the *authority* to use God's power in special and additional ways.

Let me give you an example. A policeman is given authority to use force, or power, in ways others cannot. But their authority to use a gun is different from the gun itself. The *gun* is the *real* power a policeman has. But it is a power which *anyone* can use. The only difference is that the policeman has the *authority* to use the gun and has *authority* to obtain more power (i.e., call upon more men with guns) if needed. The criminal has the same ability to use that power (a gun) but does not have the authority to use it legally or to call upon more power when needed.

The same is true with faith and the priesthood. *Anyone,* whether a member of the Church or not, can use the power of faith, if they learn how to do so. That is why many Christians of other churches experience miracles and have faith-promoting experiences. Further, *any* member of the Church, male or female, young or old, can use the power of faith to work all the miracles about which one might read in the scriptures. (Read D&C 46 and Hebrews where it talks about the gifts of the Spirit. Notice it says *nothing* about the priesthood or men only. These powers are available to *all* members who believe[4]).

This concept is easy to understand when you break it down. Make a list of all the things the priesthood can do that the general membership cannot. You will find the only thing listed is the performance of ordinances, such as baptism. Anything that pertains to *power*, such as healing the sick, miracles, etc. can be done by *anyone* with faith.

The priesthood does give us the ability to obtain more power than we could normally obtain using our own faith. Someone who is given a calling obtains special authority to use God's power to fulfill that calling when they are set apart by someone in authority. That same person will feel the withdrawal of those powers and increased spiritual ability when released. But the fact that people can obtain additional power through the priesthood does not change *what* that power really is, which is faith.

If the priesthood was a different or an additional power from faith, a priesthood holder who had no faith could perform healings and miracles, but this does not happen. A priesthood holder who is

---

[4] "No matter who believeth; these signs such as healing the sick, casting out devils, etc. should follow all that believe whether male or female." (*Words of Joseph Smith,* p. 115).

## Becoming a Great Missionary

not faithful or active might be able to baptize someone and still have it count on the records of the Church, but ordinances do not show direct power, they show authority. In order for that same priesthood holder to heal or cast out devils, he must have faith. Now, there is no question the priesthood gives us the ability to call upon *additional* power when needed, but that power is always based upon faith; whether it is God's or our own.

Let me give you an example of how faith is enhanced by using the authority of the priesthood. It is a story I have often told about the ability to cast out devils. Before I obtained the priesthood, it took a lot of prayer and effort to cast out the evil spirits that plagued me after coming into the Church. Each night, I would have to pray for a long time just to get to sleep without evil thoughts keeping me awake. My bishop, knowing my past and the problems I had with evil spirits, showed me how to cast them out the day I received the Aaronic Priesthood. This kind and wise priesthood holder told me an ancient secret: how men from the time of Adam used their priesthood to cast out devils. I used it that very night and my life has never been the same. Once I obtained the priesthood and the authority to use God's power, I found that the evil spirits were forced to leave immediately, almost instantly. It was one of the most exciting and wonderful experiences of my life!

Another example of priesthood authority enhancing the personal power of faith is the ability to call for help from God and His angels in certain situations. The ability to call upon God for more power has been translated in our daily speech as "priesthood power," but it is important to keep in mind that the real power behind it all is faith. That is why you will never hear that God used the priesthood to create the world. He used faith. Moses, on the other hand, could be said to have used both faith and the priesthood to part the Red Sea: faith was the power, but he had to use the priest-hood to obtain enough power to accomplish the act. But when actually trying to define who did what and how, so we can learn how to obtain real power and use it, it is important to remember that all power comes from faith. Even when we use our priesthood to call upon the powers of heaven to help us, when that power comes, it comes as the result of the faith that resides in that God who sent it.

Lastly, let's hear from Joseph Smith:

> *Thus says the author of the epistle to the Hebrews 11: "Through faith we understand that the worlds were framed by the word of God; so that things which are seen were not made of things which do appear."'*

> *By this we understand that the principle of power which existed in the bosom of God, by which the worlds were framed, was faith; and that it is by reason of this principle of power existing in the Deity, that all created things exist; so that all things in heaven, on earth, or under the earth exist by reason of faith as it existed in Him.*

> *Had it not been for the principle of faith the worlds would never have been framed neither would man have been formed of the dust. It is the principle by which Jehovah works, and through which he exercises power over all temporal as well as eternal things. Take this principle or attribute—for it is an attribute—from the Deity, and he would cease to exist.*

> *Who cannot see, that if God framed the worlds by faith, that it is by faith that he exercises power over them,* and that faith is the principle of power? *And if the principle of power, it must be so in man as well as in the Deity? This is the testimony of all the sacred writers, and the lesson which they have been endeavoring to teach to man.*

## Becoming a Great Missionary

*Faith, then, is the first great governing principle which has power, dominion, and authority over all things; by it they exist, by it they are upheld, by it they are changed, or by it they remain, agreeable to the will of God.* Without it there is no power, *and without power there could be no creation nor existence!"* (Lectures on Faith, *pp. 8–10, emphasis added*)

## Fighting the Powers of Darkness

Some who serve missions will have the unwanted opportunity to face the army of darkness face to face. I do not mean experiencing problems and negative consequences on your mission—those things are just a part of the life we live. I am talking about actually facing those who oppose God and his servants. This is a part of the opposition in all things that Lehi wrote about.[5] Although it is not experienced often, it is a reality that must be understood and talked about. As missionaries begin to experience success in the work of the Lord, they will find that opposition will rise against them in direct proportion to that success. Due to the authority of the priesthood we have been given, and the power of the name of Jesus Christ, this opposition is nothing to worry about. However, forewarned is forearmed. Let me give you an example.

While working one area, my companion and I faced the power of Satan head on. We had begun to find great success when, shortly afterward, everything started to go badly. Appointments fell through, good families reversed their decisions and refused to see us, cars broke down, etc. Then one night it became deadly serious.

---

[5] 2 Nephi 2:11.

That night the power of Satan came into our apartment and I was forced to use the authority of the priesthood I held to cast out this evil influence. The next morning, I tried to explain my experience to my companion. He did not believe me. I shrugged my shoulders and went back to reading—I knew what I had experienced was real. After a short while, my companion came into the kitchen where I was reading. He was white as a sheet! He told me he now believed what I had said, because he had just had a similar, but more terrifying experience. He remembered what I said concerning my experience, that I used the priesthood to cast out Satan. He used the name of Jesus Christ and was immediately released from Satan's power. That is when he came into the kitchen.

As mentioned in a previous chapter, we called President Pinnock about how to deal with this problem. He gave us the confidence to deal with it ourselves and we eventually did. The power of Satan slowly released its grip on our area and we began to find success again.

# Becoming a Great Missionary

# Seventeen
## What Happens When Things Go Wrong?

When all is said and done, success in teaching the gospel comes down to two things: a loving God who sends His Spirit to touch the hearts of men, and men who are willing to listen and accept what they hear. If one or the other is not working properly, nothing happens. In that situation, no amount of work, no amount of prayer, no amount of celestial help will make any difference. Look at Noah. He worked, he prayed, and he had God on his side, to no avail. Missionaries sent to areas already reaped of the righteous, such as Europe, have a difficult time getting anyone to listen. This chapter discusses this problem in an effort to help missionaries in such circumstances understand they aren't doing anything wrong! The bottom line is—if you are doing all you can, the rest is up to God:

> If I ask him to give me wisdom concerning any requirement in life, or in regard to my own course, or that of my friends, my family, my children, or those that I preside over, and get no answer from him, and then do the very best that my judgment

## Becoming a Great Missionary

*will teach me, he is bound to own and honor that transaction,*
*and he will do so to all intents and purposes."*
(Discourses of Brigham Young, p. 43)

## Gleaners

Some missionaries are called to countries or missions that have already been *reaped* by other missionaries. That is, most, if not all, the righteous have been found and converted. All that remains is the tedious task of gleaning through those who are left, searching for the *one* left behind or lost among the thorns. It is difficult work with few earthly rewards, but it is a necessary task for a compassionate God to require of us. Those called to these missions must endure to the end and be faithful; they will receive the same reward as those who are called to more fruitful areas of the Lord's vineyards.

## Bad Companions

Just as a missionary has no control over the area to which he is called, he has no control over the companion to whom he is assigned. If you are assigned a companion who refuses to work or has other problems that hamper the work from going forward, you will not be held responsible for the consequences. It *is* your responsibility to do everything in your power to help your companion overcome his weaknesses, but with love and compassion rather than judgment and accusations. It is also your responsibility to learn to see beyond the day-to-day problems and find good from the situation in which you find yourself. Remember, we are saved by the grace of God *after* all we can do![1]

---

[1] 2 Nephi 25:23.

## Bad Timing

The work of God *will* go forward, but according to His timetable. Sometimes we are in the right place at the right time, and sometimes we must wait patiently for that time to come. Would you expect to reap before the crop is ripe? Of course not. We must have the understanding to see the BIG PICTURE. We must be able to see there are more things going on than what we can see with our mortal eyes.

When I was first transferred to Pittsburgh, we taught less than five discussions a week. Just a few weeks before, I was teaching an average of 30 discussions a week. I was still the same person, my talents and abilities had not changed, and I knew that God's desire for me to succeed had not changed. What changed? What had changed was the time and place. The people in this new area were not yet ready to accept the gospel—the wheat was not yet ripe. But there was still work to do. A crop does not grow by itself. It needs planted, watered, fertilized, thinned, watered some more, and, when the season is right, finally reaped.

If you are doing everything right, working hard, and living the mission rules, the rest is up to God! He decides when it is time to reap. Until then, as faithful servants, we must continue to plant seeds (first contacts), water the growing plants (later contacts, member examples, advertising, etc.), and occasionally thin the crop (people who hear and then reject the gospel). When the time is right, the crop will be ready to harvest (people will accept the gospel and be baptized). Do not think for a minute your time and efforts are wasted!

## Becoming a Great Missionary

### Talents and Abilities

All of us have talents and abilities the Lord will use to bring about His purposes. It is not for us to judge how God will use those talents! We must be willing to serve God as *He* chooses.

When I served in Altoona and the Lord blessed us with so much success—far beyond what we were capable of by ourselves—I ended up disappointed! Why? Because even though we had taught literally *thousands* of people during the six months we served in that area, we ended up with only *one* baptism! Just *one*! How could that be? What was I doing wrong? Why could I not get people to commit to further discussions and to baptism? It was President Pinnock, again, who taught me the truth of missionary work: it is not up to us, it is up to God. I was a sower, sent to the area to plant seeds.

This had been tough ground (remember, the "pit" of the mission?). For *years* the members and missionaries had worked the soil, removed the stones, broken the hard ground, and prepared the area to be planted. I had been sent to plant and plant we did! However, it would be up to others to water what I had planted and still others to finally reap the crop I had helped sow.

Many years later, I discussed this concept at length with Elder Pinnock, and he told me the area we had worked so hard that summer, with such sparse results, had for *years* afterward led the mission in baptisms! Everything he had taught me so long ago had actually come true. I *had* been called to sow while others *had* been called to reap. My calling as a sower had been just as important as those who finally reaped. Those who worked for years preparing the soil before I came (and saw no results from their work) had been just as important as my sowing had been. What if the missionaries whose job it was to break up the rocky soil had given up? The seeds we sowed would never have taken root, would never have grown and matured, and *no one* would ever have been baptized!

We all have talents and abilities. My greatest talent was my testimony of the gospel. I was able to get in doors and plant the seed of the Spirit within the hearts of those with whom I came in contact. I was *good* at getting in doors and touching people's hearts. Why would God use me to break up and prepare the soil or use me to reap when my talents were clearly in sowing seeds? God knows each of us, knows our talents and abilities, and knows when it is time to sow or reap. We must trust God—and the mission president who is making decisions based upon inspiration from God—to know how and when to best use our talents.

Doctrine and Covenants section 46 talks about the gifts of the Spirit and *promises* that everyone has at least one gift of the Spirit. Your job as a missionary (or member, for that matter) is to determine which gift you have and then develop it (some people may have several gifts). It is important to realize not everyone has the same gifts so as to not become jealous or envious of the gifts and talents other people have. This would be a waste effort you could be putting into developing your own gift. Even if your gift is nothing more than the ability to believe the testimony of others, it is precious because it gives you the ability to believe the truth, which will prepare you to live with God someday. Receiving your patriarchal blessing can be a helpful step in identifying your particular gifts. You must also realize that gifts are limited in nature. Just because you have one, doesn't mean you deserve or will obtain another. We don't know the whys or hows of God's giving of gifts, we just know it is real and God has promised a gift to everyone.

## Becoming a Great Missionary

Also realize that most gifts come quietly and without much fanfare, so learn to be grateful for the knowledge and testimony you have developed, and, over time, you will not only discern the gifts you have been given by God, but you will learn to see them as the blessings they are. You must learn to enhance your ability to serve God by using those gifts.

My gift is the knowledge that Jesus Christ is the Son of God. With that gift, I became a seed planter. Over time, I was able to develop my gift so I could plant the seeds of the gospel in almost anyone with whom I came into contact. However, like all gifts, my gift is limited. I don't get to see the plant grow or be harvested. I seldom see the results of my work. During my entire mission, despite the thousands of souls to whom I was able to teach and testify, I baptized only a few. Now that I am older and wiser, I understand that such is the nature of my gift. I have learned to accept and relish it for what it is.

Other people have the gift of watering or weeding or reaping, or even making the wheat into bread (making new members productive). I suppose I could be jealous of those who get to reap the seeds I have sown, but that would be a waste of time. For every member baptized, *many* people and events have touched their lives and finally brought them to the point of conversion. It is a group effort. For any one person to say that it was he or she alone who brought someone into the Church is the height of arrogance. The important point to learn and remember is that each person must do his part for the conversion process to succeed. If someone refuses to plant, or water, or reap, or eventually make bread, the efforts of all go to waste.

# What Happens When Things Go Wrong?

Do not spend time worrying about things you cannot control. Your calling is to work hard at whatever the Lord calls you to do, whether it is planting, watering, reaping, or even gleaning the fields. Some people have stone hearts that need softened before a seed can be planted. This means they must be approached many times before they will listen. Just because you are rejected at a door does not mean you had no effect on that person. How many times have we heard stories of home teachers going to the same less-active family for years, only to have something happen and the family becomes active again. Some people simply take more time than others, which is why we continue to try even though we cannot see any results at the time.

So, be patient, continue to work hard, and you will be blessed. In time, you will see your work have an affect on the people you are meeting. Don't worry about where you are serving or to what position you may be called. You are called to *serve*, whether it is as a front-line missionary or in the office, or in some high position of authority. Remember, no matter where you serve, the pay is the same for everyone!

## It is the Spirit that Converts

At the most basic and important level, as long as you are trying as hard as you can, it does not matter what results you obtain. The results are totally up to the Lord. Only the Holy Ghost can convert. No matter how hard *you* try, if the Holy Ghost does not touch a person's heart, he will not, cannot, be converted and therefore will never be baptized. Since you have no control over whether a person will accept the gospel, how can you be held accountable, or why should you feel badly concerning the outcome?

## Becoming a Great Missionary

I am the perfect example of this principle. I was a successful missionary. I taught *thousands* of people. Even 20 years later, Elder Pinnock was still telling stories of the miraculous events that surrounded my missionary work in Pennsylvania. How many baptisms did I get? Too few to count. Yet I know that my mission was successful. It was successful because I always left the results to the Lord.

> I had only traveled a short time to testify to the people, before I learned this one fact, that you might prove doctrine from the Bible till doomsday, and it would merely convince a people, but would not convert them. You might read the Bible from Genesis to Revelation, and prove every iota that you advance, and that alone would have no converting influence upon the people. Nothing short of a testimony by the power of the Holy Ghost would bring light and knowledge to them—bring them in their hearts to repentance. Nothing short of that would ever do. You have frequently heard me say that I would rather hear an Elder, either here or in the world speak only five words accompanied by the power of God, and they would do more good than to hear long sermons without the Spirit. That is true, and we know it. (Discourses of Brigham Young, p. 330)

On a higher level, there is truth to the idea that one's personal righteousness and preparedness does have a direct relationship to his ability to touch people and be used as a tool in the Lord's hands. Enoch developed his talent of teaching to the point where no one could resist his words—his words literally had power over the very earth around him (Moses 6:34, 47). He saved a few people but most were destroyed (he lived in the same era as Noah). Ether was another prophet who had great power of speech and yet all rejected his words (Ether 13:2). Righteousness prepares us to serve the Lord in greater and greater capacities. But no matter what our personal abilities or righteousness, we cannot control whether people will accept the gospel! Even Jesus Christ could not persuade all of the people to whom he talked! This is in accordance with the eternal law of the universe which permits all men to have agency. Everyone has the divine right to choose for himself. Even though a missionary may be able to prove the gospel to be true, it does not mean that people will *choose* to accept or live it (remember Brother Brown!).

When we develop our ability to serve, and our spirit becomes powerful enough to touch others, our success will naturally increase. Obviously, the more others can feel the Spirit, the greater chance we have of touching people and subsequently obtaining positive results. It is important to understand the basic law of statistics, as well. Once we have the Spirit with us all the time, the more people we see—the more people we come into contact with physically—the more people will be touched by the Spirit, and, as a result, the more people will respond to that Spirit and be baptized. For *most* missionaries (assuming that most missionaries carry the Spirit with them), then, key to success is simply working hard. Once you have done all you can to spiritually prepare, and once you spend all the time you can doing actual missionary work, there is nothing more you can do. The rest is up to the Lord. If you have great success, good. If not, so what? It will have no affect on your eternal reward.

## Bad Things Happen to Good People

In this mortal world, bad things happen to good people. All of us suffer the pains and problems of life despite how good or bad we are. Both good and bad things have been provided by our creator to give experience to both the righteous and wicked during this life experience.[2] It is just a part of this life to experience the opposition in all things about which Lehi spoke.[3] Some may justify their poor judgment of others by talking about the karma of a person—that they deserved whatever happened to them because of the bad things they have done. You know, "what goes around comes around." Even though there is no doubt in my mind that we do reap what we sow, just because something bad happens to someone *does not* mean that the person deserves to be punished, or that they have sinned or done something wrong! This kind of thinking leads people to judge others, which the Savior has commanded us not to do.[4] This is the kind of thinking for which the Jews were condemned!

> *And as [Jesus] passed by, he saw a man which was blind from [his] birth. And his disciples asked him, saying, Master, who did sin, this man, or his parents, that he was born blind? Jesus answered, Neither hath this man sinned, nor his parents: but that the works of God should be made manifest in him.* (John 9:1–3)

If we were to believe and act like the Jews, we would condemn this blind man, assuming this terrible thing happened because of some great sin he had committed or that his parents had committed—as we often condemn our neighbors for things that happen to them, saying to ourselves that they *deserved* what happened to them because of some minor infraction or sin we may have seen them commit (or assume they had committed). But in making this judgment, it is *we* who have sinned! We have made an unrighteous judgment because we assumed things we could not possibly know—only God

---

[2] Matthew 5:45
[3] 2 Nephi 2:11
[4] Matthew 7:1–2

knows the hearts of men! The Savior made it clear there are other reasons, *righteous* reasons, for terrible things to happen. Who are we to judge? That is the whole point; we are *not* to judge people, and this includes ourselves! As individuals, we *cannot* assume the bad things we experience, or the lack of success we may have, are the consequence of some sin we have committed.

However, if you consistently break the mission rules, refuse to work, or refuse to complete assignments, then you *will* reap what you sow. Your bad karma will catch up, and you will suffer the consequences of your actions. But these two principles are totally different, and you must judge with care which principle applies.

Let me give you two examples of bad things happening to good people. The first baptism I was involved with was an older man whose wife was a faithful member of the Church. Somehow, I was the one who finally touched his heart and brought him into the Church. I was transferred just a few days before he was baptized. Several years later, he committed suicide. It was a terrible blow to everyone and, for years, I wondered what to think or how to judge what had happened. Some of my questions were answered years later, after I was married.

The teenage girl who often babysat our children committed suicide. She was a delightful person. We had never seen anything that would have led us to understand why she would do this terrible thing. It was only after her death we learned she had been addicted to alcohol as a result of abuse by her father who had given her alcohol as a young child. Before she was old enough to choose for herself, she was shackled with this terrible bond. Finally, she could not take it any more and killed herself.

## Becoming a Great Missionary

Once again I was filled with confusion and doubt. How should I judge this young woman? How should I judge this man whom I had brought into the Church? Both seemed to be righteous people but both had chosen to commit suicide. Didn't this act *prove* they were sinners?

Then the answer came, through the family of the teenage girl. In the temple, the girl's brother saw his deceased sister, smiling and happy. His heart was instantly filled with joy! All his doubts and questions were now answered. God was in control and judged a *righteous* judgment (unlike the judgment we would have made) and set all things right in the end. We must learn to trust God. We must learn not to judge according to the ways of men, according to how things *look*. We must learn to judge a righteous judgment or not judge at all.

## Illness

It is not uncommon for missionaries to get sick. Some get so sick they have to change missions or go home. Although this can be very disappointing, no missionary should feel guilty about getting sick. It is something over which you have little or no control. Once again, some people try to judge illness as a "sign" that the missionary did something wrong, or had sinned. This is both false doctrine and foolish. Sickness is a part of life. It comes upon *all men*, regardless of whether they are good or bad. You should not judge yourself or others for this natural occurrence. The only thing you *should* do is take care of yourself. Just as it would be foolish for you to put off fixing your car when broken, it is foolish to put off fixing your body if you have to see a doctor. This is part of growing up and putting things into perspective. As strict as God was with the ancient Saints,

# What Happens When Things Go Wrong?

He recognizes the importance of taking care of our animals and ourselves, even on the Sabbath day.[5] This is not just doctrinal law but common sense.

If you are required to leave your mission due to illness or accident, you may be disappointed but don't beat yourself up over it. Simply find another way to serve your Lord and Master. All things will work together for your good if you do all you can to serve God, under whatever circumstances you find yourself.

If you find yourself bedridden on your mission, there are things you can do to pass the time productively:

1.  *Phone contacting.*
Get the phone book for your immediate area and call people to introduce them to the Church and set up appointments for future discussions. This is difficult to do, and you must be careful not to offend people by your actions. Make sure you only call people at appropriate times of the day, and if they say they are not interested, don't push it.

You can also use the phone to help other missionaries set up splits with members, to set up meals for the missionaries, or to work with less-active or part-member families.

2.  *Writing letters.*
In addition to the weekly letters you should be sending to your family, you can have a wonderful and positive effect on many people by writing letters to them. You can send thank-you letters to members and investigators for meals or other things people have done for you. You can send uplifting and inspiring letters to family,

---

[5] Luke 14:5.

# Becoming a Great Missionary

friends, investigators, other missionaries, or anyone who may have a problem or need of which you are aware. The scope of this type of missionary work can go as far as your own vision. Remember, most of the scriptures we have concerning the life of Christ were first written as letters to others.

*LETTERS FROM HOME*

*Several years ago, while touring the California Mission, I interviewed a missionary who appeared rather dejected and downcast. I asked him if he had been sending a letter home to his parents each week. He replied: "Yes, Brother Monson, each week for the last five months."*

*I responded: "And do you enjoy the letters you receive from home?"*

*Came his unexpected answer: "I haven't had a letter from home since I came on my mission. You see, my Dad is inactive and Mother is a non-member. She didn't favor my accepting a mission call and said that if I went into the mission field she would never write nor send a dime." With a half smile that didn't really disguise the heartache, he said: "And she has kept her word. What can I do, Brother Monson?"*

*I prayed for inspiration. The answer came. "Keep writing, son, every week. Bear your testimony to Mother and to Dad. Let them know you love them. Tell them how much the gospel means to you. And serve the Lord with all your heart."*

*Six months later when I attended a stake conference in that area, this same elder ran up to me and asked: "Do you remember me? I'm the missionary whose parents didn't write."*

*I remembered all too well and cautiously asked if he had received a letter from home.*

# What Happens When Things Go Wrong?

*He reached into his pocket and held out to my view a large
handful of envelopes. With tears streaming down his cheeks he
declared proudly, "Not one letter, Brother Monson, but a letter
every week. Listen to the latest one: 'Son, we so much
appreciate the work you are doing. Since you left for your
mission our lives have changed. Dad attends priesthood meeting
and will soon be an elder. I have been meeting with the
missionaries and next month will be baptized. Let's make an
appointment to all be together in the Los Angeles Temple one
year from now as you conclude your mission. Sincerely,
Mother.'" (Elder Thomas S. Monson,* General Conference,
October 4, 1969)

## Bad Dreams

Almost all missionaries carry baggage on their missions—
memories and problems carried over from the lives they lived before dedicating themselves to the Lord. All of us have sinned in one
degree or another. One of the natural effects of sin can be lingering
bad dreams where we remember or relive past sins. These can be
difficult to deal with, especially if they deal with some kind of sexual
sin or pornography. These dreams can have profound and lingering
effects upon how we feel, think, and work. Even though I was considered one of the best missionaries, I was plagued by bad dreams
my whole mission. It was a constant fight to maintain my spirituality
and focus on the work. Once again President Pinnock came to the
rescue. Let me share with you part of a personal letter he wrote to
me:

*Do not worry about having evil dreams. If you will spend the
last ten or fifteen minutes of the day deeply thinking of the
Savior and His teachings, you will fill your mind with some
thoughts that will be helpful. Don't let <u>anything</u> get you down.*

## Becoming a Great Missionary

President Pinnock made it clear that I was not responsible for something I could not control. If I were wide awake and consciously decided to think evil thoughts, or to ponder pornography I had seen, or made no attempt to remove sexual thoughts from my mind during the day, then I would be held responsible for my *actions* and my *decisions*. However, since what happens when we are asleep is beyond our conscious control, we are not held responsible for those things nor should we feel guilty about the fact they happen to us. President Pinnock's advice was right on the money! *Don't let anything get you down!*

## Bad Thoughts

All missionaries will have a bad thought occasionally. These can come as memories of past sins, sexual thoughts, or bad thoughts about people. Everyone struggles with bad thoughts and learning how to deal with them—how to control them—is very important. There is no better time to learn than on a mission.

First, we need to remember how Satan tempts us. The *only* way Satan can tempt us is through our thoughts. He has no physical body. He cannot grab us by the arm and force us to do things we do not want to do. His *only* tool is to put thoughts into our minds (or into the minds of others, who then proceed to tempt us). So, if Satan's *only* tool is to put bad thoughts in our minds and it is part of God's plan for us to be tempted and tried, we *cannot entirely* prevent this from happening! Satan can, and will, place evil thoughts in our minds. From the most humble child of God to the Prophet of the Lord, all people are tempted by having bad thoughts placed in their minds. So, the fact that we occasionally have bad thoughts does not mean we are bad people or that we have sinned! A person cannot sin when he has no control over the situation; he can only sin when he *acts* or makes the *decision* to sin.

> Those evil Spirits, . . . invisible to our eyes, yet palpable to our senses, are constantly seeking to instill into our minds evil thoughts and wrong desires, to prompt us to commit sin and thereby grieve the Spirit of God and to lead us, as Cain was led, to perpetrate crime which resulted in his becoming Perdition. But there are also angels around us. Though invisible to us they are continually inviting us and pleading with us to do that which is right. The Spirit of God, too, rests upon us, and it prompts us to keep the commandments of God. By means of these influences, therefore, we are receiving experience and we are growing in knowledge. (George Q. Cannon, Gospel Truth, *Vol. 1, p. 84*)

Bad thoughts only turn to sin when we *choose* to dwell upon the evil thoughts in our minds. We sin when we *choose* to remember our sins, or take pleasure in thinking about things we should not. Then it becomes a conscious act on our part and does become a sin. There is a humorous adage I once heard that explains how this works. It goes like this:

> If you see a pretty girl and look once, that's okay, but if you look twice, it's a sin.

The point of the adage is obvious. *Everyone* will be attracted to, and look at, a pretty girl. But by looking *twice*, it means you have *chosen* to think bad thoughts about the girl. We are humans living on a telestial world filled with sin and temptation. People will come into our lives, thoughts into our minds, and memories into our dreams. This will happen whether we want it to or not, whether we choose it to or not. It is just part of the life we live and the test of this mortal life. None of this becomes a sin upon us until we *choose* to act upon those things. In the final judgment, we will be judged by our *acts*, not by our thoughts.

> *Students at our universities and elsewhere come to me and ask me for advice: "What can we do?" Perhaps I can give you some practical suggestions concerning what you can do. Evil thoughts come to every one of us. None of us are free from evil thinking, but God has given us a brain and has given us willpower to overcome this thinking, but we have to have some help to do it. We must all be prepared and be ready so that when these evil thoughts come we can have something to drive them away.*
>
> *Perhaps you might carry a poem, or a piece of scripture; something that can get your mind occupied so that you are not working in a vacuum. There are so many beautiful things that we can learn and so many beautiful things we can do, that when an evil thought comes, if we think or do beautiful things, we are saved. When an evil thought comes if you sit down and play your musical instrument, or if you can hum or whistle a tune, your mind is soon occupied with noble thoughts and the first thing you know you cannot even remember what it was that you were originally thinking about. That way we build up the protection that God gave us when we came into this world. God has given us this protection, our conscience, as an energy barrier to protect us against evil. We must not deaden it, we must not lower it. We dare not smother it and live. It is our lone protection in time of need. (Theodore M. Burton,* BYU Speeches, January 17, 1961)

How do we know when our thoughts are from Satan or from our own memories or desires? When you are in the temple, the bad thoughts you have are your own. Satan cannot come into that holy place. However, even then the evil thoughts you have do not mean you are a bad person, it is simply an indication of what kind of person you *were* at one time. We cannot erase the things we have done or seen; they are a permanent part of our memory (at judgment day we have a perfect recollection of all our sins, why they took place, and whether we did anything about them). Over time, as you concentrate on good and act righteously, the good thoughts and memories you create overcome the bad. Also, you learn to control your thoughts just as you learn to control your speech.[6] The prophets have taught us on many occasions that all you need to do is replace a bad thought with a good one—words of a hymn or a memorized scripture. Soon, after it has become a habit, it will happen almost automatically.

However, these things take time! When I came back into the Church, I spent *two years* repenting before I was ready to go on my mission. So, be patient and it will come. The most important thing to remember is that it is not your fault when these things happen! They are part of your memory, and you never know what words or thoughts might trigger those memories. After all these years of righteous living, I still have it happen to me. Someone will say something, or I will meet someone, and it will trigger a memory of bad things. Now, however, it does not bother me, because I know that I am no longer that kind of person and realize there is nothing I can do about the memories I carry, I just need to put them into context with the rest of my life and push them out of my mind as soon as they appear.

## What Happens When You Sin on Your Mission?

First of all, let us make sure we understand one another. Weaknesses are *not* sins! Just as mistakes, accidents, illnesses, and many

---

[6] *"Check Your Words*—If you first gain power to check your words, you will then begin to have power to check your judgment, and at length actually gain power to check your thoughts and reflections." (*Discourses of Brigham Young,* p. 268).

## Becoming a Great Missionary

problems that affect our daily lives in a negative way are not sins. Sins must involve a conscious decision and effort to go against your conscience. If you have weaknesses, work on them but do not feel guilty about them.

> *Let all Latter-day Saints learn that the weaknesses of their brethren are not sins. When men or women undesignedly commit a wrong, do not attribute that to them as a sin. Let us learn to be compassionate one with another; let mercy and kindness soften every angry and fretful temper, that we may become long-suffering and beneficial in all our communications one with another. (Brigham Young,* Journal of Discourses Vol. 9, p. 334)

Many people in the Church, and therefore many missionaries, do not have a correct understanding of sin. They believe that if anything negative happens to them it is a result of Satan, or the consequence of some sin they have committed. This is totally false. Sin can only be laid upon a person's soul if they consciously choose to go against their conscience. It is not an accident, it is not bad luck, and it is not bad karma. Sin must be a willful act that goes against the light and knowledge already within a person's soul.

> *There are some things allotted to us in life that have been divinely fashioned according to our ability and our capacity. When we see individuals coping with what seems to be a tragedy and making of it an opportunity, then we begin to partake of the deep wisdom in the Savior's response concerning the blind man.*
>
> *Is not our struggling amid suffering and chastening in a way like the efforts of the baby chicken still in the egg? It must painfully and patiently make its own way out of the shell. To help the chick by breaking the egg for it could be to kill it.*

# What Happens When Things Go Wrong?

*Unless it struggles itself to break outside its initial constraints, it may not have the strength to survive thereafter.*

*Afflictions can soften us and sweeten us, and can be a chastening influence. (Alma 62:41.) We often think of chastening as something being done to punish us, such as by a mortal tutor who is angry and peevish with us. Divine chastening, however, is a form of learning as it is administered at the hands of a loving Father. (Helaman 12:3.)*

*We are accustomed to noting, in connection with sin, how "one thing leads to another." And so it does. But the chain of righteous conduct operates in much the same way. Joseph, the son of Jacob, in a story that someday we shall have the full and fascinating particulars of, overcame what could have been the disabling shock of being sold into slavery. The gall of bitterness was not in him then, nor had bad breaks made him bad. He later rose to positions of trust in the household of Potiphar. His same refusal to resent "all these things" was there subsequently in the unjust imprisonment of Joseph; his resilience could not have emerged if he had been a bitter prisoner. Should we then be surprised by his later anonymous generosity to his hungry brothers—the very brothers who had sold him into slavery? Resilience begets resilience!*

*Thus, Joseph's quality service to Potiphar and his management skills even in the jail were a clear foreshadowing of his brilliant service later on as the "prime minister" of the Pharaoh. But it all sprang from within; Joseph's spiritual strength could not be shaken by things from outside.*

*Bad breaks, therefore, need not break a good man; they may with God's help even make him better! (Neal A. Maxwell,* All These Things Shall Give Thee Experience, *pp. 38–41)*

# Becoming a Great Missionary

*We may foolishly bring unhappiness and trouble, even suffering, upon ourselves. These are not regarded as penalties imposed by a displeased Creator. They are part of the lessons of life, part of the test. (Boyd K. Packer,* Conference Reports, October 29 1980)

There is one definition of sin that has stood the test of time. This definition, first written by Orson F. Whitney, has been used and reused by many prophets and apostles through the years. It gives a perfect understanding of the difference between sin and just experiencing the normal life that we all have to endure as part of our earthly existence.

*Sin is the transgression of divine law. A man sins when he violates his conscience, going contrary to light and knowledge—not the light and knowledge that has come to his neighbor, but that which has come to himself. He sins when he does the opposite of what he knows to be right. Up to that point he only blunders.* One may suffer painful consequences for only blundering, but he cannot commit sin unless he knows better than to do the thing in which the sin consists. *One must have a conscience before he can violate it. (Orson F. Whitney,* Cowley and Whitney on Doctrine, *pp. 435–436, emphasis added)*

All of us sin. None of us is perfect. Each of us has, does, and will commit sin to various degrees and measures.[7] This also will happen on your mission. Most of the time these sins are minor in nature and can be taken care of by you and the Lord during your daily

---

[7] *"Temptation*—Thousands of temptations assail, and you make a miss here and a slip there, and say that you have not lived up to all the knowledge you have. True; but often it is a marvel to me that you have lived up to so much as you have, considering the power of the enemy upon the earth. Few that have ever lived have fully understood that power. I do not fully comprehend the awful power and influence Satan has upon the earth, but I understand enough to know that it is a marvel that the Latter-day Saints are as good as they are." (*Discourses of Brigham Young,* p. 80).

prayers. However, there will occasionally be sins that will need to be addressed by those in authority or by your mission president. Even though I was considered to be one of the best missionaries, I did not go my entire mission without sinning. Once, it was serious enough that I felt the need to bring it to the attention of President Pinnock. Let me share with you his inspired response to a letter I sent to him marked "personal:"

Thank you for your letter of a few days ago. Several things you wrote show great courage and spirituality. They are:

1. You confessed a transgression—openly and honestly.
2. You have <u>not</u> given up but have promised to keep striving for perfection—which is a destination, by the way. The striving to be better is the journey. Remember that only one mortal, the Christ, achieved perfection throughout his life and he was part God.
3. You have asked for help in a <u>positive</u> way.
4. You admit Satan's influence but also realize that he can be overcome.
5. You confessed that you had stopped <u>progressing</u> and needed to get going again.

You are a wise young man but also made some mistakes in your letter—one was where you wrote, 'Because I know I can't be forgiven until I sin no more, and that every time I sin all the past sins come back.' The Savior is the most loving, forgiving, and understanding person we will ever meet. You have been forgiven for your past transgressions now—they are gone as long as you don't have further difficulties. But also remember that for over 6 months you weren't sinning. Think of it—6 months you kept a clear, clean record—Congratulations! Sure, you are having to start again—for one reason or another all of us have started over—thank goodness that is part of the plan!

You must return to some basics which are:

1. The Gospel of Christ is happy and positive—"joy" is what we, as men, are to have. Show others your positive, helpful self.
2. Satan wants you to punish yourself. He knows he can't have you so he wants you to be an unhappy servant of the Savior. Don't gratify Lucifer by being discouraged—that is Satan's spirituality.
3. Set new goals:
   A. scripture study each day
   B. bring investigators closer to baptism each day
   C. sincerely thank someone each day
   D. be known as one who is happy, positive and loving

# Becoming a Great Missionary

Elder Clawson, you are one of the best new missionaries in the mission. Now is the time for rededication. Thanks for the maturity and desire to do the Lord's work.
Sincerely, President Pinnock

You can see why I loved and admired this man so much! There was not one word of condemnation, nothing negative to further bring down my soul with grief. It was a letter filled with wisdom and encouragement that made me *want* to become a better person, *want* to become a better missionary. I *did* rededicate myself to the Lord, and it was shortly after this that miracles began to happen! Everyone will trip and fall during this long walk home to our Father in Heaven. The most important thing we can do is to get up, dust ourselves off, and keep going! It serves no purpose to wallow in our guilt, or have a pity party over how tough life is. We must become *men* who have the courage and will to do what is necessary to move forward. We must rededicate our lives to serving God with all of our heart, mind, and strength.

*To say that we are a perfect people, I can not (sic) do it, neither can I say that I am a perfect man. I am just as full of weaknesses as any other man, and so are my brethren with whom I associate; but the Elder of Israel, no matter how great his weaknesses, who humbly trusts in God and continually strives to overcome evil and to do only that which is right, will be enabled to triumph and be faithful to the end. What matters it if a man likes whisky, if he does not drink it? I do not care how much a man in this Church likes it, if he does not drink it, it makes no difference. I do not care how much he loves tobacco, or this, that or the other, that is not good, if he brings his actions and feelings into subjection to the dictates of the Spirit of God. The virtue, brethren, is in putting away or overcoming habits which you know would impede your progress in the kingdom of God. But, brethren and sisters, the idea is, to bring our actions, thoughts and feelings into complete subjection to the dictates of the Holy Spirit, and to be on hand at all times to labor as we are directed for the building up of the kingdom of God upon the earth; that should be the object with us. (Brigham Young,* Journal of Discourses, *Vol. 15, p. 139)*

## Losing the Spirit

One of the important things you will learn while on your mission is that it is impossible to be spiritual all the time. We have talked about the need to use P-days to relax, to have fun on your mission, and to not take everything too seriously. All of this is tied to the same principle— we must be well rounded and not extreme in any of our habits or actions. The same can be said about the Spirit of God. No one, not even the prophet, can maintain a high spiritual level *all the time*. It is not practical and not healthy. Once again I turn to President Pinnock and the advice he gave when I raised the same concerns about losing the Spirit while serving on my mission:

*Much of life is carrying out the assignments and responsibilities we have on a monthly, daily, or hourly basis, realizing we can't have the full Spirit of the Savior at all times. Joseph Smith mentioned on several occasions that the Spirit would not be with him for days and days but when needed he could call upon the Spirit after getting himself in tune with his calling.*

*The many general authorities that I have had the privilege talking with admit that often the Spirit is not with them, but is standing by to assist when needed. We should be righteous servants but not expect that feeling of deep spirituality at all times. Please understand what I am saying, and by understanding reduce your own anxieties about constantly needing to labor on that high spiritual plane.*

## Losing Yourself in the Work

The best way to solve a myriad of problems is to lose yourself in the work. When we focus on our personal problems or the trials we are experiencing, we lose sight of why we are on a mission in the first place: to serve others. Stop thinking about yourself and concentrate on the work. Lose yourself in the work and you will find yourself. As you focus your prayers and energy on finding and teaching people the gospel, two things will happen: you will find your daily concerns and problems will disappear, and you will finally receive the spiritual rewards you have been waiting to experience. Spiritual experiences come only as a result of God's work. If you don't work, or if you allow *anything* to impede the work, the natural result of that work–spiritual blessings and experiences–will not, and *cannot,* come. But once you begin to consistently work hard at bringing about God's work, spiritual experiences will, and *must* come. Even President Gordon B. Hinckley learned this great principle on his mission. In his biography, *Go Forward With Faith*, he talks about writing his father, complaining about his mission and desiring to come home. His father wrote back and told him to "forget yourself and go to work." He followed his father's advice and discovered the joy of missionary work.[8] The same thing can and will happen to you.

◆◆◆

---

[8] Sheri L. Dew, *Go Forward With Faith: The Biography of Gordon B. Hinckley,* p. 64.

# Eighteen
## Going Home Early

Occasionally events will arise or actions will be taken that result in a missionary being sent home early. Just as there are many appropriate reasons for not going on a mission in the first place, not all reasons missionaries go home early from a mission are inappropriate. Life is full of crazy things. No one can predict what will happen, but we can be prepared for whatever may befall us by relying on God to get us through. Perhaps nothing in life is more difficult than coming home early from a mission. It is full of mines and pitfalls, due mainly to the way members of the Church judge you, regardless of the reason you came home.

Illness, accident, or family problems may require a missionary to go home early. The missionary may choose to go home, or perhaps be sent home due to problems that occurred on his mission. Just as there are times when the best thing for a young man is to not go on a mission, sometimes the best thing a young man can do, after realizing he made a mistake by going on a mission, is to make the difficult decision to go home early. Life does not change because young men are of missionary age. Life can and will place challenges and obstacles in people's paths for which they are not ready. As mortals, we cannot judge the hows and whys of life, we can only look with compassion and understanding upon those to whom life has dealt an unfortunate blow.

We would not think a child evil who learns to walk or talk later in life than others, or children who learn at different rates or have handicaps of some kind, so we should not judge as evil young men who are not ready or able to fulfill missionary service. If a young man has the courage to try, but after arriving in the mission field finds he is not prepared for the problems he has to face or is simply incapable of dealing with the challenge of missionary work, how can we judge him harshly? We should honor him for his willingness to try. The point is, especially for members of the Church at home, do not judge those who come home early from their missions.

There are any number of reasons why missionaries might be *sent* home from their missions. Sin, homesickness, refusal to work and/ or obey the mission rules, girlfriends, etc. Any of these things can create such problems for a missionary the only way they can be re-solved is to send him home. This action is always a last resort, and except in the case of sin, is usually a result of coming out on a mission unprepared in the first place.

As hard as it might be to be sent home early from your mission, there are some measures that can be taken which will make a bad situation better, *measures that will bring some integrity and honor to a situation that usually destroys both.* There are honorable things that can and should be done by both the missionary and those leaders involved in bringing the missionary home to keep him active once he gets home.

*1. Be up front and honest.*

If you have made a mistake, if you have committed a sin, if your effectiveness as a missionary is being totally compromised by a girl-friend or homesickness, then the honorable thing to do is to bring this to the attention of your mission president. Everyone has problems at times. Everyone has weaknesses and commits sin. We *all* make mistakes. God knew well ahead of time we would all have to go through the process of repentance. He provided laws and procedures that give us a way to cleanse ourselves of these sins. The first step is to recognize you have sinned and have the *courage* and *integrity* to admit and confess those sins to your priesthood leader. It does not take any moral effort to be caught by someone and forced to leave the mission as a result. However, there is honor in acting like a man and taking responsibility for your actions, no matter how grievous the consequences may be. It takes courage to admit when you were wrong to begin a mission and ask to go home, knowing the consequence of taking that step. Do not compound your problems or sins by lying and trying to hide these serious issues from your mission president. Stand up and take your stripes like a man. This will not only provide you with some honor but will be a giant step toward receiving redemption.

*2. Accept the consequences.*

Once you have taken the first step of honor—being honest about your mistakes and sins—the next step is to willingly accept the consequences of your actions. All *real men* clean up their own messes, never let others suffer for their mistakes, and immediately repair any damage they may have created by their actions. This will not change when you get off your mission. In fact, what you do on your mission and how you handle your problems will set a pattern

# Becoming a Great Missionary

for the rest of your life. What will happen when you are at work and make a mistake? Will you act like a child and try to hide what you have done, or lie, or try to pass off your mistake upon others? Or, will you act like a *real man* and be honest about the mistake you have made, come forward, and accept responsibility for what you have done? One path leads to disgrace; the other is the path of integrity and honor. *We all make mistakes;* it is how we handle those mistakes that make the difference, both here and in eternity.

3. *Stay active in the Church.*

In spite of the difficulties you will face when you come home early from your mission, you will simply make things worse if you reject the one thing that can bring honor and peace back into your life. If you sin or make mistakes, there are two roads you can take: You can compound those mistakes by leaving the Church or further progressing in your sins, or you can regain your honor and position by following the well-worn path of repentance—a path we have *all* traveled. The Church is there to help you.

# What Members and Priesthood Leaders Should Do When Missionaries are Sent Home

It is always difficult for a missionary to come home from a successful mission. His entire life, and sometimes even his character, has changed. It is doubly hard for a missionary to come home from an unsuccessful mission. He doesn't get any of the wonderful things he has witnessed others get: crowds at the airport to greet him, a huge family party to celebrate his homecoming, the opportunity to talk in Church and sometimes in the stake, and general acclaim and warm greetings from ward members. Instead, he comes home alone and is pushed into a dark corner of the ward. Instead of his heart being full of self-confidence and pride, he is filled with doubt and regret. Instead of being filled with joy, he is filled with sadness.

Unfortunately, for the many young men who have made mistakes and go home to make amends, or simply choose to go home early, the very people who should be reaching out to him with love and support often reject him, shun him, and make life even more difficult. One young man who came home was "debriefed" by his priesthood leaders and never heard from them again. The home teachers assigned to the family refused to come for fear of being "tainted" by this young man and his family. So, at a time when both the young man and his family needed the Church most, they were not there.

> *No power or influence can or ought to be maintained by virtue of the priesthood, only by persuasion, by long-suffering, by gentleness and meekness, and by love unfeigned; by kindness, and pure knowledge, which shall greatly enlarge the soul without hypocrisy, and without guile—reproving betimes with sharpness, when moved upon by the Holy Ghost; and then showing forth afterwards an increase of love toward him whom thou hast reproved, lest he esteem thee to be his enemy; that he may know that thy faithfulness is stronger than the cords of death. (D&C 121:41–44)*

The Church deals well with members who have committed serious sin or simply have problems fitting in. For example, the Church no longer announces to the general congregation the results of Church courts, and priesthood leaders are directed to spend additional time counseling and friendshipping the person and his family to insure they come back into the fold of the Church. As a general rule, if any family or family member is having problems of any kind, the Church rallies its forces to help in any way it can. But in many cases, this is not happening with young men who return early from their missions.

We should extend our most compassionate efforts toward those who, for whatever reason, come home early from their missions. Stake and ward priesthood leaders should set up regular times each week to meet with the returned missionary and each month to meet with his family. These don't have to be elaborate meetings, but simple gestures of love and concern that will provide a framework to insure the young man and his family are being cared for and that ward members and priesthood leaders are following through with the help and support that is being (or should be) directed toward them.

God clearly states that he wants and expects us to *increase* our love and support for those who have made mistakes or are simply having a problem dealing with the recent blows life has given them. He does not want us to shun or fear them. Let me clarify the issue in this way: if we fail to forgive those who were willing to serve God, whom will we forgive? If we fail to support and love members of the Church who have fallen, what can God expect of us when we are asked to forgive our enemies? If we fail in our responsibilities to these young men and women, what does that say about how we will treat adults who make mistakes? *We all make mistakes.* "For all have sinned, and come short of the glory of God" (Romans 3:23). Therefore, who are we to judge? We must double our efforts to make sure those who come home early from their missions *learn* from their mistakes, are able to fully repent of their sins, and return to full fellowship within the Church as quickly as possible.

# Nineteen
## Other Types of Missions/Senior Missions

O ne of the blessings of living at this time is the possibility of being assigned to one of many different types of missions. We have been speaking primarily about proselyting missions; however, these are just one of many opportunities we have to serve. There are *so* many different ways to serve the Lord now there is not room enough here to discuss all of them; however, here are a few of the most popular missions.

## Visitors' Centers

The Church maintains many Visitors' Centers around the world. These can be *independent Visitors' Center*s, such as the ones in Vermont (Joseph Smith's birthplace) and in Nauvoo (the restoration of a Mormon city). There are also *dependent* Visitors' Centers, such as those associated with temples. The primary purpose of Visitors' Centers is to provide a comfortable and interesting format for sharing the gospel with nonmembers and giving members more information

## Becoming a Great Missionary

about the Church to which they belong. They are very useful tools and *millions* of people are reached every year.

These missions are very good for older couples and those who are intimidated by the idea of going door-to-door——a proselyting mission. They are almost completely stress-free, as all the people who enter the doors *want* to hear what we have to share. They are coming to us, rather than us going to them.

These missions are also wonderful for people who have strong testimonies of the gospel but may struggle when *teaching* the gospel to others. When giving tours at the center, or at restored homes, etc., almost all the information you will be presenting is memorized prior to your starting as a tour guide. Then, at the end, you simply bear your testimony to the truthfulness of the things you have said. Very easy and simple.

The downside of serving in Visitors' Centers is dealing with the *down time*. During the summer, which is the busy season, you will be kept *very* busy and time will fly. However, during the slow periods, there is very little to do. Some days you might not have a single visitor. What will you do during those slow times? Do you like to study and read? Do you like needlework or have other hobbies that can help pass the time? These will be important questions during the slow times of the year. This does not mean you should not go on a mission to a Visitors' Center, it simply means you should be *prepared* when you go.

## Temples

Another type of mission is serving as a worker in one of more than one hundred (Wow!) temples around the world. There is probably nothing more spiritual than serving every day in a temple of the Lord. You will have the opportunity to learn every aspect of every ordinance performed within the temple. You will develop life-long friends and relationships with those with whom you serve. You will have opportunities to touch members of the Church and see them grow and mature as you teach them the wonders of eternity.

The downside of serving in temples is similar to serving in Visitors' Centers—there are going to be slow times that will need to be filled. As long as you are aware the problem exists, you can be prepared to deal with it.

## Humanitarian Missions

One of the most unique missions is a humanitarian mission. These are so varied and broad there is no way to describe them all; however, all aim to use your professional and non-professional abilities on behalf of Church members and nonmembers.

Humanitarian missions for the Church could involve working in an office, farm, temple, or Visitors' Center grounds, teaching English, building new buildings or maintaining older buildings, etc. The Church simply looks at what talents and abilities you have and try to match them with their needs. When there is a match—off you go!

Humanitarian missions also may be used for helping members through the welfare programs of the Church, or perhaps serving in callings within a small ward or branch to help bolster the leadership in the area. Once again, these are varied and the Church will try to match your abilities to the requirements of the calling.

Humanitarian missions are sometimes used to gain access to a country by the full-time missionaries. As those in the government

## Becoming a Great Missionary

gain confidence in the Church through the good works of the humanitarian missionaries, they begin permitting the Church to teach the gospel. It is a process that has opened the doors of a number of countries.

## Medical Missions

Doctors, nurses, physician assistants, and nurse practitioners are needed all over the world in numerous situations.

## Church Education System

Church Education System missions are also almost as varied as your mind can imagine. There are the obvious callings of teaching Seminary and Institute as well as other religion classes, or being placed in a position to organize or manage those same institutions in other countries.

## Part-time Missions

Another way to serve without having to wait for retirement or totally leave your home and family is to serve a part-time mission. These missions are for people who cannot dedicate all their time to a mission. They are designed for members who can serve several hours a week, working around their work and family schedule. This can involve work with local missionaries, in inner cities, prisons, church offices, genealogy, etc. There is no need to wait until you are retired to go on a mission!

# Preparing to go

When preparing to serve as a senior missionary, the requirements you need to meet are somewhat different than those for young men. You will have a family, a job, a home, cars, and other possessions, which you will need to make arrangements for prior to turning in your papers to serve on a mission.

*1.  Finances.*

You will need to be financially able to support yourself while on your mission. This can be done by saving money; by making arrangements for your retirement, pension, or Social Security check to be sent to you; by receiving help from your extended family; or even by arranging some help from the ward.

*2.  Material goods.*

You will also need to arrange for the care of your home and other material things you have accumulated over the years. Many times this is done with the help of family members—a son or daughter might stay in your home while you are gone. You could also rent out your home, which would kill two birds with one stone—providing income as well as having someone take care of your home while you are gone. But a word of caution here! According to the United States Tax Code, should you choose to rent your home, you will be unable to deduct your mission living expenses as a charitable donation. So, be certain to meet with your financial adviser and weigh your options.

*3.  Health.*

You will need to take a good look at your health before you go. Are you healthy? If you have physical problems, how do they limit what you will be able to do? This might mean you should decide to go on a 6-month mission instead of an 18-month mission. Or, it may mean you will need to stay in the U.S. or in a large city so you are within easy distance of a hospital. *Any* problem you have can be overcome, resolved, and worked around. You need not stay home because you have this or that problem! There are so many different missions available to you now, *there is no excuse not to serve!*

4. *Preparations.*

Make sure you know about the mission where you will serve. Is it cold? Is it hot? Is it a modern country? Is it a third-world country? What shots do you need? What kind of clothing do you need? These are all questions that need to be addressed in order to ensure you are well prepared to serve your mission in its entirety.


## Choose to Serve

Although this principle was touched on earlier, I believe it important to look at how it applies to senior missionaries. The principle is that we should have the desire and ability to serve anywhere God may call us, as a pawn in the hand of the Lord. As young missionaries, wide-eyed and naïve, we willingly accept assignments and direction from those in authority over us. However, as we mature in age and in the gospel, we get used to making most decisions for ourselves. We serve many years in a multitude of callings, some of which carry with them great honor and prestige. When we venture into the mission field again, we do so with a completely new perspective. We no longer need the same direction and supervision we did as young missionaries. Indeed, we may even feel a little resentment when those in authority attempt to tell us where and how to serve. After all, we may have had as much or more experience in the Church as those over us. This is what we need to discuss.

Although there may be a natural tendency to resist the direction of others as we get older, when serving on a mission we must learn to humble ourselves and accept the callings and directions we are given by inspired leaders.

I have seen and heard stories of older members who refuse callings, or refuse to accept direction within callings they have accepted, because of their status as seasoned members. These senior missionaries must find a way to humble themselves and serve when, where, and how the Lord sees fit. You have the talents and abilities that are desperately needed in the mission field. It is your privilege, and your duty, to serve your God by building up his Kingdom here on earth. Yes, you have all those special gifts, but it is up to the Lord to decide how to use them.

## There Are No More Excuses

The most important thing to recognize about missionary work now is that it is no longer just proselyting, or just for young men and women. There really is no longer *any reason* (there will always be excuses) to not go on a mission of some kind and serve the Lord.

Take time to read through the lists of opportunities available to you (these lists are hung on the bulletin board in Church buildings around the world). I promise you will be astounded at the number of different missions available. And that is not all! The length of time you are required to spend on a mission varies also. You can go on a six-month, 12-month, 18-month, or 23-month mission (the 23-month limit is due to a change in the U.S. Tax Code). So, how can

## Becoming a Great Missionary

you possibly lose? Develop *your* plan for serving a mission. Stick with your plan, so the angels can help you succeed. Prepare yourself, spiritually, financially, psychologically, and physically. Then, at the proper time, see your bishop, put in your papers, put yourself in the Lord's hands, and brace yourself for a rich, satisfying, and challenging experience that will change your life and bring showers of blessings on you and your family.

# Bibliography

The Standard Works: *The Holy Bible, The Book of Mormon, The Doctrine and Covenants, The Pearl of Great Price.*

Allred, William A. *Recollections.*

Burton, Theodore M. *BYU Speeches 01/17/61.*

Callis, Charles A. *General Conference Report, April 1942.*

Cannon, George Q. *Gospel of Truth, Life of Joseph Smith the Prophet.*

Cook, Gene R. *General Conference Report, October 1988.*

Faust, James E. *General Conference Report, April 1966; General Conference Report, April 1996.*

First Presidency. *Statement of the First Presidency regarding God's love for all mankind.*

Hinckley, Gordon B. *Go Forward With Faith: The Biography of Gordon B. Hinckley.*

*History of the Church, Volumes 2 and 4.*

Josephus, *The Antiquities of the Jews.*

*Journal of Discourses, Volumes 7, 13–15.*

Kimball, Spencer W. *General Conference Report, April 1974; Regional Representatives Seminar, April 1974 Teachings of Spencer W. Kimball.*

Maxwell, Neal A. *All These Things Shall Give Thee Experience.*

McConkie, Bruce R. *A New Witness for the Articles of Faith, Doctrinal New Testament Commentary, The Mortal Messiah, Mormon Doctrine.*

## Becoming a Great Missionary

*Missionary Preparation Manual/Religion 130.*

Monson, Thomas S. *General Conference Report, October 1969.*

Oaks, Dallin H. *Church News.*

Packer, Boyd K. *Address to New Mission Presidents; Ensign, June 1983; General Conference Report, October 1980.*

*Salt Lake Tribune 12/18/01.*

Smith, Joseph F. *Gospel Doctrine.*

Smith, Joseph Jr. *Lectures on Faith, Teachings of the Prophet Joseph Smith, The Words of Joseph Smith.*

Talmage, James E. *Articles of Faith.*

Whitney, Orson F. *Cowley and Whitney on Doctrine.*

Young, Brigham. *The Discourses of Brigham Young.*

# *Index*

# Becoming a Great Missionary

# Index

# Becoming a Great Missionary

# Index

Have you enjoyed the stories in this book?

Has this book brought back fond memories of your own missionary service?

Do *you* have any missionary-related stories you would like to share with others?

The author is putting together a collection of missionary stories in a new book and is asking anyone who might be interested to submit a written copy of their missionary story (or stories) for publication. If accepted, your story will become part of an uplifting and inspirational book that can be shared by everyone.

The stories included in this book will range the gamut of interests and feelings: inspirational, humorous, sad, scary, dangerous, uplifting, miraculous, etc.

*If you have a favorite missionary-related story, please send it to us!*

These stories can be of your own conversion, stories that happened on a full-time mission or while performing church service, or simply stories of personal missionary work—how you helped someone learn about and accept the gospel.

If your story is accepted, it will be professionally edited then sent back to you for final approval. Once we receive your approval of the final, edited story, it will be included in the book. Anyone who has a story published will received a free copy of the book after it is published.

All you need to do is send a written copy of your missionary story to:

Walking the Line Publications
P.O. Box 95645
South Jordan, Utah 84095-0645

Or you can email your story to us at:

kclawson@walkingthelinebooks.com

If you enjoyed this book, you will enjoy these other books by the same author!

# The Second Coming of Jesus Christ
## and
# Obtaining Your Calling and Election

Each of these books are available for the price of $10 (plus $2 shipping and handling) for a total cost of **$12.**

To order additional copies of *Becoming a* Great *Missionary,* send check or money order for $20 (plus $3 shipping and handling) for a total cost of **$23**:

Walking the Line Publications
P.O. Box 95645
South Jordan, UT 84095-0645

You can also order by credit card online at:

www.walkingthelinebooks.com